Contemporary Democratic Theory

Simone Chambers

polity

Copyright © Simone Chambers 2024

The right of Simone Chambers to be identified as Author of this Work has been asserted in accordance with the UK Copyright, Designs and Patents Act 1988.

First published in 2024 by Polity Press

Polity Press
65 Bridge Street
Cambridge CB2 1UR, UK

Polity Press
111 River Street
Hoboken, NJ 07030, USA

All rights reserved. Except for the quotation of short passages for the purpose of criticism and review, no part of this publication may be reproduced, stored in a retrieval system or transmitted, in any form or by any means, electronic, mechanical, photocopying, recording or otherwise, without the prior permission of the publisher.

ISBN-13: 978-1-5095-4339-7
ISBN-13: 978-1-5095-4340-3 (pb)

A catalogue record for this book is available from the British Library.

Library of Congress Control Number: 2023932770

Typeset in 11 on 13pt Plantin
by Cheshire Typesetting Ltd, Cuddington, Cheshire
Printed and bound in Great Britain by TJ Books Ltd, Padstow, Cornwall

The publisher has used its best endeavours to ensure that the URLs for external websites referred to in this book are correct and active at the time of going to press. However, the publisher has no responsibility for the websites and can make no guarantee that a site will remain live or that the content is or will remain appropriate.

Every effort has been made to trace all copyright holders, but if any have been overlooked the publisher will be pleased to include any necessary credits in any subsequent reprint or edition.

For further information on Polity, visit our website:
politybooks.com

Contemporary Democratic Theory

To Jeff, Max, and Isaac for making it all worthwhile

Contents

Acknowledgments x

1 Introduction 1
2 Justifying Democracy 24
3 Equality 36
4 Freedom 55
5 Instrumentalism 1: Realism 72
6 Instrumentalism 2: Performance Skeptics 88
7 Instrumentalism 3: Epistemic Democracy 105
8 Populism and the People 128
9 Representation 151
10 Public Sphere 177
11 Innovation and Disobedience 198
12 Conclusion 218

Notes 228
References 231
Index 257

Detailed Contents

Acknowledgments   x

1   Introduction   1
   Democracy in crisis   2
   What is democratic theory?   8
   Beyond models of democracy   11
   Chapter-by-chapter overview   14

2   Justifying Democracy   24
   A new vocabulary   25
   Value versus legitimacy   32
   Conclusion   34

3   Equality   36
   Egalitarian democrats   37
   Equality and disagreement   41
   Deep pluralists   45
   Mutual justification   47
   Public reason and disagreement   50
   Conclusion   53

4   Freedom   55
   Freedom as authorship   55
   Hans Kelsen and the freedom to be wrong   57
   Freedom as non-domination   64
   Conclusion   69

5	**Instrumentalism 1: Realism**	72
	Realism in democratic theory	73
	Minimalist realism	77
	Realism and non-domination	80
	Partisan realists	82
	Conclusion	87
6	**Instrumentalism 2: Performance Skeptics**	88
	Measuring performance	89
	Citizen competence	93
	Technocracy	96
	Epistocracy	98
	Meritocracy	101
	Conclusion	103
7	**Instrumentalism 3: Epistemic Democracy**	105
	Condorcet Jury Theorem	107
	Diversity Trumps Ability Theorem	111
	Pragmatism	114
	Epistemic proceduralism	120
	Conclusion	124
8	**Populism and the People**	128
	Populism and democratic theory	128
	Constrained democracy	133
	Left populism	138
	Democratic pluralism	142
	Conclusion	148
9	**Representation**	151
	Citizen representatives and the return of sortition	153
	Parties, partisans, and partisanship	161
	Representatives and the constructivist turn	168
	Conclusion	175
10	**Public Sphere**	177
	Deliberative democracy and the digital public sphere	178
	Technological affordances	185
	Rhetoric	189
	Conclusion	196

11	Innovation and Disobedience	198
	Democratic innovation	200
	Civil disobedience and protests	207
	Conclusion	217
12	Conclusion	218
Notes		228
References		231
Index		257

Acknowledgments

I wish I could say this book was a pleasure to write. I'm just not that kind of writer. But it has been a real pleasure to read and immerse myself in contemporary democratic theory. These might be dark times for democracy but there are bright minds illuminating our predicament with care, intelligence, and commitment. I have thoroughly enjoyed the immersive process, and I want to thank all the authors and scholars who make up this important field of research. I have also enjoyed pestering people about their views on democracy. People have been amazingly generous with their time, including answering unsolicited, and I am sure annoying, emails asking what they mean on page such-and-such of their article or if they could name me three people they admire most working on X. Here is a list of some of my victims: Sam Bagg, Robin Celikates, Maeve Cooke, Julian Culp, Yasmeen Daifallah, Carmen Dege, Lisa Disch, Kevin Elliot, Alessandro Ferrara, Daniel Ferris Hutton, Jennifer Forestal, John Gastil, Rob Goodman, Cathrine Holst, Carlo Invernizzi-Accetti, Steven Klein, Cristina Lafont, Simon Lambek, Hélène Landemore, Maria Pia Lara, Jacob Levi, Alex Livingston, Jane Mansbridge, Eduardo Mendieta, Ricardo Fabrino Mendonça, Alfred Moore, Hartmut Rosa, Enzo Rossi, Martin Saar, Igor Shoikhedbrod, Charles Taylor, Mark Warren, Melissa Williams, Fabio Wolkenstein. Special thanks to Christian Rostbøll, who read an early draft of some chapters and thankfully set me straight.

During the 2020/21 academic year when I first started working on the book, I was fortunate to be invited to join the research project GOODPOL (What is a good policy? Political morality, feasibility, and democracy) led by Cathrine Host and Jakob Elster at the University of Oslo and sponsored by the Center for Advanced Studies at Oslo. Despite Covid making physical presence in Oslo impossible, I benefited immensely from the project's virtual workshops, colloquia, and conferences, even those that took place at 4 am Pacific time. A big thank you must also go to Bill Maurer, Dean of the School of Social Sciences at UCI, who supported my 2020/21 research leave and who has been key in making UCI a happy intellectual home for me.

I wrote most of this book while serving as Chair of the Department of Political Science. This would not have been possible without the help and support of a fantastic administrative team. James Keehn and Zachary Beam are wonderful co-workers and I owe a special debt of gratitude to the amazing Claudia Cheffs, the boss of us all, who keeps the trains running and the clocks on time and makes me look good even when I'm flabbergasted. Also a big thank you to my colleagues and friends Louis DeSipio and Janet DiVincenzo for consistently good advice always served with equally good wine. A special shout-out must go to my wonderful theory colleagues at UCI, Daniel Brunstetter, Kevin Olson, Mary McThomas, and Keith Topper, who suffered through my oversharing of the agonies of the writing process. I want to thank the graduate students at UCI who challenge and push me to think through many half-baked ideas and have been patient test subjects as I try out ideas and fly arguments from the book.

I also want to thank the anonymous reviewers of the book proposal and the final draft for helpful, sensible, and doable suggestions as well as Inès Boxman, Louise Knight, and George Owers at Polity Press. It has been a pleasure to work with the team at Polity.

Thank you to Addye Susnick and Gail Ferguson for terrific and much needed copy-editing.

Thank you to my sister Susan for the weekly pep talk and debrief. It has made a difference in so many ways.

Finally, my biggest debt of thanks goes to Jeff Kopstein, who has suffered through this book with good humor, encouragement, and priceless editorial guidance. With immense gratitude and even more love, I dedicate this book to him and our two amazing children, Max and Isaac.

1
Introduction

EVERYONE loves democracy. Year after year, the World Values Survey reports on the global desire for democracy. It is a "universal value at this point in history" (World Values Survey 2020). But there is a paradox. The global aspiration for democracy goes hand in hand with sinking confidence that actual democracies can live up to that aspiration (Wike and Fetterolf 2021). Democracy has perhaps always faced one crisis or another (Runciman 2017), but the opening decades of the twenty-first century have seen an intensification of the familiar pressures on democracy alongside new challenges on the horizon. Populism, economic inequality, corrupt and/or unresponsive elites, and citizen apathy and lack of political knowledge are perennial concerns, and these are joined by climate crisis, digital threats to information, and pandemic politics. This book, however, is not about democracy in crisis. This book is about democratic theory in times of crisis. The pages to come survey, explain, and evaluate contemporary democratic theory as a response to real-world challenges facing all democratic orders in the twenty-first century. Overarching epochal forces of crisis and threat are pushing democratic theory in new directions and toward new ideas.

This book is intended as an introduction to democratic theory. Not in the sense (I hope) that it simplifies the material presented but in the sense of introducing an old friend in company. For some readers in that company, it will be a first encounter, and they can pursue any of the topics further through references and citations. For others who are already very familiar with democratic theory or who are the very theorists that I discuss in these pages – because I wrote the book for them, too – I hope it serves as a useful mirror and distillation of what they are up to.

This introduction covers some of the preliminaries and explains the organization of the book. While the book is not about democratic crisis, I read many innovations and new directions in democratic theory in the context of democratic crisis. The introduction therefore begins with a brief overview of the major challenges and threats to democracy in the twenty-first century. The next task is to delineate the book's subject matter. What is democratic *theory*? What is it that we study when we study democratic theory as opposed to studying democracy itself? After an outline of what I take theory to be, I then discuss the conceptual organization of democratic theory. A common and for a long time useful way to organize democratic theory was through comparing and contrasting models of democracy, sometimes placed in a historical sequence starting with the ancient Greeks (Held 1987). This book approaches democratic theory differently, and I explain that difference below. Finally, I end this introduction with a quick summary of the chapters.

Democracy in crisis

In the era of democratization and democratic growth that dominated the second half of the twentieth century, social science developed many different indexes to measure democracy. These indexes track and evaluate the robustness of institutions and norms considered essential to any healthy democracy. There are disagreements and differences about what is included and thought important in these instruments. Some, for example, Freedom House (https://freedomhouse.org/), rely on very basic measures of voting rights, equal opportunity to run for office, and freedom of speech and association, while others, for example, V-Dem (https://v-dem.net/), use more robust and qualitative indicators, but all of them are reporting a decline in the growth and health of democracy across the globe, with the United States, arguably the oldest and most stable constitutional democracy, receiving a downgrading for the first time (*Economist* 2022). We do not need to identify a point in time when we went from growth to decline (and of course there is still growth in some places and sectors); we only need to note a general consensus that some time in the late 1990s the bloom started to go off the democratizing rose, and scholars and observers of democracy began introducing notes of worry and sometimes alarm about the global health of democracy. This trend was then accelerated by the 2008 financial crisis and recession that further weakened trust in democratic institutions.

As I noted, this book is not about democratic crisis. It is not part of the very large and growing literature sounding the alarm bells and cataloguing the signs of decline. But we cannot understand contemporary developments and innovations in democratic theory without the backdrop of democracy in crisis. I want to briefly sketch some of the phenomena fueling concern and anxiety about democracy. This is not a theory or explanation of democratic crisis. Nor do I argue that democracy is in crisis. Instead, I describe the sorts of things people are referring to when they talk about democratic crisis or democratic erosion. I break this down into four perspectives from which to evaluate democracy. As we move through the survey of contemporary democratic theory, the exposition returns to these dimensions of crisis as points of reference.

Institutional/norm perspective

Institutional and norm decline is often what people mean when they talk about democratic backsliding (Waldner and Lust 2018; Diamond 2015). The sliding usually refers to a scale with democracy at one end and some form of authoritarianism, autocracy, or patrimonialism at the other end. There are a lot of potential data points that can fall under the category of backsliding, for example, sinking Freedom House scores, failing political parties, weakening rule of law norms, or voter suppression. Although certain declines can be seen in most democracies (falling voter turnout, for example), the epicenter of this research is the rise of populist authoritarian forces within democracies, especially in places where such forces come to power and begin to chip away at institutions thought to be essential to a healthy democracy. The chipping away is often done in the name of "the people," thus invoking democratic credentials for what some see as policies that undermine democracy. For example, many populist regimes have weakened the power and independence of constitutional courts, arguing that they have been used by unaccountable elites to block popular measures. This counts as backsliding within most democracy measures because it undermines the rule of law and protection of individual rights thought necessary to sustain a democratic order. The relationship between backsliding and populism has spawned a great deal of debate within normative theory, especially rethinking what it means to appeal to "the people" (chapter 8).

In addition to the threat posed by authoritarian populism, growing levels of inequality, combined with a lack of responsiveness to people's needs, are also part of the story of backsliding. The global expansion of democracy in the second half of the twentieth century can be seen as the expansion and strengthening of political equality. Social and economic equality, however, has not kept pace, and many think that growing disparities of wealth are beginning to undercut gains in political equality. Thus we see many normative theorists arguing that oligarchization of representative democracy – meaning the rule by the few rather than rule by the many – is the most serious form of backsliding we face (chapters 5 and 9). For many democratic theorists, we should be more worried about the rule of the rich than the rule of the populist authoritarian.

At a more abstract level, observable and documented backsliding raises questions of how we evaluate democracy in the first place. A clear new direction of democratic theory over the last 25 years has been the growing intensity of the debate focused on why we should value democracy in the first place, even under conditions where it is not performing very well (chapters 2 and 6).

Subjective/attitudinal perspective

This book began by noting a global aspiration for democracy. Democracy as a vague unspecified ideal is hugely popular. Prick the surface of this public opinion bubble and people in all democracies are unhappy with their own democratic institutions. Here we see a lot of survey data indicating a decline in trust in elections, politicians, parties, parliaments, and governments (Connaughton,

Kent, and Schumacher 2020). This is matched by sinking voter turnout rates and an uptick in protest and contestatory politics. Many people think that democracy is doing a terrible job. Politicians and parties are thought to be out of touch or corrupt; government is thought to be unresponsive to the needs and concerns of ordinary citizens. The declining trust in democratic institutions is tied both to perceived lack of responsiveness as well to poor performance. These forces came to a head in many democracies in the wake of the 2008 financial crisis. Elected governments were perceived as having stumbled into the crisis through a failure of will to regulate financial markets and then a failure to produce effective policy to stem recession and unemployment (Plattner 2015: 7). Declining trust in democracy and democratic institutions is connected to the growth in support for populist parties, but this phenomenon goes beyond the threat of authoritarian populism and affects all stable democracies, even those without a strong populist challenge. Democracy is in trouble when the people, who after all are supposed to be ruling, have lost faith in the system (Mounk 2018).

Uncovering the causes of sinking trust and how we can address and reverse that decline is motivating innovative rethinking about representation, responsiveness, trust, and corruption within normative theory. Research and theory about democratic innovation is at an all-time high with the very term morphing into a disciplinary field with its own associations, conferences, and journals (chapter 11). A radical and controversial response to sinking trust in representatives and oligarchization of electoral institutions is the growing interest in using sortition or random selection to choose citizen representatives to populate citizen legislative assemblies (chapter 9). At the other end of the spectrum are normative theories that seek to rethink traditional institutions. Here there has been an interesting revisiting of political parties, why they are essential to democracy, and how we can revitalize them (chapter 9).

Outcome perspective

A third angle of focus on democratic crisis traces the growing doubt by citizens, technocrats, experts, and academic observers that democracy can get things right and solve the most pressing problems facing contemporary societies. There is of course an overlap with the attitudinal perspective that charts citizens' sinking trust in democratic institutions and skepticism about job performance. But the output debate goes beyond survey data. This third perspective often assumes that there are objectively right and wrong or better and worse answers to policy questions and that democracy is getting sinking scores on this output scale. Here Aziz Huq articulates this concern: "As contemporary experiences with climate change, pandemic illness, and economic inequality show, democracies are not always good at recognizing serious threat" (Huq 2020: 32). The concern for output can bring about different sorts of normative theory. The climate crisis and pandemic can lead to thinking we need to take these decisions out of the hands of fickle and misinformed citizens or partisan elected officials and into the hands of scientists or technocrats (chapter 6). Output failures have spawned a growing interest in and defense of epistocracy – the rule of the knowledgeable. Nobody is advocating a full-blown philosopher king, but many theorists and philosophers are suggesting that objectively knowledgeable people should have more clout within the democratic system or more decisions should be insulated from democratic determination and handed over to experts (chapter 6). At the same time, the worry about outputs has inspired two types of responses to the champions of epistocracy or technocracy. On the one hand, there is an active anti-epistocratic wave often identified under the label epistemic democrats (chapter 7). Here normative theorists argue that democracy does in fact, or can in principle, get the right answer more often than other regimes and that the output perspective offers a strong defense of democracy despite some (inevitable) disappointments with job performance. On the other hand, there are democratic theorists who argue that evaluating democracy on output measures is deeply misguided as democracy's appeal and indeed moral superiority stem from the way its procedures treat citizens fairly and as equals, not from getting the right answer (chapters 3 and 4).

Introduction

Input perspective

The input perspective focuses on the crises of information and competence. There are two sets of problems here that converge in some people's minds. First, the digital public sphere has made the common problems of manipulation and misinformation more intractable and endemic. Perhaps we are looking at a new structural transformation of the public sphere that bodes very poorly for democracy. "Post-truth" was the 2016 word of the year, and this can't be a good thing. It is hard to see how democracy can function properly if citizens have no access to trustworthy sources of information or distrust trustworthy ones. Even more alarming is the viral and effective spread of falsehoods that go to the heart of democracy, for example, claiming electoral victory when all evidence points to defeat. This dimension of crisis is fueling a growth of theory surrounding information communication and the new digital public sphere (chapter 10). The democratization of algorithms as well as crowdsourcing content moderation are just some of the new frontiers of democratic theory spurred by the crisis of digital communication.

Parallel to the worry that the digital public sphere is creating such bad information pollution that it is disrupting the most basic processes of citizen opinion formation is a resurgence of common worries about citizen competence. Modern science – especially social psychology and neuropsychology – appears to be piling up evidence that ordinary citizens, or humans in general, are not cognitively cut out to govern themselves in mass democracies. The worry about citizen competence has been around at least since Plato, but there appears to be a growing group of scientists, social scientists, and philosophers who believe that they have hard data (mostly experimental data) that can put the final nail in the coffin of claims to citizen competence. This in turn has breathed new life into minimalist and realist theories of democracy that seek to scale back our expectations about citizen input into the democratic system (chapter 5).

The citizen competence debate is not simply about the dangers of uninformed and easily manipulated voters; it is also connected to new conceptions of representation and in turn new measures of democratic success. Constructivist ideas of representation rely on empirical studies of opinion formation to question the democratic ideal of responsiveness (chapter 9). Responsiveness is the idea that democratic governments function properly when they respond to the authentic and true interests of citizens and function poorly when they fail to respond. The new wave of normative theories of representation suggests that citizens' views, opinions, and preferences are (to some extent) constructed by representatives themselves, thus reversing the causal direction implied by ideas of input and responsiveness and indeed questioning the ideal of responsiveness as an adequate or realistic measure of democracy.

These then are some of the diagnostic details that underpin and motivate contemporary democratic theory. The next question to address is what is democratic theory?

What is democratic theory?

Every year, thousands of academic books and articles are published about democracy, and the more popular democracy-is-dying book industry is also having a growth spurt. We need to circumscribe our topic to make it manageable and coherent. This in turn requires a short foray into methodology and disciplinary divides in the study of democracy. The type of theory that is primarily surveyed in this book is normative theory. Normative here means very broadly that it is theory interested in an evaluative dimension of a subject matter, for example, why democracy is good or what makes democracy good. Although I discuss theories that are put forward by scholars in various disciplines, the two most central are political philosophy and political theory, the former coming out of philosophy departments and the latter found in political science departments. Each discipline sees the delineation of normative theory slightly differently, with philosophy connecting it tightly to moral philosophy, and political science seeing it as doing the work of conceptual clarification and value justification, leaving measurement and explanation to empirical positivist political science. Although there is something to both these ways of thinking about normative theory, it is worth taking a moment to advocate for an expansive and inclusive idea of normative theory that blurs the edges suggested by both these disciplines.

Within analytic political philosophy, normative often implies moral content. For example, Thomas Christiano and Sameer Bajaj begin their *Stanford Encyclopedia of Philosophy* entry on democracy by noting that "Normative democratic theory deals with the moral foundations of democracy and democratic institutions" (Christiano and Bajaj 2022). Democratic theories that begin from the claim that all human beings are equal, or that we ought to treat all human beings as equal, clearly have a moral starting point from which one would then elaborate what it would mean for essentially equal people to govern themselves in such a way that respects that equality. A great deal of normative democratic theory invokes or presupposes moral categories in this way. We should be careful, however, not to associate normative theory too narrowly with moral theory. Realists, for example, challenge the moral sources of political normativity, which is to say, they question whether morality can offer an adequate basis upon which to make political judgments and evaluations. Realists criticize dominant trends in analytic political philosophy (embodied to some extent in Christiano and Bajaj's definition of normative democratic theory) which, "through inappropriate idealizations, abstractions, and moralizations present a misleading, if not outright false, account of politics" (Sleat 2018: 2). Realists look for the foundation of democracy and democratic institutions in the management of power and conflict. They are often relentless critical theorists, indicting the oligarchization of democracy not on moral grounds but on instrumental grounds (Arlen and Rossi 2021; Bagg forthcoming). As I discuss in chapter 5, realism has a growing number of adherents and represents an important development in recent democratic theory. To the extent that realism offers grounds for evaluating and prescribing, it is a type of normative theory, despite rejecting moral principles as the foundation for those evaluations and prescriptions.

Within the discipline of political science, normative theory is sometimes used as a catch-all category to demark a tripartite methodological division between formal theory, empirical theory, and scholarship interested in studying the history, meaning, value, and conceptual structure of our ideas of democracy. Formal theory seeks to gain insight into political phenomena using mathematical instruments that model complex choice scenarios. Often referred to as social choice or game theory, formal theory within political science has a great deal to say about democracy, especially dimensions of democracy that lend themselves to formal modeling like voting. Empirical political science focuses on description, explanation, and measurement and often aspires to scientific accuracy and verifiability. The field of democracy studies here is immense.

What falls into the category of normative theory then? Empirical political scientists, in describing the difference between normative and empirical research, sometimes invoke some version of the fact/value distinction. Empirical political scientists deal in facts and aspire to value neutrality. Political theorists work out the value part. I am not going to rehearse the familiar arguments for why positivist social science is not, nor ever can be, value neutral in any strong, deep, or epistemological sense. And to be clear, I think empirical political science really does offer good causal explanations of political phenomena and sorts through the facts in a rigorous, evidence-driven, knowledge-producing way. I am a fan and consumer of empirical political science. So, this is not a criticism of positivism. My complaint is about the assumption that empirical positive political science deals in facts and somehow normative political theory does not, or not in a rigorous way. Associating normative theory with a simplified idea of values or conceptual clarity leads to a failure to see the ways that much of normative theory is deeply entangled with the empirical world of facts, causes, descriptions, and measurements. This, I want to argue, is especially true of the new wave of democratic theory that I chart in this book. As I describe in the next section, responding to failures, weaknesses, and crises of democracy connects democratic theory more closely to studying actual existing democracies than to seeking to build ideal types of democracy toward which we should be striving. Normative democratic theory today is more empirically informed and more closely connected to positivist social science than normative democratic theory of 50 years ago. I cannot prove this, but I hope to make a convincing case for this claim as I survey the last 25 years (or so) of democratic theory.

Where does this leave us in trying to delimit the subject matter of this book? I employ a capacious view of normative democratic theory that initially demarcates my subject matter using loose disciplinary conventions (things that are called political philosophy or political theory) that I insist do not track hard and fast methodological lines. I retain the term *normative* theory not because all the theories that I survey have a clear prescriptive or moral core but because the theories that I survey usually do not base their persuasiveness primarily on a claim of scientific fact, accuracy, or verifiability, even though they often presuppose, appeal to, incorporate, and rely on many scientific facts. Most of the theories do contain some evaluative standard, however. But that can be a low bar of normativity that many purely empirical studies also meet. A definition of democracy contains an evaluative standard that says, "This here is a democracy and that over there is not a democracy." And although the assumption that democracy is always a good thing (or that we always want more rather than less democracy) has come under question in recent democratic theory, the study of democracy (both empirical and normative) within democracies has always contained either implicitly or explicitly a normative presumption in favor of democracy. Thus saying this here is a democracy and that there is a tyranny (or an autocracy) is not the same as saying something like this here is tungsten and that there is chromium.

Beyond models of democracy

Colin Bird has noted that democracy is an adjective or perhaps an adverb masquerading as a noun (Bird 2019: 285). What I take him to mean is that, first, starting from the question "What is a democracy?" is too broad and unwieldy, and, second, democracy should initially be thought of as qualifying a certain type of collective decision procedure. In this book I too start with democracy not as a way of life or a whole society but as a method or procedure for making collective decisions. Its etymological root from the Greek means "the rule of the people." This is not yet a definition of democracy, but the idea of ruling is a good place to start. Democracy might also be conceived as a way of life, or one might want to argue that one cannot maintain "rule by the people" without the broader backing of a democratic way of life

(Anderson 2009; Dewey 1954). But, to begin, I focus on democracy as a way in which we govern ourselves. Thus the democratic system is a complex system of collective action, coordination, and decision.

There is a second way I move away from democracy as a noun. Much of my own research has been within the tradition of deliberative democracy. I have often been asked the question, "What would a deliberative democracy look like?" or "How would a deliberative democracy be different from a representative democracy?" It became clear to me that these were the wrong sorts of questions to ask. They were wrong because they assumed that normative democratic theory was about building comprehensive models of democracy that compete. But for me deliberative democracy furnished an interesting and normatively compelling way to study and evaluate any and all democracies. Thinking of it as a model (or as a noun) was not helpful. We need to and indeed already are thinking beyond a models-of-democracy conceptual framework for democratic theory (Warren 2017).

A models-of-democracy approach begins with some institution or element and then builds an ideal typical picture of democracy around that feature or institution (Warren 2017). Common models in our lexicon are direct democracy, participatory democracy, deliberative democracy, agonistic democracy, republican democracy, competitive elite democracy, liberal democracy, and of course representative democracy. All the terms qualifying democracy in this list represent important traditions and arguments within democratic theory, but I do not treat them as models, nor do I organize the discussion of contemporary democratic theory along a models-of-democracy framework. I have several reasons for departing from a models-of-democracy approach as a conceptual structure.

First, a models-of-democracy framework tends to think about models as if they were ideologies in competition. This perspective stands behind the question "How would a deliberative democracy be different from a representative democracy?" Contemporary democratic theory is full of disagreement and criticism. As is natural within such intellectual debates, people stake out positions by way of contrast and criticism. And it is sometimes useful to give a name to the position one is staking out. For example, "open democracy" (chapter 9) or "epistemic democracy" (chapter 6) are useful identifiers of types of arguments. But thinking about that disagreement and criticism in terms of models of democracy does a disservice to the complexity of the disputes (Saward 2021). Philosophers who identify as agonistic democrats (chapters 5 and 8), for example, have significant and important disagreements with many of the premises of deliberative democracy (chapters 3 and 10), but these differences do not come with competing blueprints about how we should organize the institutions of democracy. Democracy is a complex system with agonistic elements alongside deliberative elements.

Second, many contributions to and debates within contemporary democratic theory are orthogonal to contrasting and competing models. For example, the last 20 years have seen a revival of interest in rhetoric and its special and problematic place within democratic public spheres (chapter 10). Many of the contributors to this debate can be identified as working within one or another tradition, but the debate itself is not about competing models of democracy. Instead, it is better understood through a systemic approach that sees democracy as a complex system with many different dimensions and components that perform various functions.

Third, models-of-democracy as an organizing structure for discussing contemporary democratic theory sometimes fails to give adequate attention to variation and disagreement within traditions. Republican theories, for example, cannot be thought of as offering a model of democracy in any strong sense. One of the more interesting aspects of republicanism today is how its core concept of non-domination can inspire the liberal views of Phillip Pettit (chapter 4) at the same time as the radical plebeian views of John McCormick (chapter 5). The shared tradition between liberal republicanism and radical plebeianism is interesting, but there are more differences than similarities between these two strands of republican thought.

Finally, the era of models-of-democracy was tied to an era of ideology and optimism. It was tied to an era where the question was essentially "What is the best form of democracy?" and it was not unreasonable to suggest that we were approaching some end point where most of our debates and controversies would all be inside a liberal democratic paradigm aimed at perfecting that way of life (Fukuyama 1992). Today, "How can we save democracy?" is increasingly the default question we face. We still want to improve democracy, but the twenty-first century has seen some shocks to democracy and the spectacle of citizens voting for parties that seem not to care about democratic values or for a form of democracy that is very thin and teeters on the edge of authoritarianism. Rather than models of democracy, then, this book studies democratic theory through the lens of the challenges, problems, and questions facing democratic orders at the beginning of the twenty-first century. These challenges, problems, and questions overlay a deep undercurrent of existential anxiety. We have seen an explosion of doom and gloom studies of democracy with "death" as a recurring motif. This existential anxiety is reflected in a shift from defending the best form or model of democracy to a discussion of why value democracy in the first place. The substantive chapters of the book begin there.

Chapter-by-chapter overview

Chapter 2 begins by introducing the reader to the value of democracy debate. What is so good about democracy? Why do we or ought we to value it above other forms of rule? The debate has evolved to produce two types of answers. One type of answer maintains that democracy's value is to be found in the procedures themselves more than the substantive outcomes that emerge from the procedures. Here theorists defend the intrinsic value of democracy. The other set of arguments looks at democratic procedures instrumentally or from the point of view of outcome. Here democracy's value is that it produces peace, prosperity, and stability or better policy, law, and governance than other forms of decision making. The terms of this debate – intrinsic, procedural, outcome-based, and instrumental – are not always clear and so I spend some time laying out their meaning and use in normative democratic theory. I conclude the chapter with a discussion of the difference between thinking about democracy in terms of legitimacy versus value. Legitimacy asks why I should obey democratically enacted laws. Value asks why I should prefer a democratic way of making collective decisions. I argue that the second question casts a wider net and is a better reflection of trends in contemporary democratic theory.

Chapter 3 looks at procedural theories of democracy that place equality at the center of democracy's value. I look at four versions of this argument. The first group starts from egalitarian theories of social justice to argue that democracy is required by justice (Brighouse 1996; Griffin 2003; Kolodny 2014a, 2014b; Viehoff 2014). Pushing back against the apolitical bent of egalitarian distributive theories of the 1970s, 1980s, and early 1990s, this group brings democracy back into the conversation about justice. Democracy is said to have intrinsic value "on the grounds that the implementation of democratic procedures is an indispensable means of demonstrating communal recognition of the equal moral status of citizens" (Brighouse 1996: 119). What is most important about democracy is that it is a decision procedure that distributes political power equally and so contributes to a non-hierarchical relation of equality between citizens.

The next three arguments all add disagreement and pluralism to equality to defend the inherent value of democratic procedures. Thomas Christiano also defends a strongly egalitarian starting point in his democratic theory, but he adds the important condition that, although we all want justice, we cannot agree when justice has been done. Therefore, only democratic procedures and not democratic outcomes can publicly affirm equality.

Jeremy Waldron also has an equality/disagreement foundation to his view of democracy but without the strong justice theory (Waldron 1999). Waldron argues that we are faced with three facts of politics: we consider ourselves equals, our disagreements about justice and what is to be done go very deep, and we need to collectively decide what is to be done. This leads to the conclusion that majority rule decision procedures are the only fair procedures under these conditions. In the final section, I discuss the mutual justification view and the special role of public reason in addressing disagreement and pluralism. Drawing primarily on the work of John Rawls and Joshua Cohen, I outline the way that the mutual justification defense of democratic procedures differs from the first three procedural defenses while still keeping political equality as the central value.

In chapter 4, I turn to theories that still focus on the intrinsic value of procedures, but which bring questions of freedom and self-government to the fore. Here equality is not only understood as equal moral status, but also as equally free or equally our own masters. The question addressed in this chapter, then, is how can we reconcile our status as equally free with rulers enacting coercive laws? For the group of theories that I look at in this chapter, democracy is the answer to this question.

I look at two examples of the freedom argument. The first group, which I call Kelsenian proceduralism, has historically identified itself as procedural democracy. Nadia Urbinati is an exemplary figure in this group. Following many insights first articulated by Hans Kelsen, Urbinati and others see parliamentary democracy with strong protections of minority rights as the system which maximizes the freedom of all. Kelsenian proceduralists take a strong stand against any view that evaluates democracy on the quality of the outcome of the electoral/ parliamentary process. Contestatory proceduralism is the second freedom-centered argument that I analyze in chapter 4. I look at Philip Pettit's neo-republican theory of non-domination as well as Pierre Rosanvallon's idea of "counter-democracy." Both these views expand the idea of freedom-ensuring procedures beyond electoral institutions and include a wide variety of pressure points that limit domination. This chapter introduces the challenge of defending democracy on traditional grounds of rule by the people, a challenge that we return to many times in the book.

Instrumental arguments in favor of democracy look at the consequences or outcomes of democracy to assess democracy's value. In chapters 5, 6, and 7, I introduce three types of instrumental arguments. First up, in chapter 5, is realism, then, in chapter 6, I discuss a growing group of theories that give democracy low grades on performance measures, and, in chapter 7, I turn to epistemic theories that argue that democracy does or can produce good-quality outcomes. I devote chapter 5 to realism as it has a growing number of adherents in democratic theory and I often return to this perspective in the book. Instrumentalism is sometimes associated exclusively with democratic theory that is concerned with measuring output in the sense of policy and legislation, but realism is also a fundamentally instrumental assessment of democracy. Realist democratic theory claims that democracy has value to the extent that it mitigates, channels, pacifies, contains, or opposes the violence and conflict that is endemic to politics understood as power struggle. In chapter 5, I review three versions of this argument. The first and most familiar version is minimal realism (Przeworski 1999). Minimalism starts with a Schumpeterian definition of democracy – a very common definition of democracy in empirical political science – as a method of choosing rulers via competitive elections. Joining minimalism to realism results in a theory that values democracy because electoral turnover ensures that losers do not resort to violence to gain power as they have future chances to win the day. Second, I cover realist theories that argue that party democracy institutionalizes legitimate opposition in the form of minority or "loyal" opposition parties, and this is an important defense against domination (Shapiro 2016). Finally, I look at a group of theories I call partisan realists. Like the preceding argument, partisan realists value democracy as a means to curb domination, but this now involves the more radical strategy of targeting the forces of domination and *excluding* them from power, not just channeling or restraining them. Partisan realists take sides in a way that minimal and non-domination realists do not. In this section, I take up and discuss two versions of partisan realism, agonism (Medearis 2015; Mouffe 2018) and plebeian democracy (Green 2016; McCormick 2019; Vergara 2020a), as examples of this type of argument.

Chapter 6 turns to instrumental views that assess democracy's value on its output or performance. After discussing some of the challenges that performance-based theories face in measuring and defining good outcomes, I examine a range of democratic theories that are skeptical of democracy's ability to perform well. All these theories begin from a negative assessment of citizens' competence, so I too begin with a review of this literature. I sort performance skeptics into three types of solutions they have for improving democracy's performance: technocratic, epistocratic, and meritocratic solutions. Technocracy involves rule by experts, epistocracy defends rule by the knowledgeable or wise (Brennan 2016; Caplan 2007), and meritocracy is rule by the best sort of people, usually defined as a combination of being knowledgeable and public-spirited or virtuous (Bai 2019; Bell 2015). Epistocratic and meritocratic critics of democracy sometimes propose radical reform measures, for example, excluding some people from the franchise or suggesting that democracy as a whole is wrongheaded. Criticism of these views is widespread, but the fact that they are getting so much attention is in itself a reflection of deep worries about democracy.

On the other side of the performance divide are democratic theorists who argue that democracy is to be valued because it tends to get the right answer. I refer to this group generally as epistemic democrats, and I discuss four examples of this type of argument in chapter 7. All these theories share the intuition that democracy does or, if well-ordered, would tend to produce sound and reasonable outcomes. All epistemic democrats embrace some version of the adage "two (or more) heads are better than one," also articulated as a confidence in the wisdom of the multitude. But there is wide variation in how theorists defend this claim and which democratic mechanisms they think are at work to produce epistemically sound outcomes. At one end of the spectrum are theories that focus on the miracle of aggregation and pay particular attention to majority-rule voting procedures. Here the Condorcet Jury Theorem has been very influential, and I discuss that influence in the first section (Goodin and Spiekermann 2018: 52). Also on the aggregate side, examined in section 2, is the Diversity Trumps Ability Theorem that suggests that experts are not always the best problem solvers and, more generally, that human beings are better at solving problems collaboratively than individually (Landemore 2012). At the other end of the spectrum are theories that see deliberation in both the democratic public sphere as well as assemblies as doing the epistemic heavy lifting. In the third and fourth sections, I outline two versions of the deliberation-centered views, starting with pragmatism (Anderson 2006; Mizak 2008; Talisse 2007) and moving to epistemic proceduralism (Estlund 2008; Peter 2013).

Chapters 8, 9, 10, and 11 move on from the value of democracy debate and study democratic theory that is more directly responding to democratic crisis. The rise of populism has been a major theme in normative democratic theory as well as in the empirical study of democracies. We are seeing a vibrant debate about what populism is, what explains its rise, and what dangers, if any, it poses for democracy. In normative democratic theory, the debate often centers on the concept of the "people" and what it means for the people to rule. Chapter 8 investigates this dimension with special emphasis on interrogating the concept of popular sovereignty. I analyze three broad understandings of populism and then connect those assessments to underlying normative views of democracy that I label constrained democracy, left populism, and democratic pluralism. The constrained democracy view worries about illiberal democracy and sees the primary danger of populism as a weakening of constraints, guardrails, and checks on direct plebiscitary and majoritarian power (Mounk 2018). Here the underlying normative theory of democracy is skeptical and cautious regarding strong ideas of popular sovereignty and the will of the people (Riker 1988; Weale 2018). Democracy needs constraint to make it safe for liberal orders.

The second group sees the primary threat of right-wing populism not in creeping authoritarianism so much as in a problematic substantive conception of the people. Ernesto Laclau and Chantal Mouffe attempt to resuscitate some general themes of populism not on nativist, anti-immigration, or white nationalist terms, but on a coalition of those disempowered and marginalized by the forces of neoliberalism (Laclau 2005; Mouffe 2008). Thus the threat and problem with right-wing populism is not that it is populist but that it is right-wing.

The final group I canvas in chapter 8 is concerned about authoritarian-leaning populist attacks on pluralism, opposition, the public sphere, and civil society (Abts and Rummens 2007; Arato and Cohen 2022; Habermas 1996; Müller 2016; Ochoa Espejo 2017; Rosanvallon 2007, 2021; Rostbøll 2023; Rummens 2017; Urbinati 2019). I label this large group democratic pluralists because they place anti-pluralism at the center of their criticism of populism, but also because in developing alternative ideas of popular sovereignty, they stress the multiple and plural institutional means through which citizens exercise that popular sovereignty.

Chapter 9 describes and explains new developments in theories of political representation. The backdrop to this discussion is sinking trust in traditional representative institutions: elected representatives, political parties, and parliaments (Dalton 2004). Sinking trust levels are often thought to be tied to two interconnected senses in which elected representatives fail to represent citizens. The first we might call the populist complaint: elected representatives are heavily drawn from elite sectors and do not look like most ordinary citizens. The second is the corruption complaint: in developing policy agendas, elected representatives are responsive to economic heavy hitters rather than the interests of ordinary citizens.

The first set of theories I cover in this chapter under the heading "Citizen Representatives and the Return of Sortition" argue that electoral democracy, as it was conceived of at the end of the seventeenth century and then handed down to all liberal democratic orders, was never designed to be truly responsive to ordinary citizens (Guerrero 2014; Landemore 2020; Van Reybrouck 2016). Elections are inherently aristocratic, meaning they select a governing elite who are chosen because of their virtue or superior ability, or perhaps oligarchic, meaning that the rich and powerful tend to get elected and rule. In the place of election, here we see the endorsement of sortition, or random selection, as a democratic means of choosing representatives – but now citizen representatives.

The second body of work I canvas might not look like a new direction as it focuses on political parties, an ever-present institution in the study of democracy (Bonotti 2017; Muirhead 2014; Rosenblum 2008; White and Ypi 2016). But, for a long time, normative democratic theory took very little interest in parties. The new turn that I discuss here attempts to breathe new normative life into the salutary function of partisanship in democratic politics. This view is in stark contrast to the sortition view in which partisanship is one of the elements overcome by randomly selected representative assemblies.

The final view reconsiders the standard idea of responsiveness and in doing so rethinks the way we evaluate and judge whether representatives are doing a good job. This new wave of normative theories of representation, dubbed constructivism, suggests that citizens' views, opinions, and preferences are (to some extent) constructed by representatives themselves, thus reversing the causal direction implied by ideas of input and responsiveness and indeed questioning the ideal of responsiveness as an adequate or realistic measure of democracy (Disch 2021; Saward 2010).

The constructivist turn in theories of representation with which chapter 9 ends highlights the central role of political communication in preference and identity formation. Chapter 10 discusses political communication and the public sphere directly, with special attention to new digital technologies. I begin with an evaluation of the digital public sphere through the lens of deliberative democracy. Drawing on recent contributions to thinking about deliberative democracy in an age of social media, I outline the threats posed by this new media environment (Chambers 2021; Cohen and Fung 2021; Habermas 2022). This analysis begins with the centrality of the public sphere to a properly functioning democracy and ends with deep anxiety about the future of the public sphere in the wake of the digital revolution. In the second section, I turn to democratic theorists who have taken the dive into technology and come away with (relatively) positive recommendations for making the internet more hospitable to truth and democracy (Forestal 2022; Landemore 2021). Finally, I look at the revival of interest in rhetoric in democracy. This too is an old topic going back to the ancient world. Now, however, the study of rhetoric can draw on modern science of opinion formation to open the black box of persuasion. But underlying much of the debate about rhetoric is the question of the relationship between autonomy and persuasion.

The twin topics of chapter 11 are democratic innovation and civil disobedience. Although the former literature is very upbeat about democracy's future and the latter not so upbeat, I read both areas of research as future-oriented and at least implying hope that actions on the ground, whether they be setting up a citizens' climate assembly or taking to the street to protest police violence, can make a difference in the life of a democracy.

Democratic innovation has recently transitioned from a collection of case studies to a self-reflective subfield asking theoretical and normative questions about its subject matter (Elstub and Escobar 2019; Smith 2009; Hendricks 2021). What counts as innovation and how we should evaluate innovations are discussed as much as cases of innovation. The normative emphasis is on enhancing and empowering citizen participation in democratic decision making. Although several types of institution are studied as sites of innovation, the deliberative mini-public gets the most attention and theoretical unpacking in democratic innovation literature. As an illustration of this, I discuss the proliferation of citizens' climate assemblies and their value in a democratic system.

Civil disobedience is not a new topic, but it is seeing new theoretical directions, especially in the wake of the rising street and protest politics of the twenty-first century (Celikates 2016; Delmas 2018; Livingston 2020; Pineda 2021; Scheuerman 2018; Smith 2012). This new direction is highly critical of the liberal or Rawlsian justification of civil disobedience that is interpreted as too narrow, too constrained, and, in some sense, too civil to face contemporary challenges. Two themes preoccupy me in this part of the chapter. The first theme is the role and function of civil disobedience within a democratic system. Drawing on the radical democratic theories of Jacques Rancière and Etienne Balibar among others, Robin Celikates argues that civil disobedience is an expression of constituent power (Celikates 2016). This reading of civil disobedience suggests that authentic democratic action always has an anti-institutional undercurrent to it. This goes against most democratic theory that seeks to perfect and stabilize institutions of democracy. The second theme is what Alexander Livingston calls the "coercive turn" in civil disobedience theory (Livingston 2021). This turn signals a move away from seeing public acts of disobedience and protest as attempts to change the public's mind about an issue and toward seeing them as about forcing authorities to act. This type of realism ties normativity to efficacy, but efficacy, it turns out, often dictates moderation in means. Although contemporary civil disobedience theory tends to have a capacious and realist view of permissible actions and tactics, there is still a sense that the "civil" of civil disobedience sets limits.

Chapter 12 is a short conclusion that revisits the overarching approach to normative democratic theory that I take in the book. Here I discuss the two framing issues that have determined what I have and what I have not included in the analysis. The first is taking democracy as a way in which we govern ourselves, therefore focusing on the institutions of ruling. The second is reading democratic theory as a response to twenty-first-century challenges and problems. The focus on ruling means that I look mostly at vertical relations between citizens and the state at the expense of horizontal relations between citizens. And focusing on crisis has led me to concentrate on democracy at the nation-state level rather than the global level.

2

Justifying Democracy

WITHIN contemporary democratic theory, questions about why we value democracy have begun to displace questions about the best form or model of democracy. In some ways, this constitutes a return to a much older discussion. The history of democratic theory is the history of the justification of democracy, so arguments about the superiority or inferiority of democracy vis-a-vis other options are not new. But the context of the justification is new in two important respects. First, we know a great deal more today than at any time in history about how real-world democracies function, thrive, and fail. Second, democracy appears to be in trouble after a period which saw the growth and spread of democracy around the globe, in fits and starts to be sure, but with a clear trajectory. That trajectory seems to have changed from ascending to declining. The normative theoretical question "Why democracy?" cannot ignore the massive amount of empirical research on democracy nor the clear signs of precarity, despite a global love fest for the ideal.

Contemporary debates have not given up trying to make democracy the best that it can be. Identifying the core appeal of democracy will have consequences for reform and questions about how we can make democracy better, but for the most part these are not articulated in terms of promoting one type of democracy over another. Tellingly, the contrast is often about why we should value democracy over more autocratic, technocratic, meritocratic, epistocratic, oligarchic, or market-based alternatives. This, I have suggested in the introduction, is tied to deep worries about the resilience of democracy in the twenty-first century. While it is rare to see philosophers suggesting that democracy be cast aside altogether, it is not uncommon to see arguments that less rather than more democracy would be a good thing (Bell 2015; Brennan 2016; Jones 2020) or to suggest that we lower our sights when it comes to what democracy can achieve (Achen and Bartels 2016). In addition to scholarly doubt and skepticism about democracy's virtues, ordinary citizens are reporting sinking trust in democratic institutions and an apparent willingness to vote for parties and leaders who promote democratic backsliding, meaning weakening and undermining institutions and norms that constitute the conventional measures of democratic robustness. This context helps explain the shift of focus from competing models of democracy to justifications of democracy.

In this and the next five chapters, I parse out the various arguments and positions that are animating this debate and why the question of democracy's value is important. This preliminary chapter introduces some general fault lines dividing competing arguments; offers some commentary about the terms "intrinsic," "procedural," "outcome-based," and "instrumental" that are everywhere in the literature; addresses what is meant by "value" in relation to legitimacy; and finally assesses what is at stake in the value of democracy debate.

A new vocabulary

What is so good about democracy? Why do we or ought we to value it above other forms of rule? The debate has evolved to produce two types of answers. One type of answer maintains that democracy's value is to be found in the procedures themselves more than the substantive outcomes that emerge from the procedures. That is, *how* democracies make decisions is more important than *what* they decide. Democracy might not always produce the best policy. Perhaps an enlightened despot or benevolent technocrat might get it right more often than the people, and in any case, do we even have an independent standard of what counts as a good outcome to use as a yardstick that we all agree on? Democracy, however, is the only fair way to make decisions among people who see themselves as free and equal – or so it is argued. This type of theory is said to look for the intrinsic value of democracy or is described as procedural.

The other set of arguments looks at democratic procedures instrumentally or from the point of view of outcome. Here democracy's value is that it produces peace, prosperity, and stability or better policy, law, and governance than other forms of decision making. Instrumental and outcome-based views of democracy also potentially produce theory that is skeptical of overvaluing democracy. Perhaps democracy is not always the best way to make a decision. Perhaps democracy gets lots of things wrong and has bad outcomes. A strict instrumentalist will then have to say that in these cases we should rethink an unreserved enthusiasm for democracy. It is of course possible to value democracy for both intrinsic *and* instrumental reasons. And many democratic theorists fall into that category (Anderson 2009; Habermas 1996). But an interesting twist to this debate is the insistence of some philosophers that only one or the other of these perspectives is defensible. Thus champions of the intrinsic value sometimes argue that there is no objective or agreed upon measure of good outcomes (this is precisely what we argue about in democracy) and so we must abandon the good outcome approach altogether (Christiano 2008; Waldron 1999). Strict instrumentalists ask what is the point of a decision procedure if it does not have good outcomes (Arneson 2003; Wall 2007)? If democracy cannot make our lives better and solve pressing problems, then no amount of intrinsic value (which is difficult to identify and measure anyway) can make up for that fact.

This way of parsing justifications of democracy – using the vocabulary of intrinsic, procedural, outcome, and instrumental – is very widespread. In the first two pages of an essay entitled "Democracy's Value: A Conceptual Map," Elana Ziliotti cites over 50 contemporary works that draw on this vocabulary, and this list is in no way exhaustive. She admits, however, that "the basic terms of the debate are quite unclear; there are no agreed meanings attached to these terms" (Ziliotti 2020: 408). On the one hand, the terms are used differently by different theorists, and this has led to some confusion. But, on the other hand, attempts at analytic precision in these terms have tended to sidetrack the debate away from real-world political concerns and into technicalities of analytic philosophy. I hope to steer a middle course here, cleaving to ordinary language meanings as much as possible. The discussion that follows is somewhat abstract nevertheless, but I think it will be helpful for when we go deeper into the specific theories explained and analyzed in chapters 3–7.

Intrinsic value

Intrinsic value refers to something that is a good-in-itself or good for its own sake as opposed to something that is good because of some consequence or other good it might produce. This is also sometimes referred to as non-derivative value, for obvious reasons (Viehoff 2019), or content-independent value, meaning the procedure has value independent of the substantive outcome produced by the procedure. A classic example of intrinsic value might be found in Aristotle's discussion of happiness.[1] People do not value happiness because it brings some other goods, like wealth, health, or success. People want these other goods because they bring happiness. But thinking of democracy as having intrinsic value in the sense of happiness requires that we say much more about what democracy is.

We might think that free and fair elections are good, but does it make sense to think of them as good in themselves like happiness? This does not seem plausible as we can have free and fair elections for dogcatcher in one municipality and a system of appointment of dogcatcher in the next municipality without violating any intrinsic good. The intrinsic value must involve more than the technical procedures of voting and elections that we associate with democratic governance. Most defenders of the intrinsic value of democracy connect it to some other value, for example, justice, equality, or freedom. But then it looks like we value democracy not for its own sake but for the sake of, say, equality unless we want to say that democracy and equality just are the same thing. Furthermore, if something is a good-in-itself, does this mean that it must be good in all circumstances? Some classical philosophers certainly thought so. This seems implausible for democracy even before we specify what we might mean by democracy. There are clearly circumstances and situations (in a crisis, within a family, choosing a spouse) where democratic procedures or values would not be advisable, appropriate, or "good."

These sorts of puzzles have led to abstract and technical discussions about what terms like "value" and "intrinsic" really mean (Korsgaard 1996; Ziliotti 2020) and this, it seems to me, has distracted from questions about why we (real people living in the twenty-first century) might value democracy. We do not need a technically airtight conception of "intrinsic" to grasp the core intuition that procedures that treat people fairly, for example, or with equal respect can have value independent of the outcome of those procedures. We value processes and procedures independent of outcomes all the time from cooking to playing chess. In the case of democracy, however, it is usually not based on pleasure but rather on a moral or ethical good that inheres in the practice, and not the outcome. One might argue that treating people as equals is good; "one person, one vote" treats people as political equals, therefore "one person, one vote" has value independently of whether we vote for sensible laws. I will use the term "intrinsic value" loosely, then, to mean a value that inheres in the procedure itself (for example, that the procedure treats everyone as equal) rather than the outcome. Given the philosophical debates about "intrinsic value," it might appear sensible to refocus on procedure versus outcome, rather than intrinsic versus instrumental, as the main divide in the value of democracy debate. But the terms "procedure" and "outcome" also have their difficulties.

Procedural and proceduralism

Procedural-based theories are often contrasted to outcome-based theories. But here we should be careful. There are very few purely outcome-based views of democracy, and many of these have been discredited. A pure outcome-based view holds that democratic value is entirely determined by a certain set of outcomes, independent of how those outcomes were arrived at. And so, we see, for example, several authoritarian and indeed totalitarian regimes claim the mantle of democratic republics, not because any democratic procedures were followed but because state policy is purported to embody the democratic equality of all citizens and be responsive to their real interests. In December

2021, for example, China released a paper, "China: Democracy that Works," claiming to be a democracy despite having no democratic decision procedures above the local level (Bradsher and Myers 2021).

Within contemporary democratic theory, few people claim that democracy refers exclusively to a set of cultural, social, and economic arrangements independent of governance procedures. We are all proceduralists in the sense that democracy is understood to involve, at a minimum, a set of procedures for making decisions or choosing social and economic arrangements. One might want to add that this way of taking collective decisions is part of or a necessary condition of a democratic way of life (Anderson 2009; Dewey 1954), but few people suggest that we could have a democratic ethos, way of life, or set of democratic social arrangements without democratic procedures of governance. Thus debates about procedure versus outcome are really debates about why we should value (or perhaps be suspicious of) this *way* of making decisions, that is, why we should value democratic *procedures* (however these are defined). We can value the procedures because of some inherent or intrinsic quality of the procedure, as we saw above, or we can value the procedure because it produces the right sort of outcome. But what is the right sort of outcome?

Outcome-based views

The possibility of bad outcomes to democratic decisions introduces a complication to the procedure-versus-outcome debate. Here the question becomes "What standard ought we to use to evaluate outcomes?" Do we work with the procedure itself or introduce some substantive standard independent of the procedure? On this question, a *pure* proceduralist will say that we must go with or be bound by whatever is the outcome of the procedure. On a pure proceduralist view, there are no independent standards to evaluate outcomes and so the right or correct outcome can only be determined by the question of whether the procedures were properly followed. If we think that flipping a coin is the fairest way to take a particular decision, then whatever is the outcome of that flip is the correct outcome, and it is correct only to the extent that the procedure was properly followed, meaning there was no cheating or interfering. In democratic theory, this translates into the view that following the democratic procedure (free and fair elections for example) is the only criterion we have for evaluating the correctness of the outcome. This might seem counterintuitive as we can all think of outcomes, especially in hindsight, that seem obviously disastrous. But pure proceduralists will say that although we all have made such judgments, we do not have a shared or agreed upon set of criteria for identifying good and bad outcomes, and that is precisely why we take votes. For pure proceduralists, democracy is a procedure to decide issues among people who disagree deeply. We will look at this view in more detail in chapter 3.

But I do want to point out a confusion in terminology here. Pure proceduralism is not necessarily the same thing as a procedural-based theory of the value of democracy or what some people just call proceduralism. Pure proceduralism is about the grounds for determining legitimate or good outcomes. Proceduralism is about where to locate the more general value of democracy. This sounds very confusing. Here is an example. I could believe that democracy has value because its procedures respect the equality of citizens but also think that democratic procedures may on occasion (or perhaps often) produce bad decisions according to a procedure-independent standard, say of justice. Free and fair elections or a properly run referendum may result in a majority limiting the rights of a minority, for example, and I believe this to be an unacceptable outcome. These decisions are democratic. But, in this situation, I might insist that we need substantive limits on outcomes in the form of constitutional rights and judicial review. Thus I would endorse a court striking down a democratically enacted law because it is unjust. In this case, I have a procedural-based theory of the value of democracy (value inheres in the procedure), but I am not a pure proceduralist (because simply following the procedure is not enough to say that this was the right outcome). Pure proceduralism adds something quite controversial to proceduralism in its rejection of any procedurally independent standards to evaluate the legitimacy and acceptability of democratic outcomes. For now, it is only important to keep in mind the idea that pure proceduralism is not the same thing as a procedural-based theory of democracy; the first is about evaluating outcomes and the second is about evaluating democracy as a whole.

Instrumental value

Instrumental value means that one values democracy not for its own sake but because it produces some other good. Often that other good will be understood as good outcomes of the procedure in the sense of laws and policies. But not always. Thus outcome-based views of democracy are a subset of the larger category of instrumental value. Here is an example. Some realists argue that democracy has value because it reduces and channels conflict and violence (Przeworski 1999). These realists value democracy for instrumental reasons. If there were another collective decision procedure that did just as good or a better job at channeling and reducing uncertainty, conflict, and violence, then we should or could value that form of decision making, perhaps even more than democracy. But realists generally do not think that we should value democracy because it produces better outcomes (laws and policies) on any substantive or objective standard. We can contrast realists to defenders of epistemic democracy. "Epistemic" is another term that has become central in the discourse on democracy over the last 25 years. Epistemic means relating to knowledge, but in democratic theory it means relating to the quality of the outcome of democratic procedures. One way to think about how to get from epistemic to quality is through the question, "Can democracies produce correct answers to collective problems?" Epistemic democrats tend to answer yes to this question. They value democracy because it produces epistemically sounder laws and policies (truer or more correct) than other types of collective decision procedures (Goodin and Spiekermann 2018). Epistemic democrats are both instrumental *and* outcome based. The difference then is whether one thinks that the good consequences of democratic procedures are tied to claims about performance or whether the good consequences are tied to the fact that democratic procedures channel and mitigate conflict and violence. I will go into all of this in more detail in chapters 4, 5, and 6.

These distinctions will become clearer once we take a closer look at the more detailed arguments that furnish examples of these types of theories. In the following five chapters, I look at two categories of intrinsic/procedural value arguments and three categories of instrumental arguments. But before proceeding, there are a few more things to say about the "value of democracy" debate.

Value versus legitimacy

Legitimacy is a common conceptual lens through which to theorize about democracy. Legitimacy is not identical to value, but in democratic theory they are closely connected. Questions of legitimacy often focus on coercion – what justifies the exercise of coercive power over citizens and subjects. All political rule involves the use of force as part of collective action coordination. Laws, even laws we would follow freely because we agree with them, are in principle coercive as they have sanctions attached to them. Laws are not suggestions; they are requirements. Almost all political rule, certainly all political rule within modern democracies, involves some people having more power to rule (to make and administer the laws) than others. All political rule – both premodern and modern – must involve some account of why this person (and not that person), this group of people (and not that group of people), or this system of rules (and not that system of rules) has the right to coerce and demand obedience. Brute arbitrary force with no attempt to offer justification is always a possibility, but it is rarely stable and often unrecognizable as *political* rule. Of course, some justifications may simply be camouflage for brute arbitrary force. Nevertheless, legitimate ruling is justified ruling or justified to some group. One can understand that justification in descriptive or normative terms. Descriptively, we might be interested in the substantive justifications employed in actual regimes. Empirical social science sometimes approaches legitimacy purely descriptively and asks questions like "How many Saudi Arabians consider their regime legitimate and for what reasons?" without then adding any normative judgments about whether they ought to or have good reasons to consider the regime legitimate. Max Weber, the early twentieth-century German social theorist who first discussed the concept of legitimacy, used scare quotes around the word "legitimacy" to denote this empirical or descriptive focus.

Normative democratic theory, not surprisingly, usually takes the normative perspective. Theorists are interested in what are good, compelling, or moral justifications of power and coercion. Again, not surprisingly, the answer is often (but not always) democracy. Only democratic rule is legitimate (Peter 2009). Although what makes a regime legitimate is a question one can ask about any regime past or present, normative democratic theorists tend to think it is a hard and interesting question only in the modern era. For moderns, the question is not simply what justifies this person or that group possessing coercive power; the question is what justifies this person or that group having coercive power over individuals who are equals to this person or that group. Starting from the modern premise that individuals are not naturally subject to the authority of others but are in some fundamental pre-political sense their own masters makes the job of justifying coercion and power *over others* much more challenging and difficult. Here many people think that only democracy can solve the problem of what justifies the exercise of coercive power between persons who are or who think of themselves as free and equal.

Thus some theorists value democracy because it is legitimate, and it is legitimate because ... and then various reasons are brought forth that justify democracy's claim to legitimacy, for example, because only democracy allows all citizens to have a say in making the laws that coerce them. So here we see that value and legitimacy collapse into each other. Many discussions of legitimacy in the literature are transparently discussions about what makes democracy good and worth protecting. But starting from the question "Why might we value or prefer democracy?" as I do in this book casts a wider net than asking what feature of democracy makes it legitimate. It is possible, for example, to prefer democracy without thinking that only democracies are legitimate. Also, legitimacy focuses on questions of the right to rule and the obligation to obey, often casting the value of democracy in the moral language of liberalism. Thus I frame the justification of democracy in terms of value and not in the first instance in terms of legitimacy. However, I note and discuss when a theory or philosopher understands the value of democracy in terms of legitimacy.

There is another way that the language of value and the language of legitimacy might diverge. For Kantians, the question "Why do I value democracy?" might be misleading in the way that the question "Why do I value doing the morally right thing?" might be misleading. For Kantians, doing the right thing is independent of whether one prefers it or personally values it. Helping someone in distress or dealing honestly with others is just what morality demands of us, and whether we like it, value it, or prefer it is not the important question. For a Kantian, democracy embodies a moral obligation to respect each other's status as free, equal, and co-authors of the laws (Rostbøll 2020). It is wrong for me to impose my will on others; thus democracy is, in this sense, what we owe each other. Asking yourself why I *value* respecting other people's autonomy is, for a Kantian, one question too many and appears to introduce a type of instrumentalism or second-order questioning of moral obligation. I am not unsympathetic to a Kantian approach to democracy, but I do not think that the language of value necessarily undercuts the moral perspective. Furthermore, in the context of democratic crisis, all theories of democracy need to grapple with the question of why real people in the real world will or ought to stick to, uphold, or embrace democracy. Thus even Kantians need to answer the question "Why should we do the right thing?" and not focus exclusively on the question "What is the right thing to do?" Democracy might be the right thing to do, but if it has failed to listen to your grievances or answer your calls for help, then you might need more arguments to stick by it in times of crisis.

Conclusion

I have up to this point resisted offering a definition of democracy. One reason for this is that there is a great deal of variation within contemporary theory about what makes a regime democratic, and this variation is often tied in turn to what one thinks is the value of democracy. As we move through different arguments pertaining to the value of democracy, these will in turn become connected to different definitions of democracy. We will be reviewing philosophical and theoretical arguments that often have other competing philosophical and theoretical arguments in their sights. The audience for these theories is not usually ordinary citizens living in real-world democracies. I try, as much as possible, however, to connect these arguments to reasons that ordinary citizens might have to stick by and defend, or at least not actively scupper, democracy.

3
Equality

IN this chapter, I discuss theories that connect the value of democracy to ways that democratic procedures instantiate equality. It is important to note that all theories of democracy – indeed all definitions of democracy – place political equality somewhere at the center. But not all theories of democracy rely on political equality to furnish the exclusive value of democracy (Beitz 1989). Political equality can be distinguished from, on the one hand, moral or fundamental equality, and, on the other hand, social equality. Moral or fundamental equality involves some recognition of the equal status of all human beings abstracted from their contingent circumstances. Moral equality can be justified in different ways (for example, by appeal to God, self-evident truth, or a "fact of reason"), and it can result in different sets of moral obligations on individuals depending on the fuller moral theory to develop from the fundamental commitment to equality.

Political equality is the core principle of democracy and refers to the equality of persons qua citizens. The justification of political equality may be connected to fundamental equality, but it need not be. Ancient Athenians understood democracy to involve equal political power among citizens, but they did not justify it with a universalist moral concept of equality (Ober 2017). This works the other way too. Christianity embraces a fundamental (eschatological) equality of all human beings, but this did not translate into a defense of political equality until the twentieth century. Many modern conceptions of political equality, however, do rest on some embrace of fundamental moral equality. This is especially true for the first group of democratic theorists I look at who connect democracy to a larger egalitarian theory of social justice.

Social equality has traditionally referred to questions of the distribution of goods, opportunities, or welfare within civil society broadly understood. Recently, however, we see a shift from thinking about social equality in distributional terms to thinking about social equality in relational terms (Anderson 1999). Here status and power become the central categories. The shift to relational equality has brought democracy within the purview of egalitarian social justice theories. I begin with these egalitarians as they make the strongest claim for the intrinsic value of political equality (Brighouse 1996; Griffin 2003; Kolodny 2014a, 2014b; Viehoff 2014).

Egalitarian democrats

Social justice theory was for a long time dominated by questions of fair distribution. This debate tended to be abstract, ideal (what principles would guide the ideal distribution of goods?), and apolitical. Here is a helpful thought experiment to illustrate the political problem (Brighouse 1996). Imagine if you thought an egalitarian distribution of welfare or the opportunities to achieve adequate levels of welfare was by far the most important task facing modern societies. In this situation, what would be wrong if a dictator brought that welfare about? Defenders of relational equality argue that a society that has a fair or egalitarian distribution of goods but is not democratic is not fully just because it fails to address inequalities embedded in status and power, which is to say, it fails to treat each person with an appropriate type of equal respect (Anderson 2009; Brighouse 1996). Levels and distribution of welfare are not irrelevant to status and power, of course, but nor are they sufficient. Egalitarian social justice involves more than the distribution of things; it involves "a society whose members relate to each other as equals, rather than as occupants of different ranks in a social hierarchy" (Ingham 2022: 689).

Beginning in the late 1990s, one sees the growing insistence that democracy is a necessary condition of justice, or political equality is a necessary condition of social equality. Although the democratization of social justice theory developed as a criticism of the distributional questions that had dominated justice theory since the publication of John Rawls's *A Theory of Justice* in 1971, in another way this strand of democratic theory is a continuation of the domination of questions of justice within political philosophy more generally as democracy is folded into justice. Pushed aside are ideas of self-government or popular rule as well as arguments that connect democracy to the satisfaction of popular demands. In their place is the idea that democracy ensures an equality of political power, and that equality of political power has intrinsic value independent of outcomes or performance.

> What is to be said for democracy? Not that it gives people what they want. Not that it realizes a kind of autonomy or self-government. Not that it provides people with the opportunity of valuable activities of civic engagement . . . the justification of democracy rests instead on the fact that democracy is a particularly important constituent of society in which people are related to one another as social equals, as opposed to social inferiors or superiors. (Kolodny 2014b: 287)

This argument is then parasitic on the defense of relational social justice.

"One person one vote," the equal right to run for office, and equal participation rights such as freedom of speech and assembly are "a public affirmation of one's basic social status in the context of jointly deciding the basic ground rules of a common social life" (Griffin 2003: 119). The role of public affirmation is central. Equal voting rights give each citizen an equal say or equal opportunity to influence public decisions, but the public affirmation involved in enshrining and protecting those rights embodies respect for persons in a special way. Flipping a coin (a favorite example in debates about how we value fair procedures) might treat people fairly, impartially, or even equally in a decision procedure. But flipping a coin does not respect each person's judgment in the way that democratic procedures do. The intrinsic value here is not only in the equal distribution of power embodied in the universal franchise, but in the value of the public recognition of equal respect that equal voting rights articulates. Democracy is said to have intrinsic value "on the grounds that the implementation of democratic procedures is an indispensable means of demonstrating communal recognition of equal moral status of citizens" (Brighouse 1996: 119). What is most important about democracy is that it is a decision procedure that distributes political power equally. The inherent value of democratic procedures rests in these two elements then: the equal opportunity to influence decisions, and the public affirmation of respect for the judgments of each citizen.

One might think that the "public affirmation" argument does not seem like a very strong justification for a system of government. Some have suggested that this argument reduces the value of equality to a mere symbolic value (Brennan 2016). But public affirmation of political equality is a necessary condition for any equality of power. The struggle for voting rights is arguably the most important political struggle of the nineteenth and twentieth centuries. The suffragette movement was not simply a demand that women be permitted to influence policy, pursue their interests, or demand that the state respond to their concerns and claims; it was a demand for the public recognition of the equal *status* of women. Status and standing are power. The suffragette struggle, and every struggle to get the vote and to protect the vote, is a struggle for the public respect and recognition that underpins and makes possible equalizing power and influence.

In many ways the "public affirmation" argument has stronger legs to stand on than the "equal opportunity to influence" argument, which introduces questions of the exact nature of the power each citizen has in casting a ballot. The equal opportunity to influence is a negative and individual principle. What this means is that it is about not allowing any other person to have more power than one has. "The concern for democracy is rooted in a concern not to have anyone else 'above' – or, for that matter, 'below' – us: in the aspiration for a society in which none rules over any other" (Kolodny 2014a: 196). This principle does not say how much power individual votes have, only that no one is to have more than anyone else.

One possible weakness of this argument is that in representative democracies, elected officials appear to have more and better opportunity to influence decisions than ordinary citizens. In response, egalitarians introduce a strongly delegated idea of representation in which elected legislators are only channeling majority preferences and so not adding any of their own influence (Kolodny 2014b: 317–18). This view does not tally very well with the observed behavior of elected representatives, but egalitarian theories of democracy are ideal theories about how democracies ought to function.

A second set of criticisms interrogates the fact that the equal opportunity to influence collective decisions requires significant and substantial background conditions to be operationalized. Thus, rather than looking at how the mediation of representatives might skew the equal opportunity to influence, this second set of criticisms looks at the social and economic factors that undermine the formal equality of "one person, one vote." From unequal access to the media and public sphere to economic factors that impact voter turnout, there are many substantive background factors that affect equal opportunity to influence authoritative decisions. Egalitarians are not unaware of this fact, and indeed they focus a great deal on the conditions of social justice that would have to be in place to realize the ideal of equal opportunity to influence. Nico Kolodny admits that "If social equality demands deflatingly little of formal procedures, it demands a great deal, perhaps impossibly much of informal conditions" (Kolodny 2014b: 332). The oversized role of informal background conditions leads to two criticisms. The first is that the focus on background background conditions makes for a thick social justice theory but a thin democratic theory. The formal institutions of equal voting rights, equal opportunity to run for office, and freedom of speech and assembly are adequate political procedures to realize political equality, and egalitarians do not go beyond these basic principles in thinking about democracy. Thus egalitarians never interrogate status quo democratic institutions very deeply (Bagg forthcoming). They do not entertain the possibility, developed by more radical theories of democracy, that the formal procedures of modern representative democracy might contain anti-egalitarian or oligarchic biases (Landemore 2020; see chapter 9).

The final problem with this view is not so much a criticism as an observation. According to egalitarians, democracy can only deliver on its egalitarian promise, which is to say create the equal opportunity to influence decisions, within a system that has achieved significant levels of social justice. The problem according to some critics is that modern democracies not only have not achieved adequate levels of social justice, but many of them also appear to be backsliding with increasing levels of inequality. If this is the case then egalitarian theories of democracy, rather than articulating the core value of democracy, articulate why no existing democracy has achieved or can achieve that value.

Equality and disagreement

I want to briefly return to our social justice dictator and to the question, what would be wrong about handing power to such an actor if one thought that justice and well-being were the most important ends for humans to pursue? One answer, outlined in the previous section, is that such a system would neither treat citizens with equal respect nor publicly affirm that respect and so would not be just. Another and perhaps more common answer questions the premise of the thought experiment. Is it possible that any one actor could ever be in possession of the truth about what social justice requires? Is there only one answer to what social justice requires? The problem here is that, although we might all embrace the ideal of social justice, we disagree fundamentally about which social and economic arrangements meet that standard of social justice. This is the problem of pluralism and disagreement, and it offers a second set of reasons for the inherent value of a procedure that treats people fairly and as equals.

The core of this argument goes something like this: "Democracy is what equal respect (procedurally) requires when there is thick reasonable disagreement about what equal respect substantially requires" (Valentini 2012: 193). There are several ways that this core idea can be elaborated and defended. Here I look at three: Thomas Christiano's egalitarian view, Jeremy Waldron's deep pluralist view, and in the final section the mutual justification view and the special role of public reason in addressing disagreement and pluralism. None of these theories begins with or endorses any form of skepticism about the truth or embraces a metaphysical principle of value pluralism. The issue is not whether there is truth or whether there are multiple incommensurable values in the world, but whether we can agree on the truth or agree on values. In addition, all these views understand that the disagreement that poses a problem for which democracy is the solution is not synonymous with any or all disagreement that we might meet in the empirical world. For example, every society has a certain number of mentally ill or just irrationally contrary people who will not agree to anything. We need to respect these people as persons, but to the extent that their disagreement is arbitrary we need not accommodate their disagreement. Thus the disagreement that matters is what is often called reasonable disagreement.

Reasonable disagreement has an epistemic and a moral meaning. John Rawls articulates one of the most influential epistemic meanings through the idea of "the burdens of judgment." Even if there were one right way to proceed or a correct answer, there are "many hazards involved in the correct (and conscientious) exercise of our powers of reason and judgment in the ordinary course of political life" (Rawls 2005: 56). Questions about what we ought to do or how we should organize society are complex with many potential points of disagreement from the interpretation of evidence to different moral starting points. Absent coercion or domination, disagreement is inevitable and unavoidable, and this causes a challenge for collective action between individuals who consider themselves free and equal. Here the assumption is that thoroughly reasonable and rational people of goodwill who are committed to impartiality in judgment (in other words, even idealized reasoners) will still disagree honestly about many questions that are relevant for making decisions for a complex society.

The second way reasonable disagreement is used introduces a normative or moral dimension. If we understand democracy as a decision procedure among equals to choose rules that will govern their collective lives and honor and respect that equal status, then certain arguments or claims seem off the table from the very beginning. So, for example, arguing that "some are worth less than others or that the interests of one group are to count for less than those of others" (Cohen 1997a: 415) is out from the start – it would be unreasonable to expect that such arguments could be the basis of any fair system, just as it would be unreasonable to expect obviously false claims (the earth is flat) to be the basis of public policy. Or so the normative argument goes. Thomas Christiano and Jeremy Waldron embrace some version of the epistemic argument (even though they are hesitant to embrace the language of reasonability) but reject any strong version of the normative argument, while mutual justification theorists embrace both versions of reasonableness in their theory. But this needs more explanation.

Thomas Christiano defends the value of democracy as part of a larger egalitarian view of justice. Thus his theory exhibits similarities with the egalitarian views I discussed in the preceding section, but he adds disagreement as a central feature to his argument – something that relational egalitarians usually do not do. Relational egalitarians argue that democracy, understood as the instantiation and public affirmation of equal power and status of every citizen, is a necessary condition of a just social order. Hierarchy is the enemy of justice (Kolodny 2023). Christiano begins his defense of democracy not with a relational view of equality but with the claim that justice requires "the public realization of equal advancement of interest" (2004: 269). Unequal advancement of interests is the enemy of justice in Christiano's view. This principle yields the intuition that laws and policies ought to advance the interests of each member of society equally and, further, that it must be publicly known or acknowledged that laws and policies advance the equal interest of all. It is not simply that justice should be done, but also that justice should be shown to be done to fulfill the principle that each person is treated equally and sees and recognizes that she is treated equally.

Christiano concedes that widespread and ubiquitous disagreement poses a challenge for this standard of justice. We are fallible in our judgments, we are subject to biases in our thinking, and we often fail to be impartial in weighing our interests against others.[1] To complicate this picture of judgment, we know these things about ourselves and others, so we are unlikely to agree that the outcomes of our collective decision procedures do in fact treat everyone's interests equally. The problem then is not simply that we may and most certainly will disagree about, say, which tax system is the most just. That disagreement makes it impossible for the democratically chosen tax system (even if it was the most just on some independent standard) to stand as a public affirmation of the principle of the equal advancement of everybody's interest: "Given these natural biases, and given the prevalence of disagreement about justice, no citizen wants merely to be treated in accordance with someone else's conception of equality. Each has an interest in being treated as an equal, in at least some fundamental respects, in a way that he can agree that he is being treated as an equal" (Christiano 2004: 273).

The procedural equality of democratic decision making, as well as the public recognition of certain basic liberal rights, is uniquely suited to satisfy this interest. Unlike substantive policies and laws, the formal recognition of procedural equality (equal voting rights, etc.) can be a point of collective recognition of equal treatment. It would appear at first sight that in this argument democracy has instrumental rather than intrinsic value as it is a means to achieve justice (Campbell 2011). But here the adjective "uniquely" is important. We each have, according to Christiano, a fundamental interest in being publicly treated and affirmed as equals. *Only* democratic decision-making procedures and basic liberal rights can do that. No other institutions can do that. Furthermore, he is very clear that disagreement means that outcomes of democratic procedures can never achieve such publicity. It is important to note that disagreement is primarily focused on whether the outcomes of democratic procedures (laws and policies) treat people as equals or *establish* justice (Christiano 2008: 251). Christiano appears confident that we can agree that the procedures of democracy, as well as basic liberal rights, treat us as equals. In other words, while we cannot agree when or how justice is substantively established, we can and do agree on a formal conception of justice as equal treatment of interests.

Christiano's defense of democracy exposes an interesting tension in democratic theory that we will return to throughout the book. On the one hand, Christiano offers a very robust defense of the intrinsic value of democratic procedures, but, on the other hand, that defense is premised on the claim that democracy cannot deliver outcomes that could ever be seen to establish justice or be recognized as pursuing everybody's interest. This places the intrinsic defense of democracy at odds with traditional ideals of democracy as self-rule or rule by the people. Democratic outcomes can never succeed in being recognized as equally in everybody's interest. Any claim that we should value democracy because outcomes are the "*people*'s will" or the result of *self*-government meets with the argument that outcomes only garner the agreement of temporary majorities and never the whole people understood as each and every person. Outcomes can never instantiate equality, and democracy is to be valued precisely because it instantiates equality. This leads Christiano (and many other equality-focused theorists) to be skeptical of any defense of democracy that leans too heavily toward the claim that democracy is a form of self-government through which a collective self could see itself in and identify with the outcomes of democratic decision-making procedures (Christiano 1996: 43). What we will see as we move through various arguments is that strong concepts of political equality are in tension with strong concepts of the "people" as the agent of self-government.

Deep pluralists

A question that confronts all disagreement democrats is how deep does disagreement go? Deep pluralists[2] like Jeremy Waldron and Richard Bellamy take issue with all justice-centered defenses of democracy (this would include Christiano and the relational egalitarians) by pointing out that people disagree about fundamental questions of justice just as much as other questions (Bellamy 2007; Waldron 1999). Deep pluralists want to defend the procedural value of democracy without endorsing any (potentially controversial) theory of justice. The puzzle to be solved here, what Waldron calls "the circumstances of politics" (Waldron 1999: 108), is how to choose a collective course of action among people who sincerely disagree about what that course of action ought to be. He compares three solutions[3]: flipping a coin, handing the decision over to a "decider," or taking a majority decision in which everyone has one vote. Only the last "embodies a principle of respect for each person in the processes by which we settle on a view to be adopted as *ours* even in the face of disagreement" (1999: 109). The democratic solution to the problem posed by the circumstances of politics then must be able to meet the twin demands of respecting individual judgments and producing a course of action that we could describe as "ours." This shifts the focus from a public affirmation of equal status embodied in the equal voting rights (Christiano) to the way majority-rule voting specifically solves the problem of taking a collective decision among equals who disagree.

One might want to argue that if pluralism goes all the way down, then won't there be disagreement about the value of equal respect to begin with? The circumstances of politics are our circumstances which Waldron takes to include citizens who generally think of themselves as entitled to equal respect. In this sense, pluralism does not go all the way down. But Waldron would also stress that some decision procedure must be adopted, and majority decision is the thinnest, least demanding, and fairest, given the circumstances. Although deep pluralists often reject the language of intrinsic moral value of procedures as this seems to introduce substantive values about which we could disagree, they value democracy on purely procedural grounds. There are no agreed upon substantive criteria to evaluate the goodness or justice of the outcome independent of the fact that it was reached through fair procedures. It is important to note that deep pluralists do not value democratic procedures because they instantiate and affirm a deeper fundamental equality of persons; they value universal franchise coupled with majority rule because it solves the problem of a fair decision procedure among people *who think of themselves as equal* and who disagree deeply about the best or right thing to do. Thus majority rule plays a central role in this argument in a way that it did not for the egalitarians who focused on voting rights and not how the votes might be counted.

The deep pluralist argument then undercuts any more robust ideas of what equal respect might mean or the possibility of limiting majority outcomes because they undermine equal respect (Beitz 1989). Thus some deep pluralists are *pure* proceduralists in the sense that outcomes are legitimate to the extent and only to the extent that a fair procedure was followed. Or, to put this in more concrete terms, all we have are majority-decision procedures to resolve our disputes fairly. Introducing, for example, judicial oversight of majority decisions is to introduce a substantive set of limitations about which people disagree. Deep pluralists ask why judges should have the last say when their procedures no more overcome disagreement than do majority voting procedures (Waldron 2006). Although deep pluralists and egalitarian democrats both value democratic procedures because they embody equal respect, they begin from very different starting points, the former from a claim that we cannot agree on questions of the good or justice, while the latter with a robust set of principles of justice. The most controversial aspect of deep pluralism is its embrace of pure proceduralism and rejection of judicial review.

Mutual justification

I turn now to the third way that the acknowledgment of disagreement and pluralism shapes a democratic theory. In this view, disagreement points to the special role of mutual justification as the instantiation of equal respect. Egalitarians identify the inherent value of democracy in the way that equal voting rights publicly affirm the moral status of citizens. Deep pluralists identify the inherent value of democracy in the way that majority rule is a fair way to take a decision among equals who disagree. Mutual justification democrats identify the inherent value of democracy in the way "deliberating and listening to one another's reasons [expresses] respect for each other as rational persons" (Valentini 2012: 193).

Mutual justification introduces several new ideas to our discussion of democracy. The first is that the procedures thought to instantiate equality and give value to democracy expand beyond formal voting and participation rights. Suppose we are twenty people shipwrecked on a deserted island. We need to make some collective decisions and coordinate our actions. Why should we choose democracy as the way to do that? Up till now we have understood democracy in generic and institutionally underspecified terms as "one person, one vote," the equal right to run for office, and equal participation rights, such as freedom of speech and assembly. So far, the argument has been that if we are the sort of people who think of ourselves as equal (and modern citizens generally are those sorts of people), we will choose democracy because it is fair, not because it necessarily comes to the best solution every time. The fairness among equals or the fairness among equals who disagree has its focal point in "one person, one vote" within the institutional framework of free and fair elections.

Mutual justification theories expand democratic procedures to include processes of deliberation and public discourse. Now most theories of democracy (but by no means all) value deliberation and discussion, and the theories we have looked at so far are no exception. Generally, having a well-informed electorate that has developed their opinions in respectful dialogue with fellow citizens is thought to be something positive that ought to be encouraged. We would want our twenty shipwrecked founders to talk and discuss the best options available to them before voting. But often the value of deliberation is understood instrumentally and tied to more or less sensible or thoughtful outcomes. Both Christiano and Waldron, for example, argue that democracy is better when there is good deliberation between citizens. But they defend deliberation as being instrumental to sound outcomes and reducing mistakes. For both, the inherent or intrinsic value is found in equal status as voters in a system of free and fair elections. Mutual justification theorists shift the locus of value to deliberation and make voting instrumental to the value of mutual justification. Here our shipwrecked proto-citizens treat each other with respect and as equal citizens when they exchange reasons (of a certain kind) and offer justifications (of a certain kind) for the proposals they make for organizing their collective life. Votes are eventually taken because unanimity is difficult to achieve, but the democratic moment inheres in a type of mutual problem solving in which each member treats fellow members as equal partners in the process. Our thought experiment of the twenty shipwrecked founders illustrates that we could imagine them coming to an essentially democratic decision (in the sense of equal influence, participation, and cooperation) in which no votes are taken at all. Here we would imagine each person's proposals, suggestions, and arguments would get an equal airing and consideration; the conversation would proceed respectfully; and at the end of the day the group would come to a consensus about the best course of action and everybody would feel that they were treated as an equal in the process. This is an idealized thought experiment even for a small group of twenty, and once the numbers are scaled up and one introduces complexity, then voting becomes a necessary mechanism of closure. What is important here is that cooperative and discursive collective action problem solving among equals is the core of the democratic ideal and voting is only one institutional mechanism used to operationalize it.

On the mutual justification view, equality shifts its locus from being primarily a status that each possesses in relation to everyone else to inhering in a reciprocal exchange of reasons between citizens (Gutmann and Thompson 1996: 52). For egalitarian democrats, citizens need to see their equal status publicly affirmed in formal procedures and institutions. For mutual justification democrats, citizens need to see their equal status affirmed by fellow citizens in a process of public justification – or in the sorts of reasons that are used to justify public policy. Does this mean that mutual justification theorists see voting *rights* as simply instrumentally necessary when we scale up? No. The public recognition of political equality enshrined in voting rights is essential as the foundation and prerequisite for the more robust view of full political equality embodied in mutual justification. There can be no mutual justification without the recognition of equal status, and that recognition needs to be articulated and protected in constitutions. It is not voting rights that are instrumentalized. It is elections and vote processes that punctuate the ongoing processes of mutual justification that lose their central role. The mutual justification view, then, is not an alternative to the equal status view but rather builds and extends that view.

The equal respect embodied in mutual justification is often a central element in theories of deliberative democracy. Deliberative democracy has become a very broad category, however, that encompasses a growing diversity of views (Bächtiger et al. 2018; Elstub and McLaverty 2014). At the core of all theories of deliberative democracy is some idea that public debate among equals is what democratic decision making is all about. But from there, theories diverge in radical ways. Many theories of deliberative democracy, for example, do not defend democracy on the exclusive grounds that equality is instantiated in the procedures of well-ordered deliberation and public reason giving (even though they almost always argue that equality is so instantiated). In addition, some theories also introduce ideas of freedom and collective autonomy (which we look at in the next chapter) as well as epistemic arguments regarding good outcomes (which we cover in chapter 6). Here, however, I focus narrowly on theories that begin from the challenge posed for collective decision making by reasonable disagreement among equals and the way mutual justification proposes to address that challenge. As I have suggested, this group of theories is much influenced by John Rawls and especially his ideal of public reason (Boettcher 2020; Quong 2010; Schwartzman 2011).

Public reason and disagreement

Earlier I noted that for mutual justification theorists, citizens treat each other with respect and as equal citizens when they exchange reasons (of a certain kind) and offer justifications (of a certain kind) for the proposals they make for organizing their collective life. Now we need to ask what kind of reasons. John Rawls offers a very powerful illustration of why simply requiring each participant to explain and justify their preferred course of action, while it might show a minimal level of respect, is not enough (Rawls 2005: 447). In 1553, Michael Servetus was burnt at the stake for heresy in Geneva on John Calvin's watch. Rawls remarks that Servetus no doubt understood the reasons Calvin called for his execution (and there is some evidence that Calvin might have even communicated those to Servetus in correspondence). But offering reasons for religious persecution of one group of citizens is not a reasonable proposal to make in a process of mutual justification among equals. This introduces the normative idea of reasonable that I mentioned briefly above. It would be unreasonable for a minority of our deserted islanders to propose that the majority become their slaves (even if they offered detailed justification for that proposal), given that they began from the premise that they were each as free and equal as everyone else. "Public justification," or what I have been calling mutual justification, "is not simply valid reasoning, but argument addressed to others" (Rawls 2005: 465). But what constitutes "argument *addressed* to others"?

The ideal of mutual justification suggests that democratic problem solving under modern conditions of disagreement and pluralism involves a special sort of conversation. In this conversation, "participants regard one another as equals; they aim to defend and criticize institutions and programs in terms and considerations that others have reason to accept, given the fact of reasonable pluralism" (Cohen 1997a: 413). Gutmann and Thompson incorporate this idea into their conception of deliberative democracy by insisting that citizens "appeal to reasons or principles that can be shared by fellow citizens . . . moral reasoning is in this way mutually acceptable" (1996: 55). Thus "addressed to others" here means shared or acceptable to others. Christiano thinks that we can agree that formal political equality treats each of us as equals; Waldron thinks that we can agree that majority voting rule is a fair way to take a decision; and Cohen, Gutmann, and Thompson, drawing on John Rawls's ideal of public reason, introduce a more demanding idea that we might be able to find substantive common ground within or despite pluralism in the types of reason we give each other in the processes of mutual justification. Showing respect for each other in this context means that we each seek reasons and justifications for our proposals that avoid or do not rely on claims, beliefs, or values about which there is fundamental disagreement. Public reason seeks islands of substantive agreement amid the general condition of pluralism and disagreement. Rawls thought that we could find those islands in principles of political liberalism by which he meant general principles of constitutional democracy detached from any controversial or disputed metaphysical or religious underpinnings.

The solution to disagreement among equals then is restraint. We show respect for each other as equals (we exercise a "duty of civility" to use Rawls's term) by refraining from appealing to arguments and justifications that draw on philosophies, religious views, or principles that are not shared. The pool of acceptable reasons ought to be drawn from widely shared principles and values embedded in the liberal constitutional order but detached from controversial claims about truth or metaphysics.

Why do we value democracy according to this argument? We value democracy because it embodies and instantiates equal respect for persons. How does democracy do that? Certainly, by enshrining and protecting rights of political participation. But even more so by encouraging and requiring a certain type of public justification involving a restraint of reason. Thus public reason adds a substantive ethic of citizenship to the procedural defense of democracy. This ethic is then connected to a principle of legitimacy. Legitimacy is about the justification of coercive power. Legitimacy within a liberal democratic framework is about justifying the exercise of coercive power among persons who are equal and free. A traditional answer to the question was consent. Consent is a notoriously tricky concept (I take this up in the next chapter). Rawls replaces consent with justification. "Our exercise of political power is fully proper only when it is exercised in accordance with a constitution, the essentials of which all citizens as free and equal may reasonably be expected to endorse in light of principles and ideals acceptable to their common human reasons" (Rawls 2005: 137). Joshua Cohen makes this a central plank in his democratic theory: "the deliberative conception of democracy is organized around an ideal of political justification. According to this ideal, to justify the exercise of collective political power is to proceed on the basis of a free public reasoning among equals" (Cohen 1997a: 412).

The language of mutual or public justification is a widely used idiom in contemporary democratic theory, especially, as I have noted, in deliberative democracy, and there is no doubt that Rawls is central in bringing about a "justification turn" in contemporary political philosophy (Chambers 2010). But Rawls's own version of public reason, with the central role played by restraint on reasons in search of shared foundations, is controversial. The most common criticism of this view is that, despite taking its starting point from the problem of disagreement among equals, its solution would involve restricting the pool of acceptable reasons in such a way as to fail to respect pluralism and disagreement. This criticism in effect suggests that there are no public reasons that we are all likely to find acceptable, and insisting that citizens refrain from appealing to their deeply held beliefs and convictions fails to treat everyone equally. A second criticism is that, if there are any genuinely public reasons, the pool of such reasons is likely to be small, abstract, and indeterminate. Perhaps we can assume that all reasonable people who are generally committed to liberal democracy would agree with or find acceptable the principle "everyone's interest should count equally." But how far is that going to get us in actually solving public policy challenges? It will exclude some obviously problematic solutions, but it is hardly a principle of democratic decision making. A third criticism is that because public reason involves drawing arguments from a pool of shared political principles, this ties public discourse too closely to the status quo and disqualifies many radical types of arguments and proposals. Finally, there is debate about where and when public reason ought to kick in. Rawls hinted that public reason was most appropriate for the reasoning of courts, especially constitutional courts. This would suggest that it is not part of a democratic theory at all. Others have argued that all democratic debate should be guided by public reason (Quong 2010) or that ordinary citizens should be reasoning like constitutional judges and employ public reason when they deliberate (Lafont 2020). But Rawls's ideal of public reason is by no means a defining feature of democratic theories that place mutual justification and deliberation at the center of democracy and at the center of treating each other as equals.

The biggest challenge facing mutual justification conceptions of equality is to translate this view into a concrete realistic picture of democracy. The equal status of voting rights is a more tangible, measurable, and operationalizable ideal of political equality than is the idea of mutual justification. The most common criticism of mutual justification conceptions of equality is precisely how far that ideal seems from the way citizens and elite talk to each other and champion their causes in the political public sphere. In chapter 9, we will look at some democratic theory that argues that political parties at their best are agents of public reason. But these views are aspirational and do not describe the slide into polarized discourse so evident in contemporary public spheres.

Conclusion

In this chapter, I have canvased democratic theory that starts from a principle of political equality and argues that the core value to be attached to democracy is that it is a decision process in which we each have an equal standing, and this reflects our modern embrace of a principle of moral equality. We might be tempted to trade some of that equality in for efficiency, economic growth, or law and order. But this would be a bad and costly deal. It would be a bad deal because it is a chimera to think that any alternative decision procedure can promise surefire successful political outcomes. Furthermore, there is no agreed upon standard of what counts as a good outcome. It is a costly deal because equality has an intrinsic moral value, the loss of which would be a betrayal of our deepest moral commitments.

But it is one thing to think that political equality is a necessary condition of democracy and another to think that only political equality by itself can justify democracy and by extension keep citizens committed to democracy. At some point, failure to produce results will turn people against democracy, and people will be willing to trade in some political equality for the promise of prosperity and security. But also, for many people, democracy contains the aspiration to popular control and self-government. We value universal franchise not only because it is an affirmation of our equal standing but also because it is a means to have our voice heard and to govern ourselves. Political equality by itself does not add up to popular rule if by popular rule we mean ruling in some meaningful sense. Voting is not ruling. Or perhaps more accurately, voting is not obviously governing, and so we need a story about how and why equal voting rights might add up to self-government or rule by the people. This is the topic of the next chapter.

4
Freedom

I turn now to theories that still focus on the inherent value of procedures, but which bring questions of freedom and self-government to the fore. Here equality is not only understood as equal moral status, but also as equally free. We are in some fundamental pre-political sense equally our own masters. No one is a natural ruler or subject. One of the puzzles we encountered in our discussion of equality was why we should care about the method of choosing policies so long as those policies furthered justice, equality, and the common good. Introducing freedom into the equation creates a different set of puzzles. These have to do with the coercive nature of law and how we can reconcile that coercion with our status as equally free. The dilemma that these theories focus on is the one famously articulated by Jean-Jacques Rousseau in Book I, chapter vi, of *On the Social Contract*: to "find a form of association which defends and protects with all common forces the person and goods of each associate, and by means of which each one, while uniting with all, nevertheless obeys only himself and remains as free as before" (Rousseau 1987: 24). For the group of theories that I look at in this chapter, democracy is the answer to this puzzle, but the answer is complicated.

Freedom as authorship

Rousseau argued (and many democratic theorists follow him, at least at the very general level) that to preserve our freedom while living under laws, it was necessary to give ourselves the laws. When I decide to follow a rule – no snacking after dinner, for example – I am still free when I abide by this rule and stick to it, even if I feel like I would prefer a snack. Some might say I am freer when I follow a rule I have deliberately and thoughtfully chosen for myself, rather than being pulled and pushed by fleeting desires and appetites or being directed by a superior or a master. Freedom here then has more to do with *my* choosing or willing an action, rather than with questions of interference or restrictions on my actions. This view of freedom is often called autonomy. Scaling up and thinking analogously, to be free (to exercise political autonomy) we need to adopt a system of laws that we can say we gave ourselves. But is this possible? It appears to require that all laws be unanimously and continually endorsed by all citizens. And this we know to be impossible. So now the puzzle becomes how to scale up the idea of self-determination and autonomy from the individual level to the group and political level. Indeed, the attendant difficulty of thinking about democracy as a form of collective self-determination analogous to individual self-determination is one of the reasons why equality democrats (as well as realists but for different reasons) have abandoned the ideal of self-rule or self-government in favor of fairness and equality in the decision process as the strongest defense of democracy (Christiano 1996: 42).

Authorship of the laws introduces a new element to our discussion of democracy and how we value democratic procedures. To be free in the sense of autonomy, we need to be able to recognize the laws that "coerce" us as laws we have given ourselves (Rostbøll 2015a). This now connects democratic procedures to outcomes. To be free, there must be a correspondence between my opinions, interests, desires, and the content of the laws and policies that are enacted into law – it must be as if I willed or chose them myself. This correspondence has two dimensions. The first is content or substance. To be free, I must identify with the content of the laws. As Cristina Lafont notes, "a permanent *disconnect* between the interests, reasons, and ideas of citizens and the actual laws and policies that they are bound to obey would alienate them from the political community" (Lafont 2020: 19). But simple identification is not enough because a skilled and attuned autocrat might be able to enact laws that I identify with, even laws that I would have also enacted if I had had the chance. Thus, in addition to identifying with the content, I must also be able to see a connection between my participation in the democratic procedures and the outcomes. As an individual, I am not free if my captor anticipates my every wish. As a democratic people, we are also not free if there is simple correspondence between our interests and outcomes. Both requirements (correspondence and agency), but especially the second, face many obstacles when we set out to think about how we can all be (equally) free under conditions of complexity and pluralism. Even though to be free involves a connection between outcome and procedure, the *value* of democracy still inheres in the *procedure* which facilitates that freedom and not in the outcome (Rostbøll 2015a: 273). Thus the argument is not that equal freedom results in the best laws; the argument is that equal freedom results in laws that we give ourselves. This proceduralism, as we will see below, significantly departs from Rousseau's answer to his own question, however.

I look at two examples of the freedom argument. The first group, which I call Kelsenian proceduralism, has historically identified itself as procedural democracy. Following many insights first articulated by the famous mid-twentieth-century jurist and political thinker Hans Kelsen, we see the defense of parliamentary democracy as the system which maximizes the freedom of all. Contestatory proceduralism is the second freedom-centered argument, and I focus primarily on Philip Pettit's neo-republican theory of non-domination as well as Pierre Rosanvallon's idea of "counter-democracy" as a way to maintain democratic freedom.

Hans Kelsen and the freedom to be wrong

The first group of democratic theorists self-identify as endorsing a procedural view of democracy that focuses on freedom as the value that inheres in the decision procedure, independent of the outcome. Nadia Urbinati, whose democratic theory is prominent in contemporary debates, is a proceduralist in this sense. As she draws some of her inspiration from the work of Hans Kelsen, it is with Kelsen, who is having a small renaissance in contemporary democratic theory, that I begin (Invernizzi-Accetti 2017; Saffon and Urbinati 2013; Schupmann 2022; Urbinati 2014; Wolkenstein 2019). Although Kelsen and Kelsenians refer to this view as *the* procedural view of democracy, all views canvased so far could equally claim that moniker. To distinguish this view from other forms of proceduralism, I refer to it as Kelsenian proceduralism. This view has two defining features. The first is the centrality of parliamentary democracy and the important functions played by parties and elections in instantiating freedom. Parliamentary democracy is sometimes used as a synonym for representative democracy. But citizens can be represented in many ways; Kelsenians always place a multi-party legislature at the center of the story of democracy rather than, say, a directly elected executive. The second defining feature I discuss is the strong opposition to any outcome-based view of democracy. I begin with this second feature.

The proceduralism of Kelsenians takes aim at all claims that democracy should be valued because it produces good results or that it can be evaluated against an independent standard of, say, the common good. The good of freedom, it is said, is independent of whether one uses that freedom in good or valuable ways. As an individual, I may value my freedom even though I know that I might very well make mistakes when exercising that freedom. The same can be said for democratic freedom on this view. "Procedures are legitimately democratic because they deliver what they are made for: to protect the freedom of its members to produce 'wrong' decisions" (Urbinati 2014: 98; see also Saffon and Urbinati 2013: 448).

Kelsen's proceduralism was developed in the shadow of Rousseau and the potential (some would say actual) misappropriation of Rousseau by totalitarian regimes. Contemporary Kelsenians also place their proceduralism in contrast with a certain reading of Rousseau (Invernizzi-Accetti and Oskian 2022: 5). Rousseau, as we have seen, was concerned about freedom, and he envisioned the solution to the "equally free" puzzle as a political regime in which citizens were equally the authors of the laws and so *self*-government was the only type of government that was consistent with freedom. This, as I have also mentioned, is a very powerful ideal still driving some democratic theory today.

Rousseau's next moves, however, are more controversial. The moves involve two claims. The first is that citizens themselves must be the authors of the laws, not their representatives. Electing representatives to make the laws amounts to passing one's freedom to someone else. In a much-beloved passage (primarily because it is a wonderful example of Rousseau's wit), Rousseau quips, "The English people believes itself to be free. It is greatly mistaken; it is free only during the election of members of Parliament. Once they are elected, the populace is enslaved; it is nothing. The use the English people makes of that freedom in the brief moments of its liberty certainly warrants their losing it" (Rousseau 1987: 74). Kelsen and Kelsenians reject this insistence on direct democracy as unfeasible and undesirable and reconstruct self-government as a representative system of parliamentary democracy.

The second Rousseauian claim refers to the difficult doctrine of the general will. When I give myself a rule, say, no snacking in between mealtimes, I do so presumably because I think it would be good for me not to snack between meals. We do not give ourselves rules to follow because we think following the rules will be bad for us. Here, then, is the idea that rules that I give myself and, by extension, laws we give ourselves are intended to promote our good. That is the purpose of laws, one might say. In the former case, it is what is a good for me and in the latter case it is what is a good for all, or the common good. Rousseau argued that when citizens directly legislate, they ought to aim for the common good. Now Rousseau admitted that real people coming together in an assembly to legislate might not always get it right. This was especially likely if they were being driven by selfish or factional interests. But the assumption that people can be mistaken about the common good implies that there is an objectively correct conception of the common good that democratic procedures should seek to produce. Rousseau articulated this objectively correct common good with the concept of the general will. The general will captures the ideal of the people willing or choosing what is objectively in the common good. All legislation should aim to produce a general will and not merely the aggregation of particular wills.

What happened to freedom in this picture? Citizens come together and vote for laws. Those votes are governed by majority rule. Does that mean that the outvoted minority is not free?

Rousseau's answer to that question is very controversial. If the outcome of the vote were really and truly an instantiation of the common good (really an expression of the general will), then one could assume that those who failed to vote for it were simply mistaken about what was in their objectively true interest. In this case, obeying a law that you did not vote for, but which is really and truly in the community's best interest, is being "forced to be free." Here is an analogy. I might think that overindulging in food and drink makes me happy and so is good. But nutritional science suggests that I am mistaken and that such behavior will only lead to bad consequences. Here we might want to say, if I could see the truth of the matter, I would never choose the life of the hard-drinking gourmand. An external authority that forces me on a path of sobriety and moderation, then, could be described as forcing me onto a path that I would have freely chosen myself if I had really thought properly about it. In this way, Rousseau wants to claim that if laws are really and truly in everybody's interest, then they are what everyone would choose if they were thinking from the proper perspective or with the proper information. This way of reading the general will implies that we value democratic procedures because or to the extent that they produce laws that indeed reflect the common good. This, then, would be an instrumental defense of democracy and suggest that there is a procedure-independent standard of common good. There are other interpretations of Rousseau that do not make him out to be an instrumentalist in this way (Cohen 2010), but Kelsenians often read him this way.

Kelsen set out to rescue freedom from the path that leads to "forced to be free," and this begins for him in a rejection of any claim that there is or could be an objective truth about the common good (Kelsen 2013). If there were such a thing as an objective common good, then its discovery would warrant bypassing democratic procedures. Kelsen embraced value relativism and insisted that there was no objective common good; contemporary Kelsenians tend not to embrace Kelsen's value relativism and instead fall back on the claim that we cannot agree on the common good. Thus they appeal to pluralism rather than making a philosophical truth claim: "Every individual's equal participation in fair and competitive elections for selecting political representatives and thereby contributing to the production of decisions via majority rule [is] the best way of respecting equal liberty in a context of pluralism and dissent" (Saffon and Urbinati 2013: 442).

So far, the Kelsenian view does not sound too much different than our disagreement democrats, and indeed there is a great deal of overlap between, say, Jeremy Waldron and Nadia Urbinati (Lafont 2020). But there are two important differences. First, Kelsen and contemporary Kelsenians invoke the value of freedom in a strong value-laden way that differentiates them from Waldron, who, when he invokes values, stays with equality. It also differentiates Kelsenians from minimalist procedural views often associated with Schumpeter (discussed in the next chapter) that eschew any discussion of inherent value and offer realist defenses of democracy. Second, Kelsenians are proceduralist but not pure proceduralists. They do not argue that democratic procedures are all we have to go on when evaluating outcomes. They endorse the intervention of constitutional courts and admit that some outcomes, although democratic, can be bad for democracy and so warrant constraining (Urbinati 2014).

So how do democratic procedures deliver on the freedom ideal – the ideal that I am only free when I follow laws or norms that I have given myself? Kelsen's answer is to acknowledge that this ideal is unrealizable under conditions of mass democracy and pluralism, and so we need to adopt a representative system governed by party democracy and a majority principle that can approximate the ideal of freedom. We do not need to give up on the idea of the common good, but we must allow that there will be disagreement. Thus, in Kelsenian proceduralism, "the specific conception of the common good that ought to prevail and therefore be translated into public policy is the one that is simultaneously constructed and identified through the democratic procedures of parliamentary deliberation and electoral competition" (Bickerton and Invernizzi-Accetti 2017: 189). "The popular will is defined – in a necessarily fallible and approximate way – through the process of political representation established by legally instituted procedures" (Invernizzi-Accetti and Oskian 2022: 5).

Kelsen's defense of the majority principle differs from Waldron's defense. Kelsen argues that the majority principle cannot be justified on a simple appeal to equality. Simply adding up equally weighted votes is a crude quantitative principle that amounts to "might is right." To maximize freedom, one needs to find a decision rule that maximizes the number of individuals who are free or, in other words, maximizes the number of people who can say that they were the authors of the law. Simple majority is such a rule. "Majority rule maximizes freedom because it chooses decisions that satisfy the opinion of the greater number of participants, while offering those who disagree the easiest path to change those decisions and provide power-limitation mechanisms that protect them in the meantime" (Saffon and Urbinati 2013: 459). Any threshold above 50 percent would give power to a minority to veto and so have their wills prevail. Simple majority ensures that "as many as possible shall be free" (Kelsen 1955: 25). Kelsen argues that in a democracy, outcomes correspond to the will of the majority, which in turn maximizes the number of people who are free.

In answer to the question "How can people be self-governing if their representatives make the decisions and not themselves?" Kelsen answers first that there is no choice. Modern complex polities need to be representative. Any Rousseauian model of direct democracy is unfeasible. But it is also undesirable because representatives can perform an important function of linking citizens' preferences and values to legislative output. Representatives, organized into parties, present platforms that have the best chance of corresponding with people's interests. Further, parties and representatives are in the business of seeking compromises, and that would in effect maximize the number of people who are free in the sense of seeing correspondence with their interests and the laws and policies enacted. In chapter 9, I take up the reinvigorated debate about parties which has also been influenced by Kelsen. Kelsenians are enthusiastic about the potential democratic role of parties. But, for now, I want to interrogate the idea of freedom a little further.

Kelsen argues that "Democracy must be parliamentary democracy, in which the ruling will of society is created by a majority of those who are elected by the majority of persons possessing political rights. As a result, political rights – and therefore freedom – are essentially reduced to the right to vote" (Kelsen 2013: 41). This view is echoed in Nadia Urbinati's defense of proceduralism: "democratic proceduralism is in the service of equal liberty since it presumes and claims the equal right and opportunity citizens have to participate in the formation of the majority view with their individual votes and their opinions; it is what qualifies democracy as a form of government whose citizens obey the laws they contribute in making, directly or indirectly" (Urbinati 2014: 19).

Democracy produces a series of ruling wills that represent a set of interests and concerns bundled and articulated in a party platform and then supported by a majority. Urbinati explains that majority rule for Kelsen is defined "within an overall temporal framework of continuity, involving the possibility of revising previously approved decisions, as well as formulating new ones" (Urbinati 2013: 10). "Revision" here suggests that, given pluralism and competition, regular elections over time will produce different ruling wills made up of different sets of interests. Therefore, both electoral turnover as well as shifting interests and coalitions will keep the door permanently open for the minority, or parts of the minority, to become part of the majority and so rule and participate in freedom. This picture suggests two levels of freedom. The universal right to vote, majority rule, electoral turnover, minority rights, and strong free speech and freedom of association protections create a political order or set of procedures that maximizes the potential for freedom of every citizen. The system maximizes the opportunity to contribute to the majority will. Therefore, in one sense, to be part of this order is to be free. But Kelsen's claim that freedom is not just a status but more importantly about participation in the authorship of laws means that on another level, at any given time, only the majority is free. Freedom is to be valued for its own sake, in a democracy "as many as possible shall be free," therefore democracy is the most valued regime.

Kelsenian proceduralism highlights the central challenge of reconciling majority rule voting with an ideal of equally shared political autonomy. The core institutions of this proceduralism are elections, parties, and parliaments. These institutions are kept maximally open to every citizen equally through a dense scaffolding of protections and incentives that, for example, encourage and underwrite an active and accessible public sphere. But ruling is undertaken by the majority, and there is no Rousseauian fiction that the majority represents or speaks for the whole. For Kelsen, the procedure is endorsed because it makes as many people as possible free (the majority), not because it makes everyone equally free in the sense of co-authors of the law. The mechanisms that ensure that majority rule is not majority tyranny are, on the one hand, the protection of minority rights and, on the other hand, an open and dynamic system that ensures electoral turnover and a responsive system of political parties. But this proceduralism still leaves those who do not make up the majority unable to say that they were the authors of the laws which they must obey. The next view I canvas claims that democracy is to be valued because it makes everyone equally free.

Freedom as non-domination

Freedom or liberty (I use these terms interchangeably) as non-domination is associated with a revival of republicanism sometimes called neo-republicanism in political theory. Throughout this book I discuss various philosophers who identify as neo-republican. I do not, however, attempt any definition of neo-republicanism beyond noting that all neo-republicans endorse some version of freedom as non-domination. As I noted in the introduction, neo-republicanism, although perhaps a coherent tradition, does not present a model of democracy at its core. Indeed, on some interpretations of that tradition, republicanism is not inherently friendly to democracy (Urbinati 2012). Here I focus exclusively on the ways that freedom as non-domination replaces a liberal idea of freedom as non-interference to produce a more democracy-friendly view of freedom (Rostbøll 2015b).

Liberty as non-interference suggests that all external limitations or impediments to my actions are a loss of freedom. Laws are limitations to action and so a case of interference. Such limitations are often justified by arguing that limiting certain actions will enhance overall freedom within society. But thinking of liberty as non-interference tends to introduce a liberal or perhaps even libertarian nuance to one's conception of democracy. If we begin with freedom as an intrinsic value, and if we understand freedom as non-interference, then all laws are in need of special justification in the face of individual liberty.

Rather than interference in the choices and agency of individuals, non-domination shifts the focus to the power to interfere with choice (Pettit 2012: 50). This then creates a more nuanced and politically sensitive view of liberty. On the one hand, it implies that domination may exist even if there is no actual or immediate interference. A benign and kind slave owner dominates her slaves even if she rarely or never interferes with them. On the other hand, non-domination also suggests that interference that I have sanctioned is not domination because it is under my control. Uncontrolled interference (or uncontrolled power to interfere) is a form of domination. Interference under my control is not a form of domination and therefore is not a limitation on freedom. Pettit uses the analogy of an individual who wishes to limit her drinking (2012: 57). She gives a friend the key to the liquor cabinet with instructions that he is not to hand over the key on any immediate request but only with a 24-hour warning. In this scenario, the "drinker" might have her will thwarted by her friend if she demands the key on the spot, but the friend cannot be described as dominating her or reducing her liberty if he refuses and sticks with the original deal. That there is some circumstance chosen in which the key is to be returned is very important. Giving someone the key with unlimited discretion on when, if ever, the key may be returned would introduce uncontrolled interference.

The significance of this view of liberty for democratic self-government is obvious. If we can say that we authorize or in some sense control the actions of the government, and if we get to reevaluate that control on a regular basis (elections), then coercive laws are not a form of domination. But how do we specify "control"? How do we scale up from individuals and liquor cabinets to mass democracies legislating for everybody? Pettit rejects two alternatives. The first is that we admit that those who lose elections do not "control" the interference, therefore they are in a potential situation of domination until they are part of the majority. This is the position taken by Kelsen, as we saw in the previous section, who insists that elections using majority rule ensure that "as many as possible shall be free" (Kelsen 1955: 25). Pettit insists that democracy must be "a system of equally shared control over government" (2012: 22). The second alternative is to follow Rousseau or what Pettit calls the communitarian option. Rather than admitting that the minority is not free, Rousseau folds them into a collective communal category of the people and argues that if legislation is undertaken properly and tracks the general will or common good, then those who oppose the legislation are mistaken and they are (infamously) "forced to be free." Richard Tuck follows Rousseau in this and suggests that in a healthy democracy the minority is swept along with the majority and enfolded into the majoritarian collective action. Citizens are said to commit to majority rule not simply in the sense that they abide by the outcomes, but in a deeper sense that, once outvoted, they take the majority view to be their view: "as a democrat, I agree that once the majority view is known, I accept it as my own" (Tuck forthcoming: 66). After a vote, the minority disappears and outcomes are as if passed and authorized unanimously: "the actual implementation of a vote by an assembly is unanimous; at the point at which (for example) the resolution of an assembly becomes a law, there *is* no minority" (forthcoming: 68). Both Kelsen and Rousseau see majority voting as the prime democratic procedure through which we exercise political autonomy as equals. This means that both have the challenge of explaining in what sense the minority can be said to be equally free in a democracy.

Pettit addresses this problem by looking at the procedures, processes, and institutions of democratic control (and non-domination) across multiple dimensions, spheres, and venues. Contestation is the central mechanism through which democracies can live up to the ideal of "a system of equally shared control over government." Contestation comes in two forms. The first is a mixed constitution and separation of powers in which a plurality of points of control clash and constrain each other. The second is a "contestatory citizenry" that is disposed to resist government abuse. The two most important avenues of citizen contestation are court challenges to legislative majorities[1] and old-fashioned protest, activism, and social movements. Contestation is a necessary supplement to elections in maintaining popular control of government – a control that respects and takes seriously each person's equal claim not to be dominated by fellow citizens or the state.

Pettit begins with the value of non-domination. He shows that democracy is compatible with non-domination, indeed, that only some form of democracy is compatible with non-domination. Strictly speaking, this is an instrumental argument in that the good is non-domination and the means is democracy. Furthermore, it has been criticized for being overly individualistic. What is important for Pettit is that no individual is in a situation of domination either vis-à-vis fellow citizens or vis-à-vis the government. In making non-domination an individual good, it appears that Pettit has lost sight of the ideal of co-authorship of the laws. Christian Rostbøll proposes a more intersubjective ideal of non-domination: "Democratic procedures that solicit the equal participation of everyone in collective decision making are constitutive of relations of non-domination" (Rostbøll 2015a: 276). This, he argues, would better articulate the intrinsic value of treating and seeing each other as co-authors. Rostbøll is correct that Pettit's view is semi-instrumental and individualist, but I think the problem with this is not that he makes democracy of only instrumental value, as if we could find another regime type that might do a better job at maintaining non-domination. This is clearly not an option for Pettit. Pettit's view still belongs in the category of theories that value democracy for procedural rather than outcome reasons. For Pettit, democracy (and only democracy) squares the circle of how we can be subject to coercive laws and still be free, i.e., not dominated. Democratic procedures do that by creating equal opportunities to control state interference. The procedures have value independent of whether citizens choose wisely in their exercise of control, so this theory of democracy is not instrumental in any strong sense.

Pierre Rosanvallon also develops a theory of democracy that hangs the hopes of self-government on the potential to control and contest elected majorities (Rosanvallon 2008). Using counterintuitive terminology, Rosanvallon defends institutions of "counter-democracy" as necessary to the health of democracy. By counter-democracy, he means "not the opposite of democracy but rather a form of democracy that reinforces the usual electoral democracy as a kind of buttress, a democracy of indirect powers disseminated throughout society – in other words, a durable democracy of distrust, which complements the episodic democracy of the usual electoral-representative system" (2008: 8). There are three types of practices, or forms of "organized distrust," through which society corrects and exerts pressure on representative elected institutions: oversight or vigilance; forms of prevention or sanction; and judgments (2008: 7–8). These practices can be undertaken on an informal level by, for example, protest, criticism in the press, and public rebuke. Or they can find venues that are more established, for example, bureaucracies and courts. What all these "counter-democratic" practices have in common is that they are not part of the set of institutions and practices that form parliamentary democracy. Thus, in Rosanvallon's hands, the ideal of control through contestation is even more clearly directed at the potential domination and abuse of majorities and elected elites than in Pettit's view. The suspicion of majorities is partly due to a general embrace of a principle of fallibility especially in the face of complexity. No democracy can ever achieve the full ideal of equal authorship. Therefore, we need to be vigilant and force those in power to behave properly, seek the common good, and give an account of themselves. This is the democratic politics of distrust. The politics of distrust is also motivated by actual democratic regimes that have pursued majority interests claiming that these were authentic expressions of the people's will. In chapter 8, I take a closer look at these populist claims. For now, I will just note that the rise of populism within parliamentary democracies is another reason for supporting a contestatory idea of political freedom.

I have argued that contestatory views of political freedom contain an ideal of self-government or popular rule because they expand our understanding of the sites of democracy beyond the election booth and potentially include a wider and more diverse group of citizens participating in the processes that lead to democratic decisions. Nadia Urbinati disagrees with this interpretation and reads Pettit and Rosanvallon through the lens of Kelsenian proceduralism and so sees both theorists as setting up impediments to democracy (Urbinati 2014: 106–27). Urbinati suggests that both Pettit and Rosanvallon are worried about parliaments (hence democracy) making *bad* decisions, and so their contestatory view is premised on correcting those decisions from some vantage point outside democracy, whether that be courts, bureaucracies, or citizens' assemblies. In criticizing Pettit and Rosanvallon as "democracy's critics from within," she reaffirms the centrality of party democracy and elections as the core of democracy:

> The permanent openness that any (Parliamentary) decision has in a free political community is the democratic answer to democracy's critics from within who propose narrowing the domain of politics in order to make good and true decisions. Openness to revision, rather than the interruption or containment of democratic practices, is the democratic answer to unsatisfactory democratic decisions. This is the maxim coming from a procedural conception of democracy that is normative. (Urbinati 2014: 127)

Thus Urbinati sticks to the Kelsenian view that only the clash and contest of pluralism passed through the procedures of free and fair elections can claim the mantle of democracy and self-government. But I think she misreads both Pettit and Rosanvallon when she implies that their views can be reduced to fail-safe mechanisms when majorities go off the rails. Contestation is a "system of equally shared control" (Pettit 2012: 22) and counter-democracy is a "form of democracy" (Rosanvallon 2008: 8), thus implying constitutive parts of democracy and not occasional remedial actions.

Conclusion

In the beginning of this chapter, I noted that Rousseau set the problem that freedom-focused democrats seek to solve: how to be free and self-directing at the same time as living under laws. Rousseau also articulated the solution to this problem. We must be the author of those laws to maintain our freedom. So, in these two respects, Rousseau is very much the father of a great deal of democratic theory. Rousseau's more specific answer about how to conceptualize the exercise of political autonomy is less followed and indeed much criticized, however. The crux of the problem is that Rousseau envisioned collective authorship as requiring a unified will of the people pursuing the common good, which is only possible to envision as an abstract ideal. Rousseau nevertheless argued that majority voting was the procedure to use to discover that unified will and bring the common good into law. Dissenters from those outcomes were then mistaken. Thus Rousseau's ideal of political autonomy comes up against pluralism and disagreement about what is the common good.

Kelsenian proceduralism and contestatory proceduralism represent two competing amendments to the Rousseauian idea of freedom as self-determination or self-rule. The first focuses on the ways that electoral democracy can approximate self-rule by maximizing access and opportunity of all citizens equally to be part of the majority. For Kelsenians, self-government is about making ruling majorities open, porous, and rotating over time and dispensing with any idea that there is an objectively true common good against which we measure outcomes. Important here are, on the one hand, good linkages between civil society and the representatives who enact laws and, on the other hand, strong safeguards of minorities, especially safeguarding their opportunity to be part of the majority.

Contestatory proceduralism stresses the popular means to limit and constrain power in order to ensure that we are not dominated or ruled by forces we do not control, or which have become corrupted in the pursuit of particular interests. For Pettit and Rosanvallon, democracy requires the means and institutions for citizens to contest majorities and limit them but also to have their voices heard and listened to even if they are not part of the majority. Contestatory ideas of democracy are on the rise. These democratic theories expand and diversify the sites of democratic agency beyond elections and include extra-electoral avenues for citizens to push for policy and law. The idea of dispersed popular sovereignty I discuss in chapter 8 also moves in this direction. Ultimately the picture to emerge is of a complex system with a division of democratic labor and multiple countervailing forces. But does contestatory proceduralism add up to authorship of the laws – self-rule – or simply the mitigation of domination through the dispersion of power (Bagg forthcoming)? Are the people the authors of the laws, or does this picture of multiple points of control, veto, checks, constraints, contestation, oversight, sanction, and judgment just show us how to make sure no one group (especially the elected majority) can be the exclusive author of the law?

Samuel Bagg argues that there is an important distinction between ideals of authorship or self-rule and control. Bagg suggests that contestatory theories like Pettit's:

> assume that political outcomes emerge from a complex thicket of contradictory tendencies and conflicting intentions. Democracy is thus seen not as popular rule – i.e., a creative process of collective decision-making through which the will of a sovereign people is enacted – but as popular *control* – i.e., a primarily reactive process of contestation through which those who do actually make decisions are incentivized to act in the public interests. (Bagg forthcoming: 163)

Bagg gives voice to a growing skepticism in democratic theory about strong claims that democracy is the will of the people. In other words, claims that scale up ideals of individual self-determination into ideals of collective self-determination where the collective self is a unified agent. Bagg challenges us to ask if contestatory or dispersed ideals of democratic input add up to a coherent view of joint authorship and popular rule, or only an uncoordinated rearguard action to curb the abuse of power. This contrast will come up repeatedly throughout the book. For example, does protest function to put popular demands on the democratic agenda or does it function to constrain powerful elites from misbehaving (look at chapter 11 for the answer)? How one answers this question represents a dividing line between democratic theory that sees contestation and countervailing forces as adding up to the rule of the (dispersed) people or democratic theory that argues that contestation is a means to constrain and check power. The more one's democratic theory leans toward realism, the more one is likely to endorse this second view. This is the topic of the next chapter.

5
Instrumentalism 1: Realism

INSTRUMENTAL arguments in favor of democracy look at the consequences or outcomes of democracy to assess democracy's value. In this and the next two chapters, I look at three types of instrumental arguments. First up in this chapter is realism, then in chapter 6 I discuss a growing group of theories that give democracy low grades on performance measures and, in chapter 7, I turn to epistemic theories that argue that democracy does or can produce good-quality outcomes. There is a fourth instrumental argument that I do not discuss at any length. This is the view that democracy is to be valued because it makes us morally better people. In other words, democratic participation promotes and inculcates civic virtue and sociability and checks selfishness and egotism. This argument has a long and distinguished pedigree beginning with Aristotle and continuing in the work of John Stuart Mill. Following Mill, Elizabeth Anderson, for example, argues that among other goods that attend a democratic way of life are goods of character that include moderating certain vices: "democratic equality protects the advantaged from the vices of arrogance, malice and stupidity" (Anderson 2009: 220). But Anderson does not suggest that individual moral character is a standalone reason to value democracy or that democracy is an instrumental means to some other good identifiable independent of democracy (see chapter 7 for a discussion of Elizabeth Anderson's democratic theory). A discussion of which civic or political virtues might be necessary to maintain democracy – for example, some might think that Rawls's "duty of civility" is such a virtue (Cohen and Fung 2021) – runs through some democratic theory, but there has been a steady decline in virtue talk within democratic theory that coincides with more realistic and empirically grounded views of democracy being on the ascendency (Elliott 2023). The idea that political participation in democracy makes us (morally) better people, and this is a central reason to value democracy, is not a common claim.

Realism in democratic theory

A dividing line within instrumental arguments is whether consequences are understood in terms of legislative outcomes (laws and policies) or whether the consequences are more indirect, for example, peace and security. Some tie the term "instrumentalism" in democratic theory exclusively to the first sort of argument. Brennan and Landemore, for example, argue that instrumentalism involves the claim that "(w)hat justifies the distribution of power, or a particular way of making political decisions, is (at least in part) that this distribution or method tends to get the right answer" (Brennan and Landemore 2022: 7; see also Fleuss 2021: 34). I understand instrumentalism more broadly than this and include realist theories of democracy that evaluate democratic institutions from the vantage point of how this regime type channels and structures power and conflict. Realists, I and many realists themselves argue, have an instrumental defense of democracy's value. However, they rarely base that defense on the claim that policy output can be shown to be the right answer.

Realism in contemporary democratic theory is associated with three different but overlapping types of claim and debate. The first is a methodological and sometimes broadly philosophical claim about how to study, understand, and evaluate what goes on in the world of politics of which democracy is of course a part (Rossi and Sleat 2014). Like so much of political theory beginning in the mid-1990s, this set of claims arose as a critical response to the dominance of Rawlsian political philosophy and what has come to be known as "political moralism" (Williams 2005: 2). In political moralism, the philosopher develops moral principles in the abstract, say, principles of justice, and then applies them to politics. According to realists, this ends up with "a misleading, if not outright false, account of politics" (Sleat 2018: 2). The problem with moralism is not feasibility but relevance. Moralism fails to see, as Machiavelli so famously did, that morality and doing the right thing have little to do with what really goes on in politics. Indeed, political agents following moral principles would lead to disastrous consequences for all involved, including ordinary citizens who benefit from peace and security. Politics is the domain of securing order and wielding power amid the clash of interests. Although all realists are united in opposing moralism or what Raymond Geuss called "ethics-first" theory (Geuss 2008), there is a great deal of diversity in developing full realist theories of politics, and this often focuses on questions of the source of normativity. Upon what do we base judgments about good and bad political regimes if we eschew all foundational moral principles, for example, that all persons are morally free and equal? Although debates about the source of normativity inform some democratic theory, for now I will leave these meta questions aside and focus on the second set of realist arguments that deal more directly with democracy.

Realist democratic theory claims that democracy has value to the extent that it mitigates, channels, pacifies, contains, or opposes the violence and conflict that is endemic to politics understood as power struggle (Przeworski 1999). "Modern democracy," Samuel Bagg tells us, "is not a collaborative process for making decisions, but a way of organizing competition for power." The function of democratic practices is to keep "inter-group competition from degenerating into violence" (Bagg forthcoming: 11, 5). Before going into this position in more detail, let me mention a third type of realism. This third claim, although a popular understanding of realism, is more like a claim to be realistic about citizen competence and what one can expect from mechanisms of aggregations (Achen and Bartels 2016). Here the argument is that much of normative democratic theory is based on the myth of the (potentially) rational and enlightened citizen whose preferences and opinions are transmitted to a responsive state. Against this myth, a realistic democratic theory must admit that most citizens lack the knowledge, good judgment, and motivation to make reasonable decisions, and there is no empirical evidence that democratic states do (or even ought to) respond to citizens' preferences. This last meaning of realism is often associated with a large branch of empirical political science and some libertarian political philosophy (Brennan 2016). Many theorists who count themselves as realists in this last sense, however, do not embrace realism in either of the first two senses (Brennan 2016). I discuss "realistic" assessments of citizen competence in the next chapter.

All realist democratic theory begins with a deflationary claim aimed at what it considers classic or conventional ideals of democracy as self-government or rule by the people – in other words, the view that we studied in the last chapter. Often taking Rousseau as the poster child for this view, three arguments are mustered against ideals of self-government. The first focuses on claims that democracy is a vehicle of the common good. Rousseau is often cited as the father of this view but contemporary theories, including some versions of deliberative democracy that highlight agreement or consensus (John Rawls and Joshua Cohen), are also included in this category. According to realists, the classical view supposes either that there is a common good to be discovered or that one could be constructed through democratic or deliberative procedures. Realists deny that there is any such common good to be discovered or constructed. This goes one step further than Kelsenian proceduralists who insisted that there is no *single* objective common good but did not deny that democratic procedures could construct a fallible and contestable approximation of the common good – and that we should seek to do that. For realists, it is not just that disagreement goes all the way down à la Waldron; they argue that violent conflict over those disagreements is an endemic feature of human society. The general will, common good, people's will, these are all fictions, the supposed content of which is often a factional or particular interest masquerading as a universal or collective interest. In other words, real-world appeals to these concepts always mask power.

The second set of deflationary arguments takes aim at democratic procedures of aggregation and challenges the idea that voting in mass democracies could produce an outcome that in any way reflected or expressed not just the people's will but even the majority will. Central here is Arrow's impossibility theorem that illustrates that voting procedures often result in arbitrary outcomes in the sense that, for example, they reflect no voter's first choice (Arrow 2012). Even without Arrow's social choice argument, we know that the same set of preferences in New Zealand versus Canada versus Germany will aggregate in very different ways with potentially radically different outcomes, given the different systems. This illustrates the difficulty in claiming that aggregation produces an authentic collective will or that outcomes can be justified as the general will.

Finally, there is an argument from preference formation. The naive picture of aggregation relies on a simple picture of a group of people given a choice between A and B, where if 50%+1 chose A, then A is the clear majority preference. But voting in mass democracies is not like that. First, as we saw above, electoral systems are complex *schemes* of aggregation in which only some sub-components some of the time (for example, a runoff between two directly elected presidential candidates) can be described in simple majoritarian terms. But there are further problems with claims that outcomes reflect clear voter preferences. Who set the agenda of A versus B? What if C and D would have both been preferable candidates to A and B? Is a choice between A and B then not a true expression of what the majority wants? Furthermore, how do we know that the people voting for A or B really understand what they are voting for? Lots of evidence suggests that citizens are poorly informed about their choices, easily swayed by manipulation, and subject to framing effects, meaning that expressed preference swings widely, depending on how that choice is framed or worded. This leads realists to claim that it might be difficult to say that choices in the voting booth reflect citizens' true interests or values, let alone an authentic general will or common good (Achen and Bartels 2016).

Not only do these arguments suggest the implausibility of a general will or common good, but they also seem to undermine less idealist views about responsiveness. One might agree that elections do not produce a clear "will of the people" but think that nevertheless good democratic government ought to be responsive to the interests of the majority in some way (Jacobs and Shapiro 2000). But modern scholarship and science have revealed a very murky picture of the process whereby citizens come to have preferences and then hold their representatives accountable if they fail to pursue agendas based on those preferences. There is a case to be made that realists sometimes overstate the empirical failure or logical impossibility of voting and elections transmitting genuine popular preferences to representatives (Chapman 2022; Ingham 2019; Mackie 2003). But they are correct to suggest that crude and simplistic claims that democracy magically transmits or creates a common will or that the people rule as a collective unified agent are hard to square with modern empirical social science, and that these claims sometimes hide populist power grabs.

Minimalist realism

Where do realists go from this deflationary starting point? The question then is why should we promote or value democracy if it is not a form of self-government of the people? Some realists first take up the question of "What is democracy?" before they answer the question "Why should we value democracy?" Here Joseph Schumpeter's minimalist view of democracy has been very influential (1942). Schumpeter begins with a version of the three arguments presented above and then argues that, as a descriptive matter, democracy is not and can never claim to be a system of *self*-government; it is instead a system in which rulers are chosen in competitive elections. All government is about some people ruling and having power over others. Regime types can be distinguished by the method of selecting those rulers. Democracy's method is competitive election. Market competition and consumer choice are considered the appropriate analogies, not a supra-subject named "the people" willing the common good. Schumpeter was hesitant to claim any strong normative status for his minimalist view, but many realists who follow Schumpeter's definition are less hesitant. Adam Przeworski and Ian Shapiro both defend democracy as our best bet in a world full of power, conflict, and domination.

As a method for choosing rulers, Przeworski argues that democracy has value because it avoids violence, and he takes "it as obvious that we want to avoid bloodshed" (Przeworski 1999: 45). Democracy avoids violence by the very simple mechanism of taking turns – electoral turnover. Politics is about power struggles between competing interests. Violence and bloodshed result when groups are permanently excluded from even the possibility of gaining power. Elections put a certain group in power, and, in ruling, this group coerces the group that did not win the election. Unlike Kelsenians, who also believe electoral turnover is a central selling feature of democracy, Przeworski does not appeal to the moral value of freedom. He does not say that in this system the most people possible are free, freedom is a good, therefore democracy has value. Instead, he argues that democracy can stave off civil war by giving all groups a chance to acquire power if they play by the rules. Flipping a coin every four years in a two-party system might also achieve this equilibrium, but voting adds an element of accountability. We vote the bums out of office when they do a bad job.

This seems a thin defense of democracy. On the one hand, most people hope that democracy offers more than simply the avoidance of bloodshed, and, on the other hand, there are regimes that meet this minimum requirement that do not appear to be robustly democratic. But this realist view does put its finger on something very important and observable in our present democratic crisis: the clearest and most obvious subversion of democracy is refusing to leave office after losing an election. The peaceful transfer of power is the miracle of democracy seen in light of human history and power struggles (Przeworski 1999: 49). Some of the most troubling backsliding we are seeing in contemporary democracies is that of parties trying to manufacture a permanent winning streak by changing the rules. Democracy has winners and losers. Stability requires that those winners and losers are not always the same people or the same groups.

Thus, although minimal theories set an aspirationally low bar, there is something undeniable about the minimal conception of democracy. Refusing to leave office after losing an election is a definitive and decisive abandonment of democracy. Accepting electoral turnover *is* a minimum and fundamental requirement to be in the democracy club. There are few democratic theorists who would not agree with this sense of minimum. The controversy arises when one adds, as Przeworski and others do, that this is all we need to ask from democracy because this is the fundamental mechanism that delivers the good of social peace (Hamid 2022).

Minimal realists argue that the regular transfer of power in elections and taking turns channels and mitigates conflict and avoids violence. They reject any idea that we value democratic procedures because they bring about some desired outcome, even the outcome of "this is what the majority wants." This argument might appear to belong in the preceding chapter where I discussed procedurally based defenses of democracy. And Przeworski suggests that his view of democracy can explain why elections "have value in themselves" while theories that prioritize moral values introduce those values as consequences of the procedure (1999: 24). But a minimalist realist defense of democratic procedures is qualitatively different than most of the arguments in chapters 3 and 4 for two reasons. First, all the theories we looked at in the preceding two chapters argued that democratic procedures embody or instantiate an important *moral* value, whether that be equality, respect, or freedom. Thus, even if, as some think, democratic procedures relate to moral value strictly instrumentally (for example, democracy is the means to achieving ruling without domination), democracy is valued for moral reasons. These are all ethics-first views of democracy. Realists replace moral value with the good of peaceful coexistence, stability, or constraint on power. These are desirable ends, perhaps even objectively good states of affairs, but they are usually not understood as given by morality but rather dictated by reality – for example, relying on some idea of self-preservation. For realists, politics is first and foremost about "securing order" (Williams 2005: 3) and reducing the risk of violent death.

The second difference is that equality, respect, and freedom cannot be achieved except through democratic procedures. The values of peace and order do not inhere in the procedures in quite the same way as, say, equality inheres in equal voting rights. Peaceful coexistence is clearly a *consequence* of regular elections. Further, it is possible to imagine – and indeed many realists do make this argument – that other regime types might also be able to deliver on this good (Williams 2005). It is difficult to imagine non-democratic decision procedures achieving equal respect or equal freedom as these have been outlined in chapters 3 and 4 because these values are constituted in or by the procedure.

Realism and non-domination

Ian Shapiro also endorses a Schumpeterian minimalist view of democracy (Shapiro 2016: 78). On many questions he is very close to Przeworski. But there is an interesting difference between the two views. Przeworski values democracy because it avoids violence; Shapiro values democracy because it constrains domination. Non-domination then is the normative core of this view. In Shapiro's realist hands, however, non-domination takes on a different role within the democratic theory than we saw earlier with Philip Pettit. Pettit understands non-domination as the most persuasive interpretation of freedom, and thus he defends non-domination as a moral value. Shapiro does not want to connect non-domination to a general moral or philosophical theory of freedom or to any claim that what democracies do is make people equally free. Democracy can only be said to minimize domination and only in specific instances, between specific groups rather than systemically (Shapiro 2016: 23). Rather than an ideal of freedom, non-domination is defended along lines closer to Przeworski: nobody wants to be on the receiving end of domination; that is a form of violence that is obviously bad.

The second difference is that Pettit talks about contestation and Shapiro talks about opposition. This parallels the division I mentioned at the end of the last chapter between positive views of control that can be construed in terms of authorship and negative views of control that seek a check on power. Contestation for Pettit (and for many other democratic theorists) is seen as an important way that democracies live up to the ideals of political equality and equality of influence or control. The two most common forms of contestation are, on the one hand, protest and street politics, and, on the other, court challenges to legislative outcomes. Both are cases of nay-saying but nay-saying in the service of spreading out and diversifying sources of democratic control. Thus contestation is understood as contributing to "a system of equally shared control over government" (Pettit 2012: 22). Shapiro does not think ideals of self-government or popular control are realistic. He is a Schumpeterian in this respect. The best we can do is to oppose groups who seek to dominate. Thus

Shapiro's view is negative, remedial, defensive, and targeted. It does not add up to or in any way contribute to an ideal of popular ruling. In politics, Shapiro argues, groups seek power to pursue their interests; the best we can hope for is to put roadblocks in the way of the scariest and most dangerous of these groups. We will never do away with domination. This oppositional view leads then to a different view of democratic institutions. Pettit's ideal of contestation points to multiple avenues and a fundamental principle of mixed constitutionalism, separation of powers, and checks and balances. Shapiro's view of opposition leads to a majority rule two-party system where what is important is that there is always a strong, well-organized opposition to the people who hold power. Strong and effective political parties are an important power base to safeguard against domination. Shapiro focuses on agents (elites and parties) to oppose domination, rather than constitutional constraints, which is what Pettit relies on to limit domination. The problem with Pettit's institutional vision, according to Shapiro, is that, on the one hand, the power is too dispersed to stand up to groups who want to dominate and, on the other hand, checks and balances inevitably lead to minority veto power and so opportunities to dominate. Shapiro uses American constitutional history as a cautionary tale illustrating the inadequacy of a checks-and-balances model to curb domination. There is a growing chorus of scholars and pundits who are blaming the American Constitution for making minority rule a reality in the United States (Hacker and Pierson 2020).

Like Przeworski, Shapiro identifies an important dimension of contemporary democratic crisis, especially regarding the erosion of democratic norms. Along with attempts to sow doubt about election outcomes, some political actors – especially those associated with the populism that I discuss in chapter 8 – publicly question and call out opposition (parties, movements, and voices) as obstructing democracy. Many democratic theorists have responded with renewed defense of the idea of legitime, or loyal, opposition as a necessary condition of any healthy democracy (Kirshner 2022). Questions of legitimate opposition cut two ways in our contemporary context. On the one hand, these arguments serve to remind us that opposition can perform positive functions within the system, but, on the other hand, they help us to think about what sorts of opposition step over a line of legitimacy. This has become especially salient in American discourse where events on January 6, 2021 in Washington, DC have been described by supporters as legitimate political expression while others (this includes most democratic theorists and the mainstream media) see it as illegitimate opposition or, in other words, insurrection. Only in parsing out the democratic role of opposition is it possible to make these sorts of normative distinctions.

Partisan realists

I turn now to a group of democratic theorists I call partisan realists.[1] I do not intend anything negative by the term "partisan." A partisan takes sides, has a cause, defends a principle. There would be no politics without partisanship, and it often has very good consequences when the side, cause, or principle is worth fighting for. Like minimalist realists, partisans think that politics is about power struggle. Democratic procedures then manage and constrain power struggle. But this group, unlike Przeworski and Shapiro, does not think the competition of free and fair elections alone can do that. Indeed, the metaphor of the market appealed to by Schumpeter is a good illustration of the problem these theorists are concerned with. We might think that fair market rules that treat every player the same are a neutral playing field for competition. But in real life, under capitalism, the rich keep getting richer and the poor keep getting poorer. Rather than neutral rules, partisan realists look for obstacles to set in the path of groups that seek to dominate and exploit. So not political equality (Pettit), not free and fair election turnover (Przeworski), not institutionalized legitimate opposition (Shapiro), but opposition to oligarchy (the other of democracy) is the defining and value-added feature of democracy. Even more specifically, these theorists seek to disempower and sometimes exclude actual oligarchs (the rich) and empower everyone else, that is, the majority. This form of realism has also been called radical realism or critical realism (Bagg forthcoming) because it is often tightly connected to left-leaning critiques of capitalism, neoliberalism, and growing inequality in wealth and status in western liberal democracies.

Instrumentalism 1: Realism 83

Partisan realists also begin with the deflationary stand vis-à-vis classical or Rousseauian democratic theory that appeals to the rule of a united people, but they often add to this empirical evidence of the failure of electoral competition to curb the worst forms of oligarchic domination. Przeworski thinks elections have saved us from continual civil war; Shapiro believes that elections can empower viable and effective opposition to power-hungry elites; partisan realists say that elections have made the rich richer and more powerful and the poor poorer and less powerful (chapter 9 looks at this claim in more detail). Democracy depends on targeting the forces of domination and *excluding* them from power. It is in this sense that partisanship takes center stage. Democracy is an "ongoing process of partisan opposition to whichever groups pose the greatest threats at a given time" (Bagg forthcoming: 8). The groups that pose the greatest threat at this time, our time, are wealthy elites and corporate juggernauts. Here realist democratic theory "must aggressively work to minimize oligarchic power" (Arlen and Rossi 2021: 33). Partisan realists take sides in a way that minimal realists do not. In this section, I take up and discuss two versions of partisan realism, agonism (Medearis 2015; Mouffe 2018) and plebeian democracy (Green 2016; McCormick 2019; Vergara 2020a). I focus on these two radical versions of partisan realism because they have taken the logic of this type of argument to its furthest point while at the same time gaining significant supporters along the way. But there are other versions, most notably the critical realism of Samuel Bagg, that incorporate many elements of more traditional realist theory into their defense of democracy (Bagg forthcoming).

Chantal Mouffe is not a traditional realist but with realists she shares the view that politics, or "the political," is a realm of power where moral principles have little relevance. In chapter 8, I have a longer discussion of left-wing populism defended by Ernesto Laclau and Chantal Mouffe in the context of populism. Here I focus on Mouffe's 2018 book *For a Left Populism* to highlight the partisan nature of her endorsement of democracy. Democracy is a site of contestation and struggle for sovereign power. The question becomes who wins that space and for what cause. Thus Mouffe is interested in strategies and tactics within electoral democracies but without any idealization regarding the mitigating effects of elections on power and domination. In her latest version of this view, right-wing populism is the most visible opponent; the only way to fight right-wing populism is with left-wing populism. In this view, the "people" will be constructed not on nativist terms but on egalitarian democratic terms, with calls to form a collective will to fight for social justice and against oligarchy. For Mouffe, the people have no essentialist homogenous core; instead, calling on the people is a discursive strategy in the battle against the hegemonic forces of neoliberalism (2018: 10). The left needs to make an affective appeal in order to mobilize the losers of liberal austerity, and this requires identifying an adversary. The adversaries in the left narrative are not foreigners or immigrants but the neoliberal establishment and the oligarchs.

The appeal to the "people" as the agent of self-rule might appear at odds with realist skepticism about self-government narratives. And for sure there are significant differences in the underlying political philosophy of traditional realists and the Gramscian-influenced school of left populism. But in the spirit of realism, the political and rhetorical appeal to the "the people" is described as strategic (but not cynical) and undertaken in order to gain an advantage in the competition for power. This competition takes place within the basic institutional infrastructure of electoral democracy (Mulvad and Stahl 2019). But Mouffe does not think that democratic procedures have intrinsic or moral value. Nor does she think that we should value them because they allow for regular turnover or the creation of an institutionally permanent opposition. Elections are sites that structure agonistic struggle.

Agonism is often introduced in contrast to deliberation (Scudder and White 2023). Deliberation embodies ideals of mutual justification and cooperative processes of reasoned problem solving; agonism is a form of competition or oppositional clash in which participants seek to win or gain advantage in a power struggle. Neither deliberativists nor agonists deny that both deliberation and agonism go on in modern liberal democracies. Deliberative democrats, for example, often endorse contestatory practices (protest and disruptive politics) that seek to get marginalized but important questions on the agenda. And agonists acknowledge that many political actors bring forth reasons and justifications into the public debate. Thus the difference between these two views is not about valuing certain practices but rather in understanding the deeper role of these practices. For deliberative democrats, contestation is valued because and to the extent that it furthers ideals of inclusive and rational opinion formation (more about this in chapter 10). For agonists, it is important to show that what looks like reasoned debate often overlays and partially obscures underlying power struggles which are the bedrock of politics.

The contrast between deliberation and agonism often overlooks another difference between these two views. The democratic theory embodied in agonism is not just about the generic nature of political struggle; it also contains the added and essential idea that one must take sides and that there is only one side to take (Medearis 2015). Thus Mouffe's view of democratic politics is asymmetrical and partisan. Only one side is democratic, and that side must defeat the other side. On this view, political equality is not a non-partisan individual status of every person enshrined in a constitution but rather the struggle of a specific and identifiable democratic agent, "the people," to reclaim their equality in the face of oligarchic usurpation. Democracy is preserved and deepened when that agent defeats and excludes the oligarchs from power (Mouffe 2018: 79).

A second take on partisan realism comes out of the neo-republican tradition. Like left agonists, neo-republicans see democracy as a partisan struggle in which we must take sides. The sides are clearly laid out; struggles in republics are always between the rich and the poor – these are materialist categories. Whereas Mouffe sees the people for whom we should fight as a constructed category, John McCormick (2006), Jeffrey Green (2016), and Camilla Vergara (2020a) begin with the view that democracy is always about the poor curbing the power of the rich. Plebeian neo-republicans attempt to resuscitate a view of democracy that has been in disrepute since Aristotle. Democracy, Aristotle tells us, is one of the bad regimes because rather than pursuing the common good, it pursues the good of the ruling group, that group being in principle the many but, in fact, the poor. Plebeian neo-republicans take this view of democracy and place it in a realist framework in order to conclude that there is no such thing as a common good or rule in the interest of everybody, or, even if there was, our contemporary democracies are so far skewed toward the few rich that we need to radically push them back toward the less wealthy many.

A commitment to democracy, then, is a commitment to the plebeian side of the equation. Plebeian democrats question the institutional rules of the electoral democratic game in a way that left agonists do not (Vergara 2020a). Mouffe certainly thinks that electoral politics have been corrupted by money and power but, ultimately, she wants to win elections for the left. Vergara and McCormick think elections as they have developed since the eighteenth century are essentially oligarchic and suggest that we need to develop alternative democratic institutions. This group is often frustrated with democratic theorists who focus on procedural equality and worry about the tyranny of the majority. As McCormick says, his view "prioritizes the threat posed to common liberty by wealth and renders secondary concerns about majority tyranny" (2019: 149). Plebeian neo-republicans do not think that representative electoral institutions are majoritarian *enough*, so they often suggest alternative institutions to give power to the people/many (Arlen and Rossi 2021; McCormick 2011; Mulvad and Stahl 2019; Vergara 2020b). The most radical such suggestion is the establishment of institutions and branches of government that exclude the wealthy. McCormick, for example, proposes a People's Tribunate selected through a lottery among non-wealthy citizens to exercise oversight power on elected law makers (2011: 184). Vergara proposes a plebeian branch of government connected to local and radically inclusive assemblies that would have extensive powers of oversight including impeaching public officials. Less radical but equally motivated by partisan concerns to curb the power of money are suggestions to insert randomly selected "citizen oversight juries" to "disrupt illicit private influence" (Bagg 2022: 2). For plebeian neo-republicans, democracy is understood as a form of government and set of procedures that is supposed to give power to the people, and the people is understood as a material category comprising the majority – "people-as-plebs" to use a term introduced by Vergara (Vergara 2020b: 231). What we call democracy today is oligarchy – rule by the rich – no matter the equal distribution of formal voting.

Conclusion

In this chapter, I have canvased three types of realist democratic theory. None of them fit perfectly into the "realist tradition" in political thought that is often associated with international relations and runs from Machiavelli through Thomas Hobbes into the modern era of Hans Morgenthau (McQueen 2018) and focuses on the instrumental means of ensuring peace and security. But realism as a trend in democratic theory is spilling out beyond the realist tradition. I have been using the terms "realism" and "realist" somewhat loosely to capture a concern for power, an interest in real-world struggles, a suspicion of overly ideal or moralistic theory, and a focus on the ways that democratic institutions structure competition and rivalry. Taking realism in this loose way and somewhat detached from the realist tradition, I would say that contemporary democratic theory has been having a realist moment. This means first that democratic theory in general is more realistic, pragmatic, and evidence driven today than 30 years ago. This can be seen in more interest in institutions and less interest in first principles, for example (Waldron 2016). But, secondly, it also means a growing cohort of democratic theorists focused on power. Criticism of ideal theory from the point of view of power has never been absent in democratic theory (Honig 1993). But now such criticism is less indebted to postmodern sources – often just as abstract and out of touch with real politics as Rawls – and more informed by empirical social science and problem-driven questions about the state of democratic regimes in the twenty-first century. In chapters 8 through 11, where I investigate responses to particular forms of democratic backsliding and erosion, a realist tone and take on democracy's ills is palpable.

6
Instrumentalism 2: Performance Skeptics

IT would be difficult to value democracy if it was shown that despite treating people with respect or as equals, it systematically resulted in disastrous consequences and outcomes. With democracies failing to adequately address climate change, turning a blind eye to growing inequality of wealth, putting up popular obstacles to pandemic policy, electing anti-democratic populists, and pushing for nativist legislation, many scholars as well as ordinary citizens are taking a closer look at democracy's outputs and asking tough questions about job performance. In this and the next chapter, I look at arguments that evaluate democracy from this consequentialist point of view. The field here is divided between those who argue that democracy does a good or fairly good job (certainly better than autocracies) in delivering what it promises and those who are skeptical of such claims and suggest that democracy is not always the best way to make collective decisions. Here, then, democratic decision procedures do not have value in themselves but are instruments for achieving other things that have value, for example, stability, justice, or effective public policy. "Democracies, in other words, should be regarded as a tool or instrument that is to be valued not for its own sake but entirely for what results from having it" (Arneson 2004: 42; Wall 2007). The implication is that when or if democracy does not deliver on these goods, we should seek other forms of governance that do; this then appears to introduce a contingent and defeasible commitment to democracy that makes some people very nervous (Bagg forthcoming: 188). Indeed, one of the motivating factors behind the "intrinsic value" camp is precisely the thought that instrumental defenses of democracy are weak and make commitments to democracy dependent on contingent events in the world.

Measuring performance

Performance-based views of democracy have a great deal of intuitive appeal and, at first sight anyway, come close to the way empirical political science might think about how and why we value democracy over other regime types. Why do we need government in the first place? Presumably to make our lives better and solve collective action problems. Surely how well our decision procedures accomplish those aims must take precedence over whether those procedures treat everyone as equals? Flipping a coin may be a decision procedure that treats everyone equally, but why should we think that it has intrinsic worth independent of the actual decision taken (Landemore 2016: 144)? And even if we thought that treating citizens as equals had value, do we really think that value trumps all performance questions? Can we not criticize majorities for getting it wrong? As I noted at the beginning of this chapter, it would be difficult to value democracy if it was shown that despite treating people with respect or as equals, it systematically resulted in disastrous consequences and outcomes. Performance theorists appeal to these sorts of intuitions in criticizing intrinsic theories and defending performance. "What justifies the distribution of power, or a particular way of making political decisions, is (at least in part) that this distribution or method tends to get the right answer" (Brennan and Landemore 2022: 7). The idea that there are right answers to political questions – or at least better and worse answers – also seems to have some anchor in ordinary intuitions or behavior. When we as citizens argue about policy, go to the polls to vote, and advocate for a political cause, we appear to be acting as if there are better and worse answers to political questions (Lafont 2020).

Although performance seems an intuitively sensible way to assess the value of democracy, it poses many challenges for normative democratic theory. Let's begin with the basic question:

does democracy outperform non-democracy? Instrumentalists have a complicated answer to this question.

Everybody involved in this debate, including those who are skeptical about democracy's overall performance potential, agree that democracy fared better than most of its rivals throughout the twentieth century. Democracies saw significant economic growth compared to totalitarian regimes, they did not go to war with each other, they did not let their citizens starve from famine or succumb to other natural disasters, and they had relative civil peace. The dictatorships of the twentieth century, whether on the right or the left, did poorly on all these measures.

But looking into the future, we might want to say that democracy's positive score card has had more to do with the quality of the competition than the inherent strength of democracy. The planned economies of the twentieth century were failed experiments, and right-wing dictators fared no better on performance measures. But the twenty-first century might be very different. China is showing some staggeringly impressive numbers on various performance scales. The problems we face in the twenty-first century, for example, climate change, might be different than the problems and challenges of the twentieth century. Democracies have done adequately so far, but what's to say that success continues? There might be other options to think about in addition to the ones offered by twentieth-century regimes. Empirical political science focuses on uncovering the causal mechanisms at work in democracy's relative success on performance scales. Normative democratic theory takes a different approach to performance. The comparison group does not have to be limited to existing political regimes but can include ideal-type alternatives. So, for example, some scholars have suggested that although China's regime, as an empirical matter, shows problems of corruption, it projects an ideal-type meritocracy that would outperform even properly functioning democracies (Bell 2015).

The biggest difference between normative and empirical theory, however, is that the former is hesitant to specify, in any empirical detail, what constitutes a "right answer" or offer any specific criteria to measure performance. With some exceptions I mention below, performance theorists do not in fact measure the performance of democracies. Instead, they defend performance as the correct measure and sometimes specify in general terms what would constitute good performance, for example, just laws, but they do not get into the question of evaluating the efficacy and quality of legislative agendas. First, many things might be involved in good performance in addition to democratic input. State capacity and bureaucratic corruption, for example, might be two factors that derail performance and so it might be hard to say that democracy itself was at fault. Normative theorists focus on isolating the democratic component of performance. They ask, why should we think that democratic decision procedures produce good decisions?

Second, performance theorists do not want to deny that we disagree about many things, and democratic theory cannot tell you if one piece of tax legislation is more correct than another piece of tax legislation. Furthermore, they do not want to get tangled in the empirical and possibly partisan questions of defending some specific legislative agenda as correct or better. But they do want to insist on the principle that "There are procedure-independent right answers to at least some political questions" (Brennan and Landemore 2022: 7), even if we cannot always agree on what those are. This view is often defended as analogous to how we think about scientific procedures (Brennan and Landemore 2022: 9; for a criticism of this analogy, see Ingham 2012). We do not know the right answer before the hypothesis is tested using scientific procedures, but we assume that there is a procedure-independent right answer. Following the procedure does not make the outcome correct; the outcome is correct, if it is in fact correct, because it corresponds to some independent state of affairs.

Sometimes theorists will suggest obviously bad outcomes (war, famine, economic collapse, political collapse, devastating epidemics, and genocides, for example) as a lower-end performance threshold (Estlund 2008: 163). If democracies can be shown to avoid these, then that counts in their favor on instrumental grounds. But this is a low bar and seems more like thresholds for a failed state than performance criteria that we can use to determine that democracies perform better than autocracies. There are some exceptions to the hesitancy in identifying actual outcomes as right or wrong answers. In the climate change debate, some people think that there is a clear right answer and democracies have not been very good at coming to it (Mittiga 2022; Shearman and Smith 2007). The question is not about details like whether we should be pursuing carbon credits or not. The question is more generally about addressing climate change. It is sometimes argued that democracy tends toward the wrong answer primarily because all democracies suffer from short-termism (Bell 2015; for a criticism of this argument, MacKenzie 2021). Electoral cycles make it very difficult to sell long-term policy, and future generations do not vote. Pandemic politics is sometimes presented as the opposite problem. Pandemics require fast short-term compliance and restrictions. Here the messy pluralist rights-based politics of democracy makes developing and implementing effective policy like herding cats. In both cases, then, the arguments flow from what is seen as an (obviously) bad outcome (slow movement on climate change and ineffectual public health measures). Both these problems have bolstered ideas that we need more expert/scientific input in decisions and less democratic input, as well as counterarguments warning against handing over decisions to technocrats and experts. But for now I leave aside issue-specific complaints about democratic performance and discuss theorists who take a more procedural view. Which is to say, they look at the features of democratic decision procedures and ask whether these features are likely to produce good decisions.

I begin with the skeptics and then in the next chapter take up arguments that defend democracy on "right answer" grounds. Very generally, all these arguments involve an epistemic approach to democracy. Epistemic means relating to knowledge or standards we use to evaluate knowledge and truth claims. In democratic theory this meaning is relaxed and stretched. It means that we are interested in the quality of democratic judgments or soundness of democratic decisions. The point is to get as close to the right or correct answer as possible. Quality and soundness are often quite capaciously defined. These judgments could be conceptualized in "terms of good government, human rights, social justice, a developmental index, a happiness index, or something like that, or something else entirely" (Landemore 2016: 143). Thus epistemic has come to be the umbrella term under which many types of outcomes are subsumed. For example, some people have argued that democracy is to be valued instrumentally because it can or is most

Instrumentalism 2: Performance Skeptics

likely to deliver social justice (Dworkin 1987). Social justice is not strictly speaking an epistemic value, but it can be subsumed under an epistemic approach to democracy in the sense that it is thought to be the "correct" outcome. Epistemic arguments for and against democracy focus on the quality of the democratic outcome (and not on the fairness of the procedure), but they vary on what constitutes quality outcomes.

Citizen competence

Although political philosophy has always had its fair share of democracy critics, contemporary democratic theory has seen an unprecedented uptick in democracy skepticism and, more surprisingly, a questioning of the value of elections and universal suffrage. This has, to be sure, shaken up a complacent tendency to sacralize voting and elections (Bagg forthcoming: 190). And in some ways the vehement criticism of this trend has been as interesting as the trend itself. What is this trend? Repackaging the oldest criticism of democracy that we have, namely from Plato, performance-focused democracy skeptics point to citizens' incompetence to argue against the unquestioned assumption that the people should rule. Few philosophers within the western tradition suggest that modern liberal democracies should entirely give up on democracy in favor of a philosopher-king. But many philosophers are suggesting that contemporary democracies can and ought to scale back and limit the influence of the unknowledgeable and conversely augment the role of experts and competent judges. But most controversial is that many of these theories question the value of universal suffrage. Here is where the intrinsic and instrumental values of democracy clash head-to-head. Some instrumentalists argue that "one person, one vote" only has value if it can be shown to produce better outcomes than other decision procedures.

These arguments begin from a "realistic" assessment of citizen competence. Within citizenship and democracy studies, this mounting evidence comes in four overlapping and to some extent mutually reinforcing areas of research.[1] The first area documents the fact that citizens are generally very poorly informed about politics, policies, candidates, and how government works (Caplan

2007; Converse 2000; Somin 2013). It is not so much that citizens are incapable of learning; it is that the realities of modern life make it unlikely or even impossible to suppose that large numbers of people in mass democracies are going to reach any significant level of knowledge about the important questions facing us as a political community. Ordinary citizens do inform themselves about all sorts of things that are important to them, from the mechanics of agricultural combines to the latest space launch. So why not politics? Rational ignorance is the term used to describe the problem: with so little tangible return on one's individual vote, there is little incentive to make the effort to become informed. The rational ignorance argument is then bolstered by survey research documenting the lack of knowledge.

Second, there is a body of cognitive psychological research that suggests that, at a deep level, humans are "motivated reasoners"; our motivations are not dominated by an interest in truth but instead by an interest in being right, winning, or not wanting to admit that we are wrong (Kahneman, Slovic, and Tversky 1982; Lodge and Taber 2013). Motivated reasoning comes with all sorts of biases (confirmation bias, in-group bias, observational-selection bias, and good old-fashioned rationalization, to name but a few) that skew our reasoning and make impartial, purely evidence-driven judgment very difficult without structure, training, and mechanisms of correction – for example, the structure, training, and criticism offered by a scientific community. It is worth noting that scientists, and indeed all experts, are also subject to motivated reasoning. The difference, it is sometimes argued, is that they work within a set of procedures and practices that are designed to mitigate this flaw or tendency in human reasoning. But there are studies that question whether experts really are freer of these biases than ordinary citizens (Christensen, Holst, and Molander 2022).

The third body of research focuses more on political communication than on human psychology as such and suggests that political preferences are deeply endogenous to the communicative context (Disch 2011; Druckman 2014) and fundamentally unstable (Bartels 2003). Multiple and often hidden forces shape and structure our opinions in such a radical way that it might even be difficult to say that they are either ours or real opinions. The most obvious are framing and priming. Public opinion data show that opinions on a question may change dramatically depending on how the survey question is worded. These data point to citizens' susceptibility to manipulation. I will have more to say about this particular aspect of citizens' opinions in chapters 9 and 10.

The final research area – and the one that has come to dominate American public opinion research and led many scholars down the road of realism – focuses on polarization. Here evidence is mounting that political preferences are often driven by identity rather than ideology (Iyengar, Sood, and Lelkes 2012; Mason 2018). Identity here means group attachment. In-group/out-group identification appears in some circumstances to be a more salient independent variable affecting political preferences and voting than policies, positions, or platforms put forward by candidates and parties. Under conditions of polarization, emotional or affective attachment to one's party comes to dominate all political preferences and judgment. Indeed, under these conditions it is difficult to say that any real judgment is going on. The metaphor often invoked here is that of a team booster (or rabid fan): loyalty to a team, no matter what, has very little to do with judgment or accountability.

In sum, voters do not have the knowledge to make competent judgments, their reasoning is often flawed and biased, they are susceptible to manipulation by elites, and, finally, they are easily swept up by affective polarization that detaches political preferences from processes of justification and accountability.

What should we make of the evidence that ordinary citizens lack basic competence to make political judgments? What knowledge citizens do in fact possess and what knowledge they need to possess for democracy to function properly is a complicated and contested question that, contrary to many of the theorists we are about to review, is not a settled matter in political science (Farrell, Mercier, and Schwartzberg 2023; Mackie 2012; Sides 2021). Some of the evidence is disputed because scholars have been unable to replicate the experimental data (Shaw 2017); other studies question any causal link between low information levels and low competence (Delli Carpini and Keeter 1996; Luskin 1987) and suggest that there is no clear standard of political competence and so low information is simply assumed to stand in for low competence; others have questioned whether the research is really getting at the sort of individual competence we need and expect from citizens, pointing to shortcuts and heuristics as adequate pathways to competence (Lupia and McCubbins 1998); and still others have argued that collective competence is not a matter of aggregating individual competence (Farrell, Mercer, and Schwartzberg 2023; Landemore 2013). I will return to this in more detail in the next chapter. But for now let us assume that there is some truth to this picture of ordinary citizens. If one is a full instrumentalist committed to the position that only the quality of the output can justify the decision procedure, then this body of research must surely give one pause.

In contemporary democratic theory, there are primarily three ways that theorists who are convinced that voter incompetence is a serious threat to performance mitigate this threat. I have sorted them into technocratic, epistocratic, and meritocratic solutions to low citizen competence. Technocracy is rule by experts. Epistocracy is rule by the knowledgeable or wise. Meritocracy is rule by the best sort of people, usually defined as a combination of being knowledgeable and public-spirited or virtuous. These three types of instrumental criticisms of democracy all start with a negative assessment of citizen competence and its impact on public policy and decisions. But, from there, they have differing solutions and institutional suggestions to enhance performance.

Technocracy

Investigating the tension between technocracy and democracy has a long history (Dahl 1989). Democratic theory is full of worry that complexity and the increasingly accelerated pace of change will push more and more policy questions into the hands of experts shielded from democratic oversight (Fischer 2009). Here one sees concern about "a growing concentration of power in the hands of a set of unelected 'regulatory bodies', drawing their legitimacy primarily from their technical competence and administrative expertise" (Bickerton and Invernizzi-Accetti 2017). But in this section I am not taking up the general question of the role and place of expertise in democracy (for this, see Christensen, Holst, and Molander 2022; Moore 2017; Pamuk 2021). I will have occasion to discuss that further along in the book. Here I want to focus on theories of instrumental value that are skeptical of democracy on performance grounds.

While few contributors to democratic theory voluntarily embrace the label of technocrat, I use the term to identify views that defend a sharp distinction between experts and citizens and that worry about citizens' lack of expertise, hyperpolarization, and the rise of populist rhetoric that targets experts as elite usurpers of ordinary citizens' democratic power (Nichols 2017). Unlike epistocrats, who I discuss next, technocrats usually do not suggest dismantling basic democratic procedures – for example, limiting the franchise – and consider themselves full supporters of democracy. Technocrats do suggest reducing the harmful influence of incompetent citizens, as well as partisan politics, by deferring to either expert committees and non-elected regulatory agencies or the market. "The core idea of technocracy is that political decision making is 'depoliticized' for efficiency reasons and insulated from the democratic process" (Sánchez-Cuenca 2017: 362; see also Cole 2022). Deferring to the market is a case of technocracy because it involves claims about efficiency over democracy, and because those who champion the market over democratically steered government usually do so on the grounds that this is what expert economists tell us to do (Caplan 2007).

Thus deferring to the market is really deferring to economists. Technocratic arguments are often tied to the notion that economics is a science, economic policy is crucial to performance, and ordinary citizens (and their representatives) have no clue about economics (or are driven by irrational passions) and so make disastrous policy choices (Somin 2013). There are three argumentative strategies employed against leaving decisions to markets to sort out. The first is to question whether markets can produce better outcomes than democratic procedures (Elliott 2019). Second is to question the claim to knowledge put forward by economists. There is a great deal of disagreement among economists, and they do not have particularly impressive track records for getting the right answer (Holst and Molander 2020). Finally, there is the normative argument that market-driven decisions lack legitimacy and suffer from a democratic deficit.

The discourse on democracy and technocracy is also then a discourse about markets and efficiency versus democracy and accountability. A popular arena for this discourse is the democratic deficit of EU governance often seen as out-of-touch bureaucrats in Brussels with bankers whispering in their ears (Matthijs and Blyth 2018; Sánchez-Cuenca 2017). The 2008 financial crisis is also a flash point in this debate as it is seen as empowering central banks and other unaccountable non-elected bodies governed by market logics. Although few people self-identify as technocrats, many calls for insulating policy decisions from popular control are technocratic arguments. This debate has in some sense become muddied by extravagant and sometimes alarming populist attacks on science, expertise, and bureaucracy (Hanson and Kopstein 2022). On the one hand, not all democratic theory that worries about technocratic encroachment is populist. On the other hand, defending a legitimate and important role for experts in government is not always, or even often, a problematic form of technocracy that questions democratic input. Figuring out how to distinguish the populist versions of anti-technocracy from democratic versions will have to wait until chapter 8.

Epistocracy

The term "epistocracy" has come to describe a group of theories that focus almost exclusively on voter ignorance as the threat to adequate outcomes. Jason Brennan's provocatively titled book *Against Democracy* is much cited as the leader in this area (Brennan 2016). Brennan's argument against democracy rests on three pillars. The first points to the research mapping citizen incompetence that we reviewed in the first half of this chapter. The second is a philosophical argument that regime types can be coherently defended or criticized on instrumental grounds alone, which is to say, on whether they produce or fail to produce good, or at least competent, outcomes. All attempts at procedural defenses – for example, that democratic procedures are fair, instantiate equality, or recognize each person's dignity and autonomy – fail according to Brennan. The third part of Brennan's case against democracy is a libertarian rights claim that denies an equal right to vote but defends a right of each individual not to be ruled by incompetent and unreasonable people. It is worth noting in passing that appealing to this right would appear to place Brennan's democratic theory outside of realist political philosophy, although he is often referred to as a realist.

Like Plato, Brennan and other epistocrats often use medicine as the appropriate analogy:

> Most of my fellow citizens are incompetent, ignorant, irrational and morally unreasonable about politics. Despite that they hold political power over me . . . I should not have to tolerate that. Just as it would be wrong to force me to go under the knife of an incompetent surgeon . . . it seems wrong to force me to submit to the decisions of incompetent voters. (Brennan 2016: 142)

Citizens have a presumptive right to be governed by competent decision makers, and "in realistic circumstances, universal suffrage will often violate this presumptive right. Current democracies are to that extent unjust" (Brennan 2016: 143).

This line of reasoning has led to several proposals to limit and restrict the power of incompetent citizens in the political system. Most of these involve some tinkering with and indeed limitation of universal suffrage to insure minimal levels of epistemic competence. Competency tests have been suggested (Brennan 2016), as well as plural voting schemes (Mulligan 2018) and an enfranchising lottery where those chosen to have a vote must go through a competence-building exercise (Lopez-Guerra 2011). In all cases, there is a call to either disenfranchise incompetent voters or dilute their influence by giving competent voters more votes.

Needless to say, these proposals are extremely controversial. There has been a widespread and vigorous set of counterarguments advanced to challenge epistocratic claims that target the franchise. Four types of arguments have been advanced against epistocrats. The first is what has come to be known as the demographic objection (Ingham and Wiens 2021). Here the argument is that it is impossible to isolate epistemic competence as a criterion of political power from other invidious distinctions, for example, race or income. Epistocrats insist that they oppose discrimination and injustice and claim that we can separate epistemic standards, such as those used in professional certification procedures in law and medicine, from problematic types of discrimination. The demographic objection doubts that that is possible.

The second argument questions the assumption that epistocracy would outperform democracy. Epistocrats tend to rely on a stands-to-reason sort of inference. When voters are individually and on average incompetent, it stands to reason that, as a group, they will choose sub-par policies and representatives. But is this in fact true? A number of arguments have been advanced to suggest that group dynamics might mitigate individual incompetence (Goodin and Spiekermann 2018). This suggests that studies that catalogue individual gaps in knowledge might not translate into collective suboptimal decisions. I explain this argument in more detail in the next chapter. Others point out that it is not even clear what impact individual opinions have on the policy output. Epistocrats go directly from poorly informed voters to presumptively bad policy without either explaining exactly how the opinions translate into policy or pointing out actual disastrous policy that has resulted from the input of incompetent citizens.

A third line of criticism focuses on what is argued to be a very naive idea of knowledge and competence invoked by epistocrats who suggest competency can be easily measured in "competency tests" (Gunn 2019). But, as the ongoing debate about standardized tests for admission to institutions of higher education shows, measuring knowledge is not so simple. It is not at all clear what these tests would look like or what they would actually measure.

The final criticism defends the intrinsic value of democratic procedures, especially "one person, one vote," as the core value of democracy and questions the hardcore instrumentalism that informs the epistocratic view (Elliot 2018).

The critiques of epistocracy far outnumber the defenses. There has been a bit of a pile-on phenomenon going on. It is worth pausing and taking note of this situation. Claims that were once thought beneath the attention of political philosophy – suggestions that we roll back universal suffrage, usually espoused by cranks and conservative throwbacks to the nineteenth century – are now being debated in the leading journals in the field and published by the most prestigious university presses. I am not suggesting that we ought to consider epistocratic challenges to "one person, one vote" beneath our attention. On the contrary, I am suggesting that democratic theory is facing a new era where there is real and genuine skepticism about many features of democracy that we have taken for granted. We ignore these challenges at our peril. Epistocrats offer just one challenge to the sacred cow of equal voting rights. Meritocracy, which I outline next, is an even more radical challenge, and in chapter 9 I look at lottocracy, where the radical proposals call for replacing voting entirely with selection by lot. The interest in these alternatives signals a new era in democratic theory.

Meritocracy

Meritocracy is the rule of the best sort of people. Many but not all defenses of representative democracy suggest that, if they are functioning properly, elections will select, or ought to be a mechanism for selecting, the best and the brightest. This view sees a basic compatibility – indeed, a synergy – between elections and meritocracy. The Federalists argued along these lines, suggesting that Athenian-type direct democracy was always a slippery slope to mob rule. But elections, if properly structured, would be a selection process that ensured that capable and public-spirited individuals would rise to the top and rule (Wooton 2003: 173). Against this view, the Antifederalists thought that representatives should be as much like ordinary people as possible. The meritocratic ideals of the Federalists were elitist, argued the Antifederalists, and, rather than resulting in sound policy directed at the common good, would reflect the privileged interests of a commercial class aspiring to be aristocrats (Wooton 2003: 17). Although Madison's ideal of rulers "who possess most wisdom to discern, and most virtue to pursue, the common good of society" (Wooton 2003: 259) is sometimes appealed to, contemporary debates about meritocracy have taken a surprising turn away from the merit of elected representatives. Meritocracy has come to be identified with arguments inspired by Confucianism and an aspirational picture of political regimes in China, Singapore, and Hong Kong (Bai 2019; Bell 2015; see He and Warren 2020 for an overview and critique). I draw on Daniel Bell's work as exemplary of this type of argument.

Daniel Bell begins with what he considers an uncontroversial view of good government: "voters should do their best to select wise leaders, the government should try to structure the economy so that the benefits do not accrue only (or mainly) to a small group of rich people, leaders should not enact policies that wreck the environment for future generations, and the political system should not poison social relations" (Bell 2015: 19).

These are clearly performance-based standards of evaluation. He then suggests, often using the very same evidence introduced by epistocrats, that electoral democracy does poorly on meeting these standards because of four tyrannies. Tyranny of the majority points to "irrational and self-interested majorities" (Bell 2015: 7) having pernicious influence on the policy process and bad judgment in choosing leaders; tyranny of the minority highlights the power of wealth in the political process, especially agenda setting; tyranny of the voting community raises the problem of future generations whose interests are overlooked by the short-termism of electoral cycles; and tyranny of competitive individualists suggests that electoral competition exacerbates and exploits cleavages and difference such that social fragmentation and debilitating polarization are almost inevitable. This last problem speaks to the underlying philosophy of Confucianism that values harmony as both an intrinsic good and as an instrumental goal to be achieved.

For Bell and others in this group, "one person, one vote" and the underlying principle of political equality fail to produce decisions that are in fact good for everyone equally. They embrace what might be called a democratic principle in that they think good government is government that is responsive to the real and vital interests of the people, but they suggest that achieving this goal requires skilled, socially integrated, and public-spirited individuals making the decisions, and electoral democracy fails to produce those. Few contributors to this tradition claim that China or Singapore has achieved this ideal of good government. But they often do claim that the ideals embedded in the selection process of leaders within these regimes, although often corrupted, reflect a more sensible approach to decision making than democracy does. Thus meritocrats do not argue, as democrats might, that the ills of electoral democracy are a matter of failing to live up to an ideal embedded in the institutional model. Meritocrats argue that electoral democracy is inherently flawed, while the meritocratic systems of China and Singapore are contingently flawed.

Like in the case of epistocrats, there are many critiques of meritocracy. Unlike epistocrats, Confucian-inspired meritocrats are not proposing reforms for western liberal democracies. They are seeking legitimacy for alternative decision procedures and regime types. Most of these criticisms, therefore, take issue with the argument that flaws in actual regimes that claim to be meritocratic are merely contingent (He et al. 2016). China comes under special critical scrutiny where it is argued that corruption and oppressive mechanisms of control are inherent to the regime type.

Conclusion

On the one hand, performance-based criticisms of democracy that seriously question political equality and the universal franchise are widely condemned and criticized. This suggests that some dimension of the equality argument that we looked at in chapter 3 has a hold on democratic theory as well as democratic citizens. On the other hand, the widespread engagement with these theories reflects real concern about the quality of policy being produced in democratic regimes. Part of that concern is certainly tied to citizen input into the process. But low individual competence levels might not necessarily translate into low collective competence levels, as we will see in the next chapter. Furthermore, individual-level opinion formation is a complicated process where elites – indeed knowledgeable elites – might be responsible for some of the pathologies of citizens' competence, for example, the rise in affective polarization as well as some populist policy preferences (Bartels 2023).

But, ultimately, performance-based evaluations of democracy need to measure performance and cannot rely only on questioning voter input. Here the real problem becomes clear. On the one hand, most empirical indexes of performance give democracies high scores (so far) compared to autocracies and, on the other hand, when we look at more fine-grained evaluations of policy, there is no agreement on what good policy looks like. Many performance skeptics are focused on economic policy, but, as I have already noted, there is no consensus on correct economic solutions to public problems. Thus some performance-based criticisms of democracy risk looking like they come from a partisan place of policy preference rather than a philosophical place of principled argument.

7
Instrumentalism 3: Epistemic Democracy

ON the other side of the performance divide are democratic theorists who argue that democracy is to be valued because it tends to get the right answer. I refer to this group generally as epistemic democrats because all share the view that democracy does or, if well-ordered, would tend to produce sound and reasonable outcomes. Of course, we can all point to disastrous policies and people chosen through democratic means, and therefore "tend" is an important qualifier here. All epistemic democrats embrace some version of the adage two (or more) heads are better than one, also articulated as a confidence in the wisdom of the multitude.[1] But there is large variation in how theorists defend this claim and which democratic mechanisms they think are at work to produce epistemically sound outcomes. At one end of the spectrum are theories that focus on the miracle of aggregation and pay particular attention to majority-rule voting procedures. At the other end of the spectrum are theories that see deliberation in both democratic public spheres and assemblies as doing the epistemic heavy lifting.

In some discussions of epistemic democracy, it is thought that a defining feature of such a theory is that "there exists some procedure-independent fact of the matter as to what the best or right outcome is" (Goodin and List 2001: 280; Schwartzberg 2015), and democracy is the best method of getting that outcome.[2] The role, place, and even possibility of a "procedure-independent fact of the matter" is a contested and controversial question, however, both within and outside epistemic democracy. Many people feel very uncomfortable with the idea that there are "political truths" or correct and incorrect answers to political questions, as this seems to downplay the importance of respecting democratic disagreement and pluralism and offers an invitation to bypass democratic procedures and go directly for the truth (Lafont 2020). While certain facts, evidence, and settled scientific consensus about the truth may and ought to be drawn on when taking a political decision, many democratic theorists believe that political judgment and choosing sound public policy cannot be reduced to selecting the correct option. Skepticism about political truth or correct answers to political questions has spawned considerable criticism of epistemic democracy along with, of course, even more vigorous opposition to epistocrats (Fleuss 2021; Lafont 2020; Urbinati 2014). These critics then tend to place epistemic democrats and epistocrats in the same problematic category, suggesting that epistemic democrats are on a slippery slope to epistocracy despite their radically different assessment of democratic institutions and publics.

Criticism of what is sometimes called "correctness theory" (Estlund 2008: 99) (the details of which I outline below), even if compelling, does not fit all theories of epistemic democracy, however. There are several arguments in favor of the epistemic credentials of democracy that are also skeptical about political truth and concerned about pluralism, and so do not assume that political questions have right or wrong answers or that most political questions can in any way be reduced to a matter of fact (Anderson 2006; Knight and Johnson 2011). These theories, often influenced by pragmatism, argue that we should value democracy because its procedures are good at solving practical problems for which there are no procedure-independent correct answers. In what follows, I begin with correctness theories, which do presuppose a correct answer to at least some political questions put to voters, and then move to theories that progressively relax the "procedure-independent correct answer" premise but stay within the realm of epistemic defenses of democracy.

Condorcet Jury Theorem

The Condorcet Jury Theorem (CJT) has been described as "the jewel in the crown" of epistemic democracy (List and Goodin 2001: 283). Although first suggested by the Marquis of Condorcet in 1785, it is only since the late 1980s that there has developed a sustained interest in rehabilitating this theorem as a defense of epistemic democracy and majority rule (Grofman and Feld 1988; see Schwartzberg 2015 for an overview of this development). As the name suggests, CJT is a mathematical proposition derived from the law of large numbers. The theorem states that if the average voter is even slightly more likely than random to choose the correct answer in a binary choice, then, as the number of choosers increase, so does the probability that the majority outcome will be correct. Three conditions must be met for the theorem to be correct: the average voter's competence must be better than random, votes must be statistically independent of each other, and voters must vote sincerely. There is a fourth condition not so much underlying the theorem itself but rather underlying its applicability to democratic politics: there must be a correct answer to the question being asked of the voter. All four of these conditions face challenges when we move from mathematics to democratic politics.

The assumption that voters' competence must be better than random is not an epistemically high bar, however. "Sheer ignorance [. . .] provides no reason to think that people would be worse than random on average (at least given a large number of people)" (Goodin and Spiekermann 2018: 52). On the one hand, this seems counterintuitive as one would think that knowledge (or at least not sheer ignorance) is a cornerstone of decisional competence and claims that democratic procedures produce epistemically sound outcomes. On the other hand, this is precisely the beauty of CJT: even without high levels of knowledge (perhaps an unachievable ideal in modern mass democracy), large numbers of people all addressing the same question tend to get it right in the aggregate. There is a catch, however. "It takes something like widely shared prejudices and systematic biases that people introduce into many people's judgments at the same time and in the same direction to drive individual competence below random" (Goodin and Spiekermann 2018: 52; see also Estlund 2008: 16). Thus systematic error produced by widespread social bias, propaganda, or information manipulation might significantly affect the "better than random" condition. This problem on its own does not point to the impossibility of satisfying the conditions of CJT, however. It instead points to the importance of minimizing propaganda, manipulation, and systemic prejudice.

Systemic error might be connected to a violation of the second condition – votes must be statistically independent of each other – and this condition is more challenging than the competence condition. The intuition here is straightforward, but what this might mean for evaluating real voting is not clear. Suppose a charismatic opinion leader has one million followers who vote exactly as she tells them to vote. In this situation, we do not have one million separate votes; instead, it is as if the charismatic leader votes one million times (Goodin and Spiekermann 2018: 54). Statistically independent means that one's vote for X is not affected by the probability that someone else votes for X. Much depends on how "affected by" is understood. An early criticism of CJT was to point out that independence is both unrealistic and undesirable if it implies that individual voting must be undertaken in some kind of a social and political vacuum with little communication or deliberation among voters (Estlund et al. 1989: 1327).[3] Even without the case of the charismatic or manipulative leader, the independence assumption so necessary for the math to work seems problematic in real life, where voting preferences are the result of ongoing social intersubjective processes as well as elite messaging and persuasion. Several defenders of the CJT, however, have argued that the independence condition does not require an atomistic assumption about voters (Estlund 1994; Goodin and Spiekermann 2018).[4] If millions of people are in the thrall of a single leader and this determines their voting behavior, this is a problem for CJT. But, in complex democracies with multiple messages, multiple parties, multiple elites, and millions or even hundreds of millions of voters, some level of independence can often be assumed because of the cross-cutting and multiple sources of influence that do not add up to a clear compromise of individual independence. Furthermore, persuasion in deliberation is not the same thing as slavishly following another's lead in voting and is compatible with the condition that each voter is casting an independent vote at the ballot box (Estlund et al. 1989). But, like the competence condition, independence is conditional on empirical factors that need to be assessed in order to make the case that CJT is generally applicable.

The sincerity condition means that everyone must vote for what they believe is the best or most correct outcome. This condition is undone by strategic voting. Defenders of CJT argue that real strategic voting is a very complex undertaking and there is good reason to suppose that although most voters may consider it, they vote sincerely when casting their ballot (Goodin and Spiekermann 2018: 48).

The dimension of the CJT that provokes the most concern and interest, however, is the condition that there must be a correct answer in the set of possible choices. Here it appears that the analogy with juries and democratic publics breaks down. Juries are tasked with evaluating the evidence to determine whether the defendant is guilty or not guilty according to the law. For juries, there is a fact of the matter (even if they do not always have a clear picture of it) underlying the legal question and so a correct answer to the guilty/not guilty judgment. But how often is this the case for questions facing democratic publics or elected assemblies?

Goodin and Spiekermann argue that although it is not always the case, there are many democratic decisions that can be construed as having a correct answer. The original requirement that choice needs to be binary should be relaxed, they argue, and then all that is needed is that one of the options be superior in some procedure-independent sense. Sometimes the superiority of the choice is premised on the evidence used to justify the decision. For example, one might think that mask mandates are not a straightforward correct or incorrect type of question because for some people they represent a serious violation of freedom. Should we or shouldn't we prioritize freedom is not a question for which there is a fact of the matter. But, if the anti-mask-mandate option is justified by faulty science or poor evidence, then the decision clearly has a truth-apt component to it. Thus, if a judgment involves evaluating evidence that could be determinate in the decision, CJT suggests that, if the other three conditions are approximated, then we have some confidence that majorities will come down on the answer that is backed by the facts. The theorem can be restated this way: "in so far as there are correct answers to be found politically, they are more likely to be found through democratic than through any other decision-making procedures" (Goodin 2017: 352). The "in so far as" is the crux of the matter and suggests that each decision will have a different level and type of truth aptness. In other words, there is no linear scale from yes/no matter-of-fact questions to open-ended value questions. Each judgment or decision a voter is confronted with (including choosing a representative) will have its own unique truth-apt dimension to it.

Ironically, the successful application and relevance of CJT to real democracies creates its own problems. If many of our democratic decisions have a right answer, and if the public sphere is functioning halfway properly with little manipulation or propaganda, then CJT implies that majorities will be right much of the time and minorities wrong much of the time. Indeed, under very good conditions majorities are said to be close to infallible. For juries, we would want and hope this to be true. But this seems problematic in democracies (Anderson 2006; Ingham 2012). Thinking that minorities are usually or often wrong, without an assessment of the substantive content of their claims and priorities, appears to undermine ideals of political equality that rely on respecting disagreement among equals as an important component of democracy. There is a second reason why embracing CJT might work against democracy. From an epistemic point of view, CJT evaluates the probability of a correct outcome for individual votes and not for democratic processes over time. A majority might choose the correct option on the table at the time, but it might not be the best option overall or over time. We often need feedback mechanisms (including listening to minorities) to correct earlier judgments (Anderson 2006). From this perspective it is important that every democratic decision is seen as fallible and corrigible.

Where does this leave us in assessing CJT? CJT cannot be the end of the story about the epistemic value of democracy, but it can be the beginning. First, it offers a counterweight to views that assume that competence and numbers are on a sliding scale. It suggests that even with low (but not disastrous) levels of knowledge, the law of large numbers is on the side of majorities. The problem with relying on CJT to do all the work in defending democracy on performance-outcome grounds is not that the conditions are difficult to achieve or assess or even that many of our democratic decisions do not appear to have a correct answer. It is that CJT is formal and so can't tell us *why* two heads are better than one. There is no epistemic or cognitive mechanism at work that could give us confidence that the substance of the outcome is the right answer. Its clearest illustrations have no epistemic content: if 1,000 coins are weighted to come up heads ever so slightly more often than tails, then chances are very good that heads will come up more than 50 percent of the time (Estlund 2008). But what makes heads the right answer? The cognitive emptiness of the mechanism (law of large numbers) is both unsatisfying as a theory of epistemic democracy and as a reason one might give to citizens for why majority outcomes are sound or indeed correct (Niesen 2021).

Diversity Trumps Ability Theorem

Like CJT, Diversity Trumps Ability (DTA) is a mathematical theorem for which one of its creators claims the status of "logical truth" (Page 2007: 162). Despite the math, the underlying intuition, however, has more cognitive substance than CJT and moves epistemic defenses of democratically inclusive decision procedures closer to explaining why many heads are better than one. The theorem – first presented by Lu Hong and Scott Page in a much-discussed 2004 paper in the *Proceeding of the National Academy of Sciences* – states that "a random group of intelligent problem solvers will outperform a group of best problem solvers," suggesting that cognitive diversity within the group of problem solvers is more important than expertise. The paper is highly technical (the problem solvers are algorithms) with no empirical extension and no mention of democracy, only the suggestion that the results have implications "for problem-solving firms and organizations" (Hong and Page 2004: 16389). Nevertheless, the paper has spurred a vigorous discussion regarding its relevance for democratic theory.

DTA operates under four conditions (Page 2007: 157–62). First, the problem must be difficult. If the problem is not a stumper, then the best problem solvers will get it every time. This leads to the counterintuitive conclusion that experts are fine for easy or at least straightforward and bounded problems but not for really hard ones. The problems facing democracies are often considered hard because of high levels of complexity and uncertainty. I will return to this point below. The second condition states that all the problem solvers must have some ability to solve the problem. A random selection of ordinary citizens will not solve a difficult physics problem better than physicists; but a random selection of ordinary physicists will outperform a group of Nobel Prizewinning physicists. This condition means that the mechanism at work in DTA is not aggregate guessing, but actual problem solving. The third condition is that the problem solvers must be cognitively diverse. This means that they employ different approaches and heuristics in problem solving: "When one agent gets stuck, there is always another agent that can find an improvement due to a different approach" (Hong and Page 2004: 16387). It is all about thinking outside each other's boxes. Diversity in the first instance does not refer to social, ideological, ethnic, or value diversity – in other words, what we usually think of as diversity in democratic theory. These may, however, turn out to be connected to cognitive diversity. Fourth, the randomly selected problem solvers must be drawn from a fairly large pool, and the group of problem solvers selected must also not be too small.

What does this mean for democracy? DTA does not offer a general and direct defense of democratic procedures (for example, majority rule) the way that CJT potentially does. It is instead corroborative of the general principle of the wisdom of crowds and suggests that the mechanism of that wisdom is diversity. How that might manifest itself in real democracies or be designed into democratic institutions is not self-evident.[5]

Hélène Landemore has developed a theory of epistemic democracy that relies heavily on the epistemic power of diversity as illustrated in DTA (Landemore 2012). Landemore is an instrumentalist who believes that outcome and performance offer the best defense of democracy. "Democracy does better than less inclusive and less egalitarian decision rules because, by including all voices equally, it structurally maximizes the cognitive diversity brought to bear on collective problems" (Brennan and Landemore 2022: 143; see also Landemore 2012). Landemore introduces three important extensions of DTA to make it more democratically friendly. The first is that she argues that cognitive diversity is captured by democratic inclusivity. Diversity Trumps Ability is replaced by a "numbers trump ability theorem"[6] under the assumption that involving large numbers "automatically ensures greater cognitive diversity" (Landemore 2012: 104). This extension is important because DTA could just as easily support epistocracy as democracy by suggesting that diversity within epistocratic institutions is important (Brennan 2016: 184). The second important extension is to introduce deliberation to the equation. DTA does not model deliberation per se, but there is no independence condition, and problem solvers "learn" from each other in the sense that when one is stumped, another takes the problem in a different direction. Thus, thinking about how DTA might play out in the real world, communication and deliberation between problem solvers seems a natural mechanism to optimize the process.

The third extension is to argue that in democracies, although specialized committees and groups of experts may be needed to address and problem-solve narrowly defined problems, democratic assemblies are all-purpose assemblies "for which there is ex ante uncertainty as to what the relevant diversity should be" (Landemore 2020: 42). They are debating climate change one day and lunches for preschool children the next. Pointing out that all-purpose decision bodies like parliaments require a different type of epistemic competence than specialized committees is a common argument against technocracy and epistocracy. Landemore in her most recent work takes this intuition in a radical direction. If high competence in all-purpose problem solving is what we seek in a well-performing democracy, then a random selection of the general population might be a better way to choose our representatives than electing who we think are the best and the brightest. Electing the best and brightest might mean that our elected assemblies, although showing ideological diversity on the surface, suffer from cognitive homogeneity at the level that counts. This argument is then used to defend sortition (random selection like we use for juries) as a method of choosing representatives (Landemore 2013, 2020). I discuss sortition in more detail in chapter 9. Here I just want to signal the connection between sortition and DTA.

DTA assumes that if there is a solution to the problem, then, when that solution is found, all problem solvers will recognize and agree that the solution has been found. Like fitting the last piece into a jigsaw puzzle, there will be no doubt that the goal has been achieved and all solvers will have an identical "Aha!" moment. This is analogous to CJT's assumption that there is a correct answer to the choice presented to voters. As with skepticism about correct answers to political questions, one might question the probability that political problems can be solved to the satisfaction of everyone involved. DTA has an advantage over CJT in this regard, however. Because DTA identifies a cognitive mechanism at work, it is possible to endorse the epistemic power of diversity without claiming that every outcome has achieved the optimal solution, or even that political problem solving is ever able to reach optimal solutions. Political problems are complex, multidimensional, require action over time, and display high levels of uncertainty and unpredictability. Thus not only are these problems hard (and so benefit from a diverse group of people working on them), but they are also not self-contained. Applying the lessons of DTA to politics does not hold out hope for doing away with disagreement about policy and solutions to problems. Instead, it focuses squarely on the process and suggests that group competence is not a matter of individual competence. This in turn is ammunition against democracy skeptics who do indeed reduce group competence to individual competence.

Pragmatism

CJT offers an argument for why majority rule voting under some conditions tends to get the right answer; DTA offers an argument for why optimal epistemic input to decision processes might favor democratic inclusiveness over oligarchic, technocratic, or epistocratic restrictions. In both cases, the move is from a narrowly defined, non-political formal model to messy, complex, and expansive political decisions in which the conditions of the formal model are never perfectly met. Nevertheless, the models do suggest that democratic decision procedures are not as epistemically hopeless as some critics have maintained. Rather than formal models, pragmatism uses the idea of inquiry, often epitomized in scientific inquiry, to help explicate the epistemic potential of democracy.

Contemporary pragmatists draw on two sources when developing epistemic theories of democracy: Charles Sanders Peirce and John Dewey. Peirce leads to relatively strong epistemic claims on behalf of democratic institutions, while the place of truth tracking in followers of Dewey is more contested (Festenstein 2019; MacGilvray 2014). Cheryl Mizak and Robert Talisse follow Peirce in arguing that humans have a fundamental interest in true belief, and, therefore, they have an interest in pursuing the best means of acquiring true belief (Mizak 2008; Talisse 2007). But what is the truth? For pragmatists, there is no truth out there to be discovered like a holy grail. All we have are methods that can test our truth claims. Cheryl Mizak describes Peirce's view this way: "A true belief is one that would stand up to inquiry. A true belief is one that is indefeasible – it would not be improved upon; it would forever meet the challenges of reasons, arguments, and evidence" (Mizak 2008: 95). Inquiry involves continuous, open, critical debate and deliberation. Properly structured inquiry, whether in the sciences or the realm of politics, is democratic in three senses: it is a collective, communal, and public process; inclusion of diverse points of view is an important condition of success because one wants every possible objection to be raised and answered; and it requires broad freedoms for all inquirers.

Peirce himself was not interested in politics. But in the hands of theorists who are interested in politics, this view is transformed into a justification of democracy because, of all the regimes at our disposal, democracy is the one that can come closest to instantiating the condition of inquiry. Therefore, democracy is the one that can produce the best (truest) policies. Mizak again: "democratically produced decisions are legitimate because they are produced by a procedure with a tendency to get things right" (Mizak 2008: 95). As democratic citizens and representatives, we are tasked with acting like good inquirers. This means subjecting our claims, principles, and policy proposals to the crucible of argument, reason giving, and justification. Connected to this view is a strong insistence on fallibility and revisability. All inquiry, including and perhaps especially democratic inquiry, is always open to improvement and revision in the face of new evidence, new problems, and new challenges.

When translated into political terms, ideals of inquiry do not point to voting as the core epistemic mechanism, but deliberation. Hence pragmatists are often described as, or describe themselves as, deliberative democrats – meaning that at the core of democracy is a type of collective communication, discussion, and reflection that can only be achieved among equals. For Mizak, the value of democratic equality is tied squarely to an instrumental goal of correct outcomes.

Pragmatists who follow John Dewey, although keen to outline the epistemic benefits of democracy, also often add non-epistemic goods achieved by democracy. Elizabeth Anderson argues that a Deweyan approach suggests that there are external *and* internal standards of success (Anderson 2006: 10). The external standards are performance based: "do the pollution laws enacted actually reduce pollution to acceptable levels at an acceptable cost. . . . Laws can get things right or wrong" (2006: 10). The internal standards refer to how we come to decide that something, for example reducing air pollution, is in the public interest. Here it is important that there is a procedurally fair way to give everyone a voice in determining the public good and setting the agenda. For Deweyans, "political institutions should be maximally inclusive not because this maximizes our chances of holding true beliefs" – the position held by Mizak and Talisse – "but rather because we believe that political institutions should advance the interests of everyone who is subject to them, and that everyone should have a say in judging their performance" (MacGilvray 2014: 117).

The inclusiveness of democratic procedures performs an epistemic as well as an ethical function for Deweyans. The better decision is the result of not only the deliberative process of testing claims but also diverse substantive input about what is in the public interest. The intuition underlying DTA is that problem solving requires a diversity of ways to approach problems. For pragmatists, diversity contributes substantive practical information essential to solving public policy problems that face real people who consider themselves a community of equals. For example, the nature of a problem and its solution may appear different depending on geographical location, class, occupation, education, gender, age, or race. "Surely an important part of the case for the epistemic merits of democracy rests on its ability to pool asymmetrically distributed information about the effects of problems and policies so as to devise solutions that are responsive to everyone's concerns" (Anderson 2006: 11). The ethical component is embedded in processes of deliberation and problem solving that embody mutual respect for each citizen (Anderson 2009: 220).

Critics of epistemic democracy often make no distinction between pragmatist and other types of arguments, claiming that all epistemic defenses of democracy embrace a problematic procedure-independent idea of truth (Ingham 2012; Invernizzi-Acetti 2017; Urbinati 2014; see Peter 2009 for an exception). I want to suggest, however, that pragmatist arguments avoid the dangers associated with "correctness theories." The two main reasons to worry about "political truth" are, first, that it appears to open the door to bypassing democratic procedures in favor of going straight to the truth, and thus truth has a certain anti-democratic tendency built in (Fleuss 2021; Lafont 2020). Second, it appears to stand in opposition to pluralism and reasonable disagreement. As we saw in chapter 3, many people embrace democracy precisely because we cannot agree about the truth, and so we need decision procedures that respect reasonable disagreement about the truth. Contemporary pragmatist democratic theory addresses these two worries via, on the one hand, a pragmatic understanding of truth where fallibilism, revision, and experimentalism are the most important elements and, on the other hand, an insistence that dissent and disagreement are the means through which diversity and inclusion work their epistemic magic.

Knight and Johnson, for example, although denying they have an epistemic theory of democracy, nevertheless defend the epistemic power of democratic procedures but distance themselves from the view that "democratic institutional mechanisms are in some sense truth tracking, where truth is posited as existing independently of the democratic process." In contrast to this, the authors "do not presume that in politics there is a truth of the matter waiting to be discovered" (Knight and Johnson 2011: 37–8, n. 48). Instead, there are problems to be solved in more or less efficacious and satisfactory ways. Better and worse outcomes replace true/false or correct/incorrect outcomes (Knight et al. 2016: 138). But how do we know outcomes are better or worse? Pragmatists appeal to ideas of experimentalism and reflexivity or learning to insist that epistemically better and worse can be recognized without positing procedure-independent standards of truth. We determine public goals, design policy to address those goals, implement the policy, assess the results, go back to the drawing board, learn from failures, and do it again. "The true epistemic virtues of democracy are not found in the static outcomes of voting but rather in the dynamic process of discussion and feedback to government policies already implemented" (Anderson 2009: 222). Rather than a procedure-independent standard of truth, pragmatists appeal to internal standards of comparison, correction, improvement, and learning in relation to past decisions and policies. Democracy, so the argument goes, is the best regime to instantiate this ideal because of the epistemic power of inclusiveness *and* dissent. Criticism, dissent, and challenge, are "epistemically productive, not merely a matter of error" (Anderson 2006: 9). Under non-ideal conditions, that dissent might need to be loud and disruptive. Alexander Livingston insists that, for Dewey, "coercive means can serve democratic ends when they are used to *provoke* rather than *resolve* democratic inquiry in the face of habits, ideologies, and institutions obstructing the public's inquiry into its problems" (Livingston 2017: 523).

Pragmatists agree that democracy has epistemic merits that recommend it over less inclusive forms of government. But pragmatists disagree on how much weight to give the epistemic argument as well as how much weight to give other reasons to value democracy. Chief among these other reasons is the value of equality and fairness, independent of its epistemic function. "Sometimes we want everyone's voice to be heard because we think that will make a better decision as a result, and sometimes we want everyone's voice to be heard simply because we think that everyone has a right to be heard" (MacGilvray 2014: 106). Although MacGilvray's appeal to "a right to be heard" has affinities with intrinsic defenses of democracy, ultimately Deweyan pragmatists do not value political equality and fairness as ends in themselves or as being derived from abstract principles of moral equality. Their arguments are consequentialist, which means that we learn through experience (or from the consequences of our actions) that respecting each other as equals in pursuing our common projects is good for all of us. Valuing democracy for pragmatic consequentialist reasons cannot be reduced to valuing democracy for narrowly instrumental reasons. Democracy's value is ascertained through living and practicing a democratic life and assessing the benefits – both material and moral – of that life for all of us. "We test our principles by living in accordance with them, seeing whether doing so solves the problems we were trying to solve, and delivers other consequences we find acceptable" (Anderson 2009: 224). When Deweyan pragmatists say "living in accordance with" democratic principles, they mean more than respecting voting and participation rights; they mean living according to democratic principles at a deep cultural level. To really see the value of democracy (indeed for democracy to have true value) it must become a way of life and inform our "habits and affects" (Anderson 2009). On this view, the epistemic benefits of democracy are not a standalone argument for why democracy is to be preferred to other regime types but are folded into a thicker ideal of democracy that encompasses social relations, culture, and attitudes. This also suggests that those benefits are produced only when we have developed a sufficiently democratic culture.

One criticism of pragmatism is that consequentialism runs afoul of pluralism (Peter 2009: 121). In order for the internal epistemic standards of comparison, correction, improvement, and learning to have purchase, democratic citizens must agree (to some extent) on shared goals. Without some shared goals, how can we evaluate whether our experiments in living (the consequences of collective problem solving) are successful or not? For pragmatists, dissent and disagreement are important epistemic forces in testing our attempts to reach our goals, but without a shared view of those goals or of the public good it is difficult to imagine the basis for evaluating epistemic improvement. Proceduralists like Fabienne Peter (whose views I look at below) argue that pragmatists must posit a public good about which there will be reasonable disagreement. This proceduralist critique once again raises the twin questions of "How deep does disagreement go?" and "How much underlying agreement in the form of shared values do we need to make democracy work?" For Deweyan pragmatists, democracy requires quite substantial shared commitments for it to work. This is a highly aspirational picture of democracy. Democracy is a work in progress aspiring to achieve a society where equality is deeply and widely embodied as a way of life. The proper criticism of this view (if criticism is even the correct word) is not that people can reasonably disagree with the goal of promoting a culture of equality but rather that it sadly seems out of our grasp and unrealistic.

Epistemic proceduralism

The final two versions of epistemic democracy I discuss in this section, David Estlund's and Fabienne Peter's contributions, reject pragmatist consequentialism and reintroduce strongly procedural elements to defending democracy on epistemic grounds. This brings us full circle to the opening arguments of chapter 3.

David Estlund's work has come to be associated very closely with epistemic democracy. He makes relatively modest claims, however, about the epistemic merits of democracy and outright rejects the idea that democratic legitimacy can be directly tied to performance. Estlund is primarily concerned with legitimacy and not with the value of democracy. Let's recap the difference. The value of democracy debate is about reasons one might have to support democracy over other forms of decision making or governance. Legitimacy is about the reasons one might have to obey the laws. Or, to put this another way, legitimacy is about what gives someone or some regime the right to rule over others. Estlund's most comprehensive statement defending his version of epistemic democracy, *Democratic Authority: A Philosophical Framework*, does not have the word "epistemic" in the title. Estlund's view of legitimacy or what justifies the authority to make laws is Rawlsian. A regime or collective decision procedure is legitimate if it can be found acceptable or be justified to all reasonable people. So the question that motivates Estlund is, in what ways can or ought epistemic considerations be part of the justification of regimes? Estlund argues that many traditional defenses of epistemic ideas of legitimacy are unjustifiable because they make a direct connection between knowledge and the right to rule. Even if we think that it would be a very good thing to have knowledgeable people in charge, this is not the same thing as showing that knowledge in and of itself gives someone the moral *right* to rule over others. The correctness of the outcome cannot generate a moral obligation to obey the law. The reason why is that special knowledge possessed by special people would never be acceptable to all as a source of legitimate power primarily because people disagree on what counts as a correct answer (Estlund 2008: 99). Nevertheless, he insists that epistemic considerations are important. A procedure that was shown to be fair but had no, or random, epistemic benefit would also be unjustifiable. Legitimacy requires a fair system that is epistemically better than random: "Democratically produced laws are legitimate and authoritative because they are produced by a procedure with a tendency to make correct decisions. It is not an infallible procedure and there might even be more accurate procedures. But democracy is better than random and is epistemically the best among those that are generally acceptable in the way that political legitimacy requires" (Estlund 2008: 8).

Estlund calls this view epistemic proceduralism. On this view, we do have to assume that there are better and worse (correct and incorrect) answers to political questions. But we do not need to specify those. We only need to find a procedure that *tends* to get the right answer.

Estlund views democracy through the prism of justifiability or what decision procedure is generally acceptable to an idealized group of reasoners. If democracy did not tend toward the right answer but only instantiated fairness, then why not just flip a coin? Flipping a coin is clearly unjustifiable among people who are free and equal. He uses this argument to challenge the non-epistemic procedural views canvased in chapter 3. Fairness or equal consideration cannot be the only grounds justifying democracy.

Estlund, unlike pragmatists for example, is not primarily interested in mapping how the procedures of democracy may get things right. Instead, he is interested in how epistemic considerations may indirectly generate obligation. Furthermore, his bar is very low. All we need to show is that democracy is better than random. In some of his early work, he endorsed the Condorcet Jury Theorem as a promising backup to the better-than-random claim, although he has since introduced some skepticism about CJT (Estlund 1994, 2008). He does suggest that exchanging views and deliberation are positive epistemic forces, but he does not hang his theory on establishing this as a fact. Finally, he admits that there might be non-democratic decision procedures that are much more likely to get epistemically right answers, but these must be rejected on moral and fairness grounds. He is more interested in showing at a conceptual level that democratic legitimacy involves both procedural and epistemic dimensions than in showing how or even whether actual democracies achieve better-than-random outcomes (Anderson 2018).

Fabienne Peter has proposed what she calls *pure* epistemic proceduralism (Peter 2013). Pure proceduralism (introduced in chapter 2) is the view that there are no procedure-independent standards of right answer. Citizens disagree profoundly about questions of justice and the common good, and there are simply no external sources of authority that can resolve that disagreement. We need to take collective decisions. Therefore, we ought to design procedures to be as fair as possible, knowing that no answer will please everyone. On this view, the fairness of the procedure is the sole criterion we can use to evaluate the legitimacy and binding power of the outcome – not whether it is just or the correct solution to the problem, only whether the proper procedures were followed. Peter builds an epistemic version of this view.

Like Estlund, Peter rejects the "correctness view" – the view that democratic procedures are justified to the extent that they make correct decisions or produce correct outcomes. Both Estlund and Peter agree that such a criterion is impossible because there is no agreement on what the correct outcome would be. Peter also rejects the weaker view embraced by Estlund that we should choose procedures that we think will *tend* toward the correct answer even if we cannot agree what that right answer might be. She insists that we need to forget about the golden apple of a correct answer even as an unspecified ideal. Instead, we need to focus exclusively on inherent epistemic/moral qualities of the procedure. Waldron, we will remember, said majority-rule voting is preferable because it is a fair way to take a decision among equals who disagree. Peter wants to make a similar argument, but now it is not just about fairness, it is also about epistemic relations and knowledge creation, and the procedure is not voting but deliberation. This is a bit harder to get one's head around.

Properly structured deliberation and processes of mutual justification do not just constitute relations of mutual respect; they also constitute relations of mutual, inclusive, egalitarian knowledge building. Peter embraces a specific type of social epistemology that embeds knowledge in evolving social interactions that are always open to dissent and pluralism.

This seems somewhat alarming and radically constructivist, as if deliberation among equals could somehow make it true that the sun revolves around the earth. But this is not what she is saying. Not unlike pragmatists (but minus the strong underlying ideal of public good), she is making a higher-level point that the soundness of all our truth claims ultimately rests on the soundness of our procedures as no one has a god's eye view of truth against which we can check our conclusions. We just have other discourses and critical exchanges. Furthermore, the discourses and critical exchanges through which we produce knowledge always have a social dimension. It is not possible to immunize epistemic discourses, even at the highest level of science, from being impacted by social forces (for example, biases or hierarchies). Thus what we as a society take as true is (to some extent) the product of social forces, not simply epistemic forces. Or more accurately, social forces and epistemic forces are irrevocably intertwined because we are not brains in vats but social creatures interacting even when we are pursuing the truth. Peter concludes from this that we really need to focus all our attention on the epistemic fairness of the procedures. What is important is that in deliberation we are treated as epistemic equals and that the process is maximally open to pluralism and disagreement. This requires that we accept a type of epistemic open-endedness in our political conversations.

The upshot is that, although Peter wants to claim that democracy has value and can command obedience on epistemic grounds, she rejects all forms of instrumentalism and wants to maintain that her view is not just compatible with but respects and promotes deep pluralism. Peter brings us full circle back to the procedural theories of chapter 3 and far from the original intuition that the quality of outcome must count for something in our evaluation of democracy.

Conclusion

There has been a tremendous surge of interest in the epistemic dimension of democracy, starting somewhere in the mid-nineties. Like many of the trends that I trace in this book, some of this interest can be seen as, on the one hand, a response to the domination of Rawlsian political philosophy and, on the other hand, a response to new real-world pressures on democracy.

Rawls's later work placed disagreement and pluralism as the central challenges facing liberal democratic orders. To respect the free and equal status of each person entails respecting their reasonable disagreement about worthwhile ends to pursue in politics. This in turn led Rawls to argue that we should banish truth claims from public debate. Referencing science and evidence was of course encouraged, but all claims that proposals deserved to be adopted because they were true or correct fell under suspicion with the new focus on respecting reasonable pluralism. This, as we saw in chapter 3, pushes in the direction of valuing democracy for procedural and not outcome reasons. But, starting in the late 1990s, one sees the growing conviction that it is neither possible nor desirable to exclude truth claims from public debate. This is Mizak's point: we defend things in the public sphere because we do think they are true or right in a non-relativist way. Furthermore, democratic citizens care a lot about whether democracies get it right or produce better answers on some objective standard. Thus Rawls's epistemic abstinence (Raz 1990) gave way (for some democratic theorists) to an investigation of how we could theorize and justify the value of getting it right.

Alongside reactions to Rawls's bracketing truth claims in public debate have been real-world developments that suggest than non-democracies are gaining ground on performance scales. The failures of the twentieth century planned economies have given way to redistributive authoritarianism that often delivers economic and welfare benefits widely and efficiently. Democracies can no longer assume with not much argument that they will outperform non-democracies. This has led to investigations of the underlying logic of good performance (rather than empirical comparison between outcomes). What is it about democracy that can give us confidence that, over the long run anyway, outcomes will tend to be strong? Epistemic democrats identify different mechanisms at work that produce that tendency or would produce that tendency if we strengthened our democracies. Performance skeptics of course argue that our confidence in democracy's epistemic potential is unfounded.

The starkest contrast between epistemic democrats and performance skeptics is that the latter start from democracy at its worst, one might say, and the former look to what democracy could be at its best. Although democracy skeptics usually do not point to actual legislative agendas or electoral outcomes, this branch of democratic theory is tied closely to empirical research, especially research on citizen incompetence. More specifically, some of the research is drawn from the last 15 years in the United States, which has seen relatively higher levels of affective polarization than other contexts. The principal message is that democracy is not working very well, and we might need to rethink some basic assumptions. Epistemic theories of democracy are all, to one degree or another, aspirational theories. Thus the focus is on the epistemic *potential* of democracy when certain conditions are met. Democracy, if well-functioning or under the right conditions, can produce sound and sensible policy, sounder and more sensible than autocracies.

A final word about instrumental versus intrinsic or procedural defenses of democracy. Instrumental defenses of democracy that focus exclusively on outcome and performance are in some sense weaker defenses of democracy than intrinsic defenses. They do in principle open the door to trading in political equality for welfare. On the other hand, purely intrinsic defenses of democracy are also weak because people cannot thrive on political equality alone, nor can it save them from climate disaster or pandemics. It is not just unrealistic to think that citizens ought to value political equality no matter what; it is also unfair to expect that of citizens – even though we see citizens regularly putting their lives on the line by demanding political equality in authoritarian regimes. A strong defense of democracy needs both types of arguments working together.

Chapters 3 through 7 have looked at a variety of arguments for why we should value democratic procedures over other methods of making collective decisions. I have suggested that the intense interest in this question is tied to a growing worry and insecurity about democracy's resilience in the face of challenges and erosion. Except for performance skeptics, all the theories that we have looked at see value in the principle of democracy, independent of how actual democracies perform or function. Epistemic democrats, although arguing that democracy ought to be evaluated on the quality of outcome, make an argument for why democracy is in principle not a bad way to make a decision and often is the best way to make decisions. This leaves aside more empirically grounded reasons why particular democracies have not made good decisions. Something similar can be said for all the theories. Equality democrats insist that the procedural equality of democratic rights is a moral good that far outweighs any illusory and contestable idea of effective government. But they often do not address the question of whether our actual democracies can still be considered to be constituted by political equality. Thus they tell us why democracy matters but not whether we are still living in real democracies. The same I think can be said for freedom-based theories. Political autonomy and self-government are valuable ideals, but can they be approximated in mass complex democracies of the twenty-first century? Realists, too, have an argument about democracy's value when it is working correctly. Of course, this is a book about normative democratic theory, so it is appropriate to start with theories that set out the ideal of democracy. As Charles Taylor has noted many times, democracy is a necessarily "telic" concept, which is to say, it aims to become something better. "It denotes not just a set of conditions but also commitments and aspirations; it is defined by purposes even if those are never perfectly met ... To participate in democracy is to work for more and better democracy" (Calhoun, Gaonkar, and Taylor 2022: 8). In the next four chapters, I do not abandon the telic dimension of democratic theory, but I do turn to theory that more directly addresses present conditions, pathologies, and crises of democracy in the twenty-first century.

8
Populism and the People

THE rise of populism has been a major theme in normative democratic theory as well as in the empirical study of democracies. This has led to a vibrant debate about what populism is, what explains its rise, and what dangers, if any, it poses for democracy. In normative democratic theory, the debate often centers on the concept of the "people" and what it means for the people to rule. This in turn resolves itself into two axes of analysis. One has to do with the contrast between the people and an elite. Populism always champions people power and spotlights the ways elite actors undermine or usurp that power. On this axis, parliaments, representatives, and parties as well as economic and technocratic elites come under particular scrutiny and suspicion. The second axis focuses on popular sovereignty and identifying who exactly are the people and how do they rule. In this chapter, I take up this second debate. In the next chapter, I take up the first question of representation and political parties.

Populism and democratic theory

Populism as a political phenomenon and an object of academic study has been around a long time. But until recently it had been thought to arise with threatening force mainly in fragile and new democracies, primarily in the global South (de la Torre 2019). It is generally associated with direct appeals to the masses, often couched in nationalist rhetoric that circumvents representative institutions, weakens checks and balances, and empowers a strong, directly mandated charismatic leader. Juan Perón in Argentina is a classic example from the middle of the twentieth century. What is new – and what has sparked an extraordinary explosion of scholarship and debate about this phenomenon – has been its significant inroads and successes within established and consolidated democracies, from which it had long faded until recently. For both champions and critics alike, the rise of populism beginning in the 1990s and continuing into the first decades of the twenty-first century is a sign of deep crisis within democratic orders (Kaltwasser et al. 2017).

Populism has very few champions in the field of normative democratic theory. Ernesto Laclau (2005), Chantal Mouffe (2018), and perhaps Margaret Canovan (1999) are exceptions defending theoretical versions of populism (rather than actual populist regimes) that they argue promote and enhance democracy. Others seek a type of neutrality, arguing that populism can be good or bad for democracy depending on many variables (Mudde and Kaltwasser 2012). But criticism, anxiety, and concern are the more common responses to populism within democratic theory. These criticisms sometimes take aim at the theory of populism, but more often populism is seen as a political phenomenon sweeping over, or at least on the rise within, liberal democracies. As a political phenomenon, normative democratic theory reconstructs populism into a set of underlying principles, logic, or defining features and then evaluates those principles, logic, or features from some point within a larger theory or ideal of democracy.

The literature on populism has been growing at an exponential rate, and our purpose here is not to review this entire field of research. Instead, this chapter concentrates on normative democratic theory's response to populism. The debate about "What is populism and what is bad/good about it?" is also a debate about "What is democracy?" because the two are so closely linked. Populism is a political phenomenon that thrives and takes root only in democracies and is steeped in a "democratic imaginary" that includes a central appeal to popular sovereignty and the rule and power of the people (Arato and Cohen 2022: 107). Rather than begin with my own full definition of populism, I start instead with identifying the political phenomena that have many people concerned and worried about the future of democracy without committing myself to saying that these phenomena represent the true character of populism.

The phenomena in question are right-wing (and sometimes left-wing) populists who have come to power within established or stable democracies and who deploy democratic appeals and concepts to justify authoritarian-leaning institutional reforms. Some twenty-first-century examples are Recep Erdoğan (Turkey), Viktor Orbán (Hungary), Narendra Modi (India), Nicolás Maduro (Venezuela), and Donald Trump (United States). These cases and more are what has democratic theory in a lather because it is not simply that these regimes and leaders are toying with and perhaps sliding into authoritarianism; it is that they defend those moves with appeals to the people, popular sovereignty, democratic participation, and majority rule. In effect, they challenge democratic theory to deny that they are not fully democratic and simply exercising their own and legitimate forms of political autonomy. For now, I stay agnostic about whether these cases, as Andrew Arato and Jean Cohen argue, illustrate the inherent authoritarian logic of all populisms (Arato and Cohen 2022). There might be other movements and parties that could be described as populist which do not or have not headed down authoritarian paths (Mansbridge and Macedo 2019). Or populism as an opposition movement may represent salutary correctives to a representative system of government deeply out of touch with the people (Mudde and Kaltwasser 2012). Or right-wing populists in power may in theory be a subset of populism or populism gone wrong, as Chantal Mouffe argues (Mouffe 2018). Or, finally, there is a widespread dissatisfaction with institutions of representative democracy and political elite, for example, leading to the uptick in referendums and support for citizens' assemblies. This dissatisfaction is not inaccurately described as a populist sentiment, even though it need not be connected to support for authoritarian-leaning right-wing populists. Despite the lack of agreement on what is the core of populism, all democratic theory is united in acknowledging that the rise and popularity of a Donald Trump, Victor Orbán, Marine Le Pen, or Geert Wilders are signs of a crisis and pose a threat to the health of democracy.

What is the nature of the threat posed by this group of twenty-first-century leaders? In what follows, I look at three broad understandings of the core features of the threat under the headings of constrained democracy, left populism, and democratic pluralism. I then connect those assessments to underlying normative views of democracy, especially views about popular sovereignty and the rule or role of the "people" in a well-ordered democracy.

Popular sovereignty is the doctrine that the people possess ultimate authority or power. The nature and site of that authority, as well as who or what is the entity the "people," are highly contested questions. Although these questions have been on the agenda of political theory since at least the sixteenth century (Tuck 2016), the threat of populism in the twenty-first century has given new life and relevance to this debate.[1]

At the core of the debate are two issues. The first has to do with how upstream or downstream (or in the background or foreground, to use a different metaphor) one understands the idea of "ultimate authority," invoked by ideas of popular sovereignty, to be. An upstream view would be something like this: although ultimate authority can be traced to rare and exceptional founding moments undertaken in the name of the people, this ultimate authority to constitute a government has little or no role to play in everyday decision making, which in modern democracies is majoritarian, representative, indirect, and mediated. Here popular sovereignty is part of an origin story but not part of governing. Far downstream from this is the view, often associated with populism, that the people's ultimate authority to constitute (that is, to make and change constitutions) is or ought to be ever present in day-to-day decision making. On the downstream view, popular sovereignty is not limited to a background constitutional principle embodied in constitutional preambles like "We the people of the United States," but is a principle of democratic governance and legislation. For the downstream view, the people exercise ultimate authority, which is to say they rule, via plebiscitary and electoral mechanisms. The use of a referendum to amend the Turkish Constitution in 2017, for example, was defended on this downstream view: "Now for the first time the people will make its own constitution" (Yazici 2017). Constituent power (the power to make and change constitutions) and constituted power (the power of majorities to act within the constitution) are joined in the idea of the rule of the people.

The second and connected issue is who or what is the "people," and in what sense can the people rule, act, or will. Even syntax points to the dilemma. Do we think of the people in the singular or plural? Does the people act, or do they act? Is the people a universal category that encompasses all citizens as equals, or does the people refer to the common folk or the masses to be distinguished from the elite? Do we associate the people with an historically identifiable group as in the French people/nation, or can it be divorced from any strong collective identity? The people is always something that must be invoked in some way (Olson 2017). This means first that someone has to speak on behalf of the people. The people cannot speak the way, say, a head of state can speak. Even appeals to the people that point to concrete visible events, for example, declaring that in a referendum the people have spoken or identifying mass protest as the people rising up, are contestable claims, not descriptive statements. When a king speaks, we might question his claim to be the rightful king or indeed the claim that kings have a right to rule at all, but there is no question that he spoke (Morgan 1989: 153). The obvious problems with conferring sovereignty (meaning having the final say) to a collective agent have led some to talk about the people as fiction, myth, or imagined (Olson 2017). But for others who want to operationalize the rule of the people in concrete terms, it has led them to identify the people with concrete segments of the population. This is often referred to as the problem of embodiment. Are the people an abstract concept underpinning our theories of democracy, or are the people flesh-and-blood voters having the final say?

The embodiment/non-embodiment question is connected to a second dilemma about the people. As we have seen in other parts of this book, political equality is a central principle of democracy. Can political equality be squared with the idea of the rule of the people? Political equality suggests that the people must be everybody. But in modern democracies characterized by pluralism, disagreement, and competition, it is difficult to imagine the whole people acting, willing, or choosing anything as one unified agent. But the moment one identifies the people with some part rather than the whole, one introduces exclusions from the people, and this seems to violate the principle of political equality.

These then are the issues that animate the debates that have arisen in response to populisms. I now outline three broad approaches to the ideals of popular sovereignty and the rule of the people.

Constrained democracy

A widespread concern among many students of democracy has been the rise of illiberal democracy associated with populism. The term "illiberal democracy" was coined by Fareed Zakaria in 1997 to describe regimes in which competitive multi-party elections produce governments that tout their democratic credentials at the same time as they pursue policies that chip away at the liberal guardrails, constraints, and checks and balances that make democracy safe for modern constitutional orders (Zakaria 1997). The trend is to move toward strong executives under the banner of direct popular mandates and to weaken civil and constitutional protections in the name of the exercise of popular sovereignty (Waldner and Lust 2018). Often riding waves of nationalist or anti-immigrant sentiment, these regimes depict liberal constraints (for example, minority rights enforced by an independent judiciary) as roadblocks and obstacles put in the path of the people's will by unaccountable or "cosmopolitan" elites who are out of touch with and unresponsive to the real people. Also in evidence is the gradual dampening and stifling of the full force of civil society and the public sphere as instruments of opposition and criticism. The weakening of oppositional and contestatory voices often falls short of doing away with free speech and freedom of association altogether but aims to tilt the playing field in the public sphere in favor of the populist party or leader in power.

Identifying the primary danger of populism as a weakening of constraints, guardrails, and checks on direct plebiscitary and majoritarian power has its roots in democratic theory that has a skeptical and cautious view regarding strong ideas of popular sovereignty and the will of the people (Riker 1988; Weale 2018). The very term "illiberal democracy" offers a hint of that skepticism. The term suggests that there is a regime type that is indeed a democracy but simply not a liberal one and that liberalism is something added and external to democracy that restrains and checks the popular will (Mounk 2018). The view that liberalism and democracy, or constitutionalism and popular sovereignty, are in inherent tension with each other is shared by both the liberal critics of populism as well as populists themselves. Indeed, some populist leaders are happy to divorce democracy from liberalism, arguing that throwing off stifling liberal constraints on the people's will is precisely what they seek. As Hungarian Prime Minister Viktor Orbán put it in a much-quoted 2014 speech, "We need to state that a democracy is not necessarily liberal. Just because something is not liberal, it still can be a democracy" (Tóth 2014).

The illiberal democracy critics of populism have then what could be called a "constrained" view of democracy, where democracy is primarily embodied in the representative institutions of electoral democracy that channel and aggregate majority preferences but operate within strong constitutional limits (Wolkenstein 2019). Although this reproduces the same tension between liberalism and democracy that is embraced by populists, the underlying idea of democracy is very different. Two features of the populist view of democracy are particularly problematic from the "constrained democracy" view. The first is that the people rule through majoritarian institutions with as little mediation as possible. The second is that the people (now understood as speaking through the majority) have ultimate authority (sovereignty) in establishing all rules, procedures, and laws with little constraint on this authority.

For populists, democracy is rule by and for the people, and representative institutions are only democratic to the extent that they directly express or channel the people's will. Despite some rhetoric about the superiority of direct democracy to representative democracy, modern forms of populism are all representative in some sense (Urbinati 2019). A directly elected president is still a representative, no matter how charismatically they embody the aspirations of the people. Referendums and plebiscites are shaped and dominated by the voices of party and movement leaders – in other words, representatives – who speak for the people. Populist regimes do not for the most part seek to overthrow representative democracy. They seek to make representative democracy more responsive to the people and sometimes more "like" the people.

Thus the people rule through majoritarian-decision procedures, and this in turn leads to a conflation of majoritarian outcomes with the people's will. So, for example, in the aftermath of the 2016 Brexit referendum in which a slim majority approved the UK exit from the European Union, critics of the outcome and procedure were branded as "enemies of the people" by pro-Brexit press and political representatives (Van Crombrugge 2020: 7). This conflation is weaponized when attached to a strong idea of popular sovereignty. As Margaret Canovan notes, "once the notion of popular sovereignty is available in politics it is hard to avoid attempts to translate the abstract constituent sovereignty of a collective people into political action by concrete individuals" (Canovan 2005: 93; Yack 2001). Populism thus gives rise to constitutional change and amendment legitimized by simple majority mechanisms – referendums, directly elected executives, or majorities in parliament – that undermine the liberal logic of constitutions which, among other things, limits the power of majorities. Conferring constituent power to majorities also undermines strong ideas of the rule of law.

As I noted above, overarching concern with the need to constrain democracy is often rooted in a democratic theory skeptical or anxious about investing the people with too much power or a more extreme view that implies that democracy is inherently populist (Riker 1988). I outline two theoretical strategies open to liberals to underpin and justify the constrained democracy view. The first alternative questions the coherence of any ideas of popular sovereignty. Here we will briefly return to minimalist ideas of democracy discussed in chapter 5. The second strategy does not give up on popular sovereignty, and indeed often champions it as the most important founding principle of modern democratic orders, but limits popular sovereignty to a hypothetical status with only very limited availability for workaday majoritarian politics. I draw on some arguments of public reason liberals as an illustration of this second strategy.

Minimalist theories of democracy argue that, as an empirical fact and metaphysical principle, there is no popular will, only various competing ways to aggregate individual wills, and that no aggregative mechanisms can plausibly construct a collective will. Ideas of popular sovereignty are dangerous fictions because they always amount to some group's arbitrary claim to ultimate authority or power. Democracy is not actual rule by the people; democracy is one way to choose rulers that is stable, relatively peaceful, and compatible with modern commitments to human rights. Thus, from one point of view, minimalists completely reject populist claims to be instantiating the will of the people but, from another point of view, they often have no democratic reasons to criticize populist actors. As Adam Przeworski puts it, "populist parties are not anti-democratic in the sense that they do not advocate replacing elections by some other method of selecting governments" (Przeworski 2019: 88). Populist parties in power are often, however, decreasingly liberal, and to the extent that stabilizing rules of the game – for example, a neutral umpire in the form of an independent judiciary – are weakened, these regimes threaten the delicate balance of power that maintains peace. Although the rhetoric in populist regimes draws on the democratic imaginary of participation and people power, the intent of many reforms is to solidify the populists in power (Müller 2016). Minimalists' democratic bottom line is electoral turnover. As soon as populist attempts to solidify power threaten electoral turnover, most obviously by refusing to leave office or claiming victory where there was none, they have stepped over into anti-democratic territory.

Minimalists do not offer much conceptual help in combatting the appeal of populist claims. Part of the success of populist parties within established democracies is certainly that they tap into a common understanding of democracy as rule by and for the people. That is to say, they tap into popular frustration that government is not responsive to ordinary people (not "for" the people) and that the people have no or little control over what governments do (not "by" the people). Minimalist theories, which are also sometimes called elitist theories, of democracy need not stand against responsiveness, but they usually do stand against any strong idea of popular control. Indeed, as the name elitist theory suggests, they often side with leaving as much of the governing as possible to competent elites.

A second line of liberal argument to address the problems raised by populist appeals to the ultimate sovereignty of the people does not jettison popular sovereignty but constitutionalizes it. The "people" is the final source of authority, but the people as a truly inclusive category encompassing all citizens as equal members can only be thought of in hypothetical, counterfactual terms and never as an embodied agent acting in the political world. The people appear in the preamble to constitutions or embodied in a set of principles and arguments but not on the political stage of day-to-day politics. This can be seen in the arguments of public reason liberals. Public reason, we will recall from chapter 3, is a form of reasoning or a set of reasons that "all can reasonably accept." Public reason shifts the grounds of legitimacy from consent and will to a type of justification that is inclusive of all reasonable interests and claims and looks for a point of consensus. Public reason is the reason of the "people" understood not as an aggregation of natural individuals but rather as a hypothetical construction of reasonable persons guiding and constraining the sorts of proposals and claims we can legitimately make. Rather than consult all the real people, public reason asks us to incorporate the idea of all people as equals into our reasoning. The ideal is that laws and policies should be grounded as much as possible in principles that everyone can reasonably accept. In modern, complex, pluralist democracies, those principles will be few and very general. They will be constitutional principles.

Public reason liberals then tend to constitutionalize the people. Christopher Eisgruber, for example, describes the Supreme Court as "a kind of representative institution well-shaped to speak on behalf of the people about questions of moral and political principle" (Eisgruber 2001: 3). Samuel Freeman argues that for a Rawlsian "when the court effectively maintains the higher law enacted by the people, it cannot be said to be anti-democratic for it executes the people's will in matters of basic justice" (Freeman 1994: 661). But talk of "willing" and "enacting" is somewhat misleading or highly metaphorical because the higher law, or the constitution, is the expression of the people's will only to the extent that constitutional principles can be justified by public reason, not because any actual people endorsed it in a vote. This view flips the populist logic. Populists see the modern liberal constitution as a counter-majoritarian and so counter-democratic institution. Public reason liberals see the modern liberal constitution as the ultimate expression of the sovereign people. Constitutions are only legitimate to the extent that their principles and applications can be mutually justifiable or acceptable to all. This view then places the abstract, universal, and hypothetical will of the people (what all could accept) against the empirical, partial, and temporal will of the majority. The former, because it can come closer to inclusivity and universality, is a more morally acceptable view of the people while the latter is always potentially exclusionary and partial (Ochoa Espejo 2017). On this view, then, "We the people of the United States" sets limits to constrain the future actions of majorities which cannot claim the mantle of the people. From this view, populists are wrong to think that liberal constraints are external to the exercise of popular sovereignty; constitutional constraints are justified and flow from the proper view of popular sovereignty.

What these two liberal views have in common is the rejection of the claim that outcomes of majoritarian voting can embody the will of the people. For minimalists, this is because there is no will of the people, and, for public reason liberals, this is because only a hypothetical people can be inclusive. Strong constitutions and liberal constraints are important principles for both views but for slightly different reasons. Minimalists see the constraints as guaranteeing the rules of the game that maintain stability; public reason liberals see these principles as publicly justified, that is, as acceptable to all (the people).

The constrained democracy view seeks to reinstate liberal constraints and stop or reverse the backsliding in populist-led regimes. Critics of this view often point out that there is an assumption here that things were fine before the backsliding. The thrust of the illiberal democracy argument is that we need to return to some status quo ante. This fails to take seriously the democratic deficits that have contributed to the rise of populism in the first place. I turn now to two alternative responses to populism, both of which explicitly address democratic deficit.

Left populism

"The effacement of the theme of popular sovereignty in liberal democratic societies constitutes the first important element for apprehending the current rise of right-wing populism" (Mouffe

2008: 54). For Chantal Mouffe and Ernesto Laclau, right-wing populism taps into and is energized by an anger and frustration with the democratic deficit of liberal democratic orders, a deficit that Mouffe and Laclau think has been facilitated by many of the arguments that I have just canvased. They want to replace right-wing populism with left-wing populism. The primary threat of right-wing populism is not in the "people" overriding constitutional limits in the name of popular sovereignty but in a problematic substantive conception of the people. "The problem lies in the way this 'people' is constructed. What makes this populist discourse right-wing is its strongly xenophobic character, and the fact that in all cases immigrants are presented as a threat to the identity of the people" (Mouffe 2008: 69). In *For a Left Populism* (2018), Mouffe attempts to construct an idea of the people not on nativist, anti-immigration, or white nationalist terms, but on a coalition of those disempowered and marginalized by the forces of neoliberalism. Thus the threat and problem with right-wing populism is not that it invests the people with too much constituent power but that it constructs the people on a right-wing narrative that ultimately reproduces the structural pathologies of neoliberalism. In *For a Left Populism*, Mouffe gives clear ideological and normative content to populism. She is *for* left-wing populism and *against* right-wing populism. This view, however, is built on a broader understanding of populism that she shares with Ernesto Laclau that is normatively neutral (it would appear) between different types of populisms. From this broader perspective, both right-wing and left-wing populism are fundamentally democratic.

In *On Populist Reason*, Laclau does not consider populism to be merely a movement or a political phenomenon among other political phenomena (2005: 117). Instead, he argues that populism is what politics and democracy are all about. Indeed, only populism can revive the political and invigorate authentic democracy. In order to understand this, we need to start with his critique of representative democracy and the welfare state, which he argues have depoliticized and de-democratized modern governance structures.

In the normal course of events, individuals and groups develop grievances and claims for which they seek redress from the state either via institutions of representative democracy or by making claims on the welfare state (Laclau 2005: 75). These grievances are heterogenous, meaning that there is a great deal of variation and difference among the grievances. Think about the sorts of claims made by, for example, the urban poor, ethnic minorities, parents of school-age children, steel workers, farmers, the list could go on indefinitely. Representative democracy, as well as the technocratic welfare order, treats these grievances and demands as differentiated and so addresses them as so many separate if interconnected problems to solve. The extreme of differentiation is to think about and treat the grievances that arise in society as individual demands that can be bundled by way of mediating institutions like parties, the public sphere, and parliaments.

What is wrong with this way of doing things? Laclau says, first, it is neither political nor democratic. The more that the modern state deals with grievances in a differentiated way – as so many memos crossing someone's desk – the less this process is political and the more it is technocratic. Politics, or the political, is essentially about struggle and clashing of power. Liberalism and technocracy both seek non-antagonistic strategies to resolve problems, the former seeking consensus and the latter rational and efficient policy solutions. Thus both liberalism and technocracy seek to exclude the political from governance.

Now one might think that the depoliticized administrative state might not seem such a bad thing if it did indeed meet all the demands and answered all the grievances that society threw at it. But the crisis of representative democracy sees growing inability and unwillingness to answer demands. This failure has a lot to do with the lack of politics. The more grievances are presented as differentiated and segmented, the less political power they have. Differentiation creates a power vacuum that is exploited by neoliberal elites who pursue their own agenda and are unresponsive to ordinary people's grievances. That agenda involves globalization that further multiplies the grievances of ordinary people. The liberal state is eventually unable to adequately address grievances, and we see a crisis of representative democracy developing to which populism is the response. Populism replaces differentiated and powerless heterogenous grievances circulating in society with the united will of the people (Laclau 2005: 85). Only in uniting into a powerful actor on the political stage – that is, only in turning grievances into something political – can ordinary people back their demands for redress with the power needed to get results.

Power requires a united homogenous actor: the people. But the question now is how to create the people out of all these heterogenous claims and grievances? Laclau argues that it is possible to link heterogenous grievances together – to make them equivalent to each other but not identical to each other – by first identifying an "antagonistic frontier" and, second, articulating a set of (sometimes vague) demands that, although only articulating part of all those grievances, can stand in for the whole (Laclau 2005: 74).

> If I refer to a set of social grievances, to widespread injustice, and attribute its source to the "oligarchy", for instance, . . . I am constituting the "people" by finding the common identity of a set of social claims in their opposition to oligarchy . . . This is why an equivalential chain *has* to be expressed through the cathexis of a *singular* element: because we are dealing not with a conceptual operation of *finding* a common feature underlying all social grievances, but with a performative operation constituting the chain as such. (Laclau 2005: 97)

The people only exist to the extent that they are mobilized, and they are mobilized only by the image of an antagonist ("enemy") that is viewed as an obstacle to the achievement of redress. The second move is to place a vague and under-specified set of demands to stand in for the whole. This Laclau refers to as the empty signifier (2005: 69–71).

The "people" is constructed via a narrative. Laclau wants to insist that it is a mistake, however, to think of that narrative as a mere fiction or as having no embodiment or presence. He challenges the common trope that I used above that contrasts the concrete presence of a king to the invoked fiction of the people. For Laclau, the difference is between one body and many bodies, but there are always bodies. In other words, the narrative brings the people into being as a concrete embodied force in politics. Bringing the people into being as a political actor is bringing democracy into being. "So the very possibility of democracy depends on the constitution of a democratic people" (Laclau 2005: 171). Democracy is rule by the people. To be *for* democracy and popular sovereignty, one must be *for* populism that is for the creation of the people. "[D]emocracy is grounded only on the existence of a democratic subject, whose emergence depends on the horizontal articulation between equivalent demands. An ensemble of equivalential demands articulated by an empty signifier is what constitutes a 'people'" (2005: 171).

The rise of populism within liberal democratic orders has spurred and given content to a particular critique of that order. The left-populist response has two important features. The first is that it suggests that the most effective way to combat right-wing populism is to mobilize the very same frustrated and angry citizens but for progressive causes, including and especially the environment. The second is that it offers a criticism of the liberal administrative state and the depoliticizing and disempowering rise of technocratic governance. These two dimensions of the argument are appealing to many theorists as well as political activists. Leading figures in left-wing opposition parties in Europe (Syriza in Greece and Podemos in Spain) have claimed to be influenced by Laclau (Peruzzotti 2019: 40).

What is highly criticized is the claim that the people and hence democracy can only be brought into being through an antagonistic frontier. The concept of "antagonistic frontier" draws on two sources. One is Saussurean semiotic theory, which postulates that linguistic systems depend on contrast and opposition between signs to produce meaning and value. And second is the work of Carl Schmitt, who argued that all politics involves drawing lines between friend/enemy. As we have seen, this opens the door for the vilification of "enemies of the people." This runs up against ideals of political equality and inclusion, on the one hand, and democratic pluralism and disagreement, on the other hand. The next group of democratic theorists I discuss explicitly challenge the idea of an "antagonistic frontier."

Democratic pluralism

In the face of populism, this final group I canvas reconceives popular sovereignty as dispersed across time and space and proceduralized through an interdependence of democracy and constitutionalism (Abts and Rummens 2007; Arato and Cohen 2022;

Habermas 1996; Müller 2016; Ochoa Espejo 2017; Rosanvallon 2007, 2021; Rostbøll 2023; Rummens 2017; Urbinati 2019). This critique of populism focuses on authoritarian-leaning populist attacks on pluralism, opposition, the public sphere, and civil society. I label this group democratic pluralists because they place anti-pluralism at the center of their criticism of populism, but also because, in developing alternative ideas of popular sovereignty, they stress the multiple and plural institutional means through which citizens exercise popular sovereignty. I call this dispersed popular sovereignty. This idea of dispersed popular sovereignty has many affinities with "contestatory proceduralism," which I discussed in chapter 4. Both dispersed popular sovereignty and contestatory proceduralism are part of a trend in contemporary democratic theory to decenter ideas of ruling and weaken but not abandon the place of majorities in democratic rule.

Although many in the democratic pluralism group, like the constrained democrats we looked at above, are worried about the erosion of rule of law and constitutional limits, they do not articulate that worry in terms of an inherent danger to a liberal order from unchecked popular sovereignty or people power. They take issue with the idea of "illiberal democracy," arguing that democracy and liberalism are mutually constitutive. Like left populists, democratic pluralists worry that we are in a crisis of representation in which popular sovereignty is losing ground as technocracy and financial interests steer governance and neutralize the voice of the people. But they reject and find dangerous the left-populist story about the constitution of the people as a democratic agent. As we will see, they find the invocation of an "enemy," as well as the part standing for the whole, particularly problematic.

This group begins its critique of populism not with the dangers of backsliding but with the dangers of populist conceptions of the people. They start here because their goal is to reinvigorate popular sovereignty, strong democracy, and even conceptions of the people that are democratic (or popular) but not populist. "To proceduralize the notion of popular sovereignty is not to abandon the idea that the people can and should rule themselves, but to provide a very different interpretation of the idea than we find in populism" (Rostbøll 2023: 141). The problem with populism then is not that it is illiberal, but that it is a false, disfigured, or counterfeit view of democracy (Rosanvallon 2021; Urbinati 2019).

Several scholars in this group have zeroed in on a particular way that the people are invoked as a defining feature of contemporary populism (Arato and Cohen 2022; Müller 2016; Rummens 2017; Urbinati 2019). There are four features of the populist idea of the people that come under criticism. The first is the most important and the very thing that Laclau sees as essential in constituting the people as an agent of democracy: embodiment. For Laclau, the people can only be sovereign to the extent that it has power, and it has power only to the extent that it is an agential and agonistic force in the political world. The problem with embodiment is that the acting agential people will always only be a part of the whole people, who are never a singular agent but a plural amorphous idea. Here pluralists often invoke Claude Lefort's famous dictum that a "revolutionary and unprecedented feature of democracy" is that "the locus of power becomes *an empty space*" (1988: 17). This means, first, that the people are a permanently contested, negotiated, plural, ever-changing fiction that can never be fully or unitarily embodied. And, second, modern democracies are made up of complex counterbalancing institutions, electoral turnover, competition, revisability, mediation, and generally an institutional structure that seeks to disperse power.

Populists reject Lefort's view of democracy, explicitly in the case of Laclau (2005: 170), and seek to fill up that space. Populists seek "the closure of that place of power in favor of a fictitious image of the people as a homogeneous and sovereign body" (Abts and Rummens 2007: 415). "The claim to exclusive moral representation of real or authentic people is at the core of populism" (Müller 2017: 592). Populism involves "the symbolic representation of the whole of 'the people' by a mobilized part" (Arato and Cohen 2022: 13). "Populism is a phenomenology that involves replacing the whole with one of its parts" (Urbinati 2019: 13).

The second problematic feature of a populist conception of the people is that populists in power make their claim to be pursuing the will of the people by pointing to success at the polls, whether that be elections or plebiscites and referendums. Thus there is always a conflation between the majority and the people. Third, the mobilizing power of appeals to the people is maintained via

Populism and the People

a rhetoric of enemies of the people. Those enemies are often identified as any and all opposition voices in the public sphere, and this results in and feeds off of polarization. Finally, this view of the people is loaded into a strong idea of popular sovereignty. Populists, it is argued, invest the people with a type of permanent constituent power such that referendums and simple electoral majorities are used to amend constitutions. All constitutional limits and constraints exist at the pleasure of the people, and if these are thwarting the people and limiting their ability to act, then they can be removed.

These four elements of populist appeal to the people then result in a type of democracy that is exclusionary, majoritarian, anti-pluralist, and claims an almost unlimited constituent authority of majorities to lay down the rules of the game. Democratic pluralists propose an alternative view of the people. Given the criticism of populism, this alternative conception of the people would have to have four features. The people would have to refer to the whole, meaning it is inclusive of all citizens as political equals; majority outcomes could not be identified with the will of the people; opposition and contestation would have to be folded into the exercise of popular sovereignty and rule by the people; and popular sovereignty would have to be conceptualized as self-limiting in some way or, as Arato and Cohen put it, as "self-government under law" (Arato and Cohen 2022: 111). Attempts to meet these four criteria are the defining feature of the group I call democratic pluralists. The first three criteria are met through the introduction of a dispersed or proceduralized conception of the people. The fourth criterion is met by a proceduralized view of the people that attempts to reconcile the tension between liberalism and democracy by making them co-dependent.

Jürgen Habermas is a contemporary German social and political philosopher whose discursive conception of democracy is probably the most prominent example of a dispersed and proceduralized conception of the people and is an important influence on many in this group. In his reconceptualization of democracy, "popular sovereignty is no longer embodied in a visible identifiable gathering of autonomous citizens. It pulls back into the, as it were, 'Subjectless' forms of communication circulating through forums and legislative bodies" (Habermas 1996: 135–6). Habermas also calls this idea "fully dispersed sovereignty" and "intersubjectively dissolved popular sovereignty" (1996: 486). This conception of sovereignty forgoes "overly concrete notions of a 'people' as an entity" (1996: 185), and can be described as "communicatively fluid sovereignty" (1996: 186). Rosanvallon refers to "a generalized and expansive sovereignty of the people" (Rosanvallon 2021: 11) and Paulina Ochoa Espejo describes it this way:

> [the people are] not a collection of individuals, but a procedure of decision-making and opinion formation, by which individuals interact with each other mediated by legal civil society institutions that channel popular demands and force representatives to adopt views and make decisions. In the long term, these procedures can be recognized as "the Popular will" and, thus, we can eventually think of them as popular sovereignty. (Ochoa Espejo 2017: 615)

Christian Rostbøll recently echoed this view: "the people never appear as one, but only as a dispersed and diverse plurality. They act together only through shared procedures that connect millions of diverse and dispersed citizens, their opinion formation in civil society, and their will formation in elections and formal representative institutions" (Rostbøll 2023: 141).

The dispersed idea of popular sovereignty is not the same as the hypothetical idea of popular sovereignty we looked at above. This brings us back to the idea of embodiment and Lefort's empty space. The hypothetical popular sovereignty of "We the people" is rarely embodied in everyday democratic politics and does not add up to the rule of the people. It is an upstream view of popular sovereignty. Dispersed popular sovereignty is exercised in everyday democratic politics by real people, so in this sense it is embodied. But that embodiment is understood synchronically across multiple institutions and locations as well as diachronically across time in which elections, for example, punctuate an ongoing open-ended process. Elections are important, but so are citizens challenging state actors through the courts; a critical and free press that asks hard questions; an active civil society that can organize and identify salient issues; street politics and protests that channel, articulate, and publicize grievances and injustice; innovative and effective forms of citizen consultation at all levels of government (for example, citizens' assemblies); and independently minded bureaucrats pursuing public goods. These are just some of the ways that citizens exercise constraint on and demand responsiveness from the state, which is to say exercise and protect popular sovereignty. Populists attempt to simplify democracy and have all power pass through the ballot box; democratic pluralists suggest that "democratic progress implies making democracy more complex, multiplying its forms" (Rosanvallon 2021: 159).

Democratic pluralism presupposes an interdependence between constitutionalism and democracy that makes the concept of illiberal democracy nonsensical. Koen Abts and Stefan Rummens have a clear articulation of this somewhat complex idea:

[L]iberal *individual rights* are constitutive elements of the constitutional democratic logic because they guarantee the irreducibility of the diversity of society and prevent the despotic imposition of a tyrannical will of the majority. The *sovereignty of the people*, on the other hand, refers to the fact that the democratic process generates temporary interpretations of the essentially open identity of the people. This identity does not reflect the singular will of the people as a collective but rather reflects the identity of a community which respects the irreducible individuality and diversity of its citizens ... Only the mutual interdependence of individual rights and the democratic construction of temporary interpretations of the will of the people allow for the realization of the *diversity-in-unity* which defines constitutional democracies. (Abts and Rummens 2007: 413)

Something like this view is endorsed by all democratic pluralists. As Arato and Cohen note, rights and rule of law are "functionally intertwined institutional predicates of a democracy today (call it democratic constitutionalism or constitutionalist democracy) that must be guaranteed if one is to speak of a democratic regime" (Arato and Cohen 2022: 118).

Democratic pluralists often acknowledge that twenty-first-century democracies are suffering from multiple deficits that have pushed many into the arms of populists. The democratic deficit means that citizens "are not being heard, not being included in decision-making processes; it signifies that ministers are not assuming their responsibilities, that leaders are telling lies with impunity; it signifies that corruption reigns, that there is a political class living in a bubble and failing to account adequately for its actions, that the administrative function remains opaque" (Rosanvallon 2021: 158).

How to address these deficits? The solution is complex – literally. Dispersed popular sovereignty involves "a plurality of avenues for voice, action, and participation while refusing both the restriction of popular sovereignty to acts of voting and its remythologization in populist imaginary of the unitary people incarnate and acting in and through a leader" (Arato and Cohen 2022: 188). Intermediary institutions, for example, social movements (Arato and Cohen 2022), reimagined political parties (Müller 2021), interactive representation (Rosanvallon 2021), regulated public sphere and media (Habermas 2009, 2022), and redesigned referendums (Chambers 2019), are on this pluralist agenda. In the next three chapters, I look at some proposals for institutional renovation to address democratic deficits.

Conclusion

Contemporary democratic theory is shaken by but also obsessed with populism. I have only reviewed a small fraction of the scholarship and research that attempts to pin down this troubling phenomenon. Part of what is driving this scholarship is the thought – made palpable by the January 6, 2021, violent attempt to overturn a presidential election in the oldest stable democracy in the world – that populism might spell the end of democracy. Less dramatically, this scholarship – including those who are positively disposed toward populism – is motivated by the idea that if we can get a handle on the rise of populism, we can get a handle on what really ails our democracies. Much more would need to be said to come close to explaining the rise of populism. Indeed, I did not set out to explain the causes of populism or investigate the economic, social, and cultural forces that have contributed to citizens being open to and mobilized by the rhetoric of the people taking back power from a corrupt elite. Instead, I analyzed alternative understandings of popular sovereignty and suggested that democratic theory must take seriously the popular appeal of giving power back to the people. In doing that, democratic theory is tasked with thinking through and laying out how the rule by the people can be squared with equality and pluralism. Although I have not talked about economic and cultural sources of distress and anti-system anger, I have suggested that a real lack of responsiveness on the part of our democratic institutions is certainly part of the story and a legitimate complaint in many democratic systems.

Before turning directly to questions of responsiveness, there is one more dimension to debates about the people that I wish to mention, if only to explain why I do not take up this question in any detail. A perennial puzzle in democratic theory has been dubbed the boundary problem (Song 2012). The boundary problem is about how to decide who is to be included (given a say) in democratic decisions. The territorial borders of nation-states are the products of contingent historical factors. Therefore, the boundaries of our citizen bodies or the demos are also the product of arbitrary historical factors that created the present system of nation-states. Is using the borders of a territorial nation-state as the boundary of the people legitimate or morally justified? Broadly speaking, there are two competing principles put forward to solve the boundary problem: the all-subjected principle and the all-affected principle (Fung and Gray forthcoming). The former states that all people who are subject to coercive laws ought to have a say in the making of those laws. The latter and more widely accepted principle – at least in political and moral philosophy – states that all those affected by a decision should have a say in that decision. The all-affected principle pushes in a cosmopolitan direction but can have minimal impact on present arrangements or offer a radical critique of nation-states. On the minimal view, an all-affected principle might suggest that citizens and representatives in nation-states ought to take the concerns and interests of all affected, which might include persons outside the borders of the nation-state or future unborn generations, into consideration in decisions. The all-affected principle does not in itself stipulate if all affected must have an equal say. At the other end of the spectrum is the idea that many national-level decisions have repercussions for people outside national borders and those people ought to have a real say, a vote. At the extreme, then, the all-affected principle suggests that "the demos is unbounded and that virtually everyone in the world ought to be included" (Song 2012).

This chapter has focused on the question of the people in relation to populism, and the boundary problem is not directly raised by the populist challenge. The boundary problem is particularly salient when we think about democracies making decisions about their borders, immigration, asylum seekers, and refugee policies (Abizadeh 2008). It is also relevant in thinking about different ways to determine voting rights, for example, giving residents in cities voting rights in municipal elections irrespective of their citizenship status at the national level (Lenard 2021). But ultimately the boundary problem points outward to questions of globalization and our cosmopolitan moral obligation to people, irrespective of what passport they hold. As I discuss briefly in the conclusion of this book, I have not thematized questions of transnational democracy or the challenges of globalization. I have focused on democratic crisis and erosion within the nation-state, assuming that there is no future for global democratization without strong – or at least not failing – democracy at the national level.

9

Representation

THIS chapter describes and explains new developments in theories of political representation, including the ways that political parties represent citizens within electoral democracy. The backdrop to this discussion is sinking trust in traditional representative institutions: elected representatives, political parties, and parliaments (Dalton 2004). Sinking trust levels are often thought to be tied to two interconnected senses in which elected representatives fail to represent citizens. The first we might call the populist complaint: elected representatives are heavily drawn from elite sectors and do not look like most ordinary citizens. The second is the corruption complaint: in developing policy agendas, elected representatives are responsive to economic heavy hitters rather than the interests of ordinary citizens.

Mass democracies are representative democracies in the sense that citizens do not, or do not often, directly rule themselves, but rather they elect legislators and support parties that represent their interests, aspirations, or identities. Sinking trust in these institutions has led to an uptick in support for referendums and plebiscites. Traditionally (and also in the popular imagination), referendums and plebiscites have been thought to be examples of direct democracy, meaning a democracy where citizens rule themselves directly and bypass the need for representation. Ancient Athens, in which every adult male citizen could participate in legislation, is often the template for this imaginary in which direct democracy is presented as a challenge and an alternative to representative democracy. Much of recent democratic theory questions this stark contrast, however, with many theorists suggesting that all politics involves representation (el-Wakil and MacKay 2020; Landemore 2020). Referendums and plebiscites are deeply entangled with representation, first because campaigns for and against questions on the ballot are led by people who claim to represent one side or another in the contest, but also because these mechanisms need to be integrated into the larger representative system (Invernizzi-Accetti and Oskian 2022). Many referendums, for example, are consultative, which means that any action to result from the referendum must be undertaken by elected representatives; special one-off referendums, as in the case of Brexit, have to be brought into being by votes of Parliament; binding plebiscites have to be designed and questions set (that is, what people will actually be voting on), often with no citizen input; bottom-up initiatives that begin with a signature campaign can be captured by wealthy stakeholders. Thus the study and conceptualization of referendums and plebiscites falls more and more within the broader study of representative democracy rather than within a competing model of direct democracy (Van Crombrugge 2021).

Rather than positing a contrast between direct and representative democracy, another way to approach falling trust levels in representatives is to posit that governing always involves the creation of a political elite. Ancient Athens had its powerful and influential orators, for example. According to a simple but intuitively appealing model of democracy, this elite should be responsive to the interests, concerns, and grievances of citizens. On this view, then, the crisis of representation involves both the failure of the elite to be adequately responsive to citizens and the growing perception on the part of citizens of this lack of responsiveness. In this chapter, I look at three new directions in democratic theory that speak to this crisis of responsiveness.

The first set of theories, and in some ways the most radical, argues that electoral democracy, as it was conceived of at the end of the seventeenth century and then handed down to all liberal democratic orders, was never designed to be truly responsive to ordinary citizens. Elections are inherently aristocratic, meaning they select a governing elite who are chosen because of their virtue or superior ability, or perhaps oligarchic, meaning that the rich and powerful tend to get elected and rule. In the place of election, here we see the endorsement of sortition, or random selection, as a democratic means of choosing representatives. These theories introduce the idea of citizen representatives.

The second body of work I canvas might not look like a new direction as it focuses on political parties, an ever-present institution in the study of democracy. But, for a long time, normative democratic theory had very little interest in parties. The new turn that I discuss here attempts to breathe new normative life into the salutary function of partisanship in democratic politics. This view is in stark contrast to the sortition view in which partisanship is one of the elements overcome by randomly selected representative assemblies.

The final view reconsiders the standard idea of responsiveness and, in doing so, rethinks the way we evaluate and judge whether representatives are doing a good job. This new wave of normative theories of representation, dubbed constructivism, suggests that citizens' views, opinions, and preferences are (to some extent) constructed by representatives themselves, thus reversing the causal direction implied by ideas of input and responsiveness and indeed questioning the ideal of responsiveness as an adequate or realistic measure of democracy.

Citizen representatives and the return of sortition

Sortition is a method of choosing members – of an assembly, jury, or committee, for example – by drawing lots or random selection. Its most common use today is in the selection of a jury pool. There is currently a great deal of interest in sortition, and that interest spans many areas of democratic theory (Sintomer 2018). Assemblies or deliberative bodies chosen by random selection are called deliberative mini-publics or citizens' assemblies. Their use within representative democracies to address all sorts of problems is growing, as is their popularity among ordinary citizens (Curato et al. 2021; Wike et al. 2021). In chapter 11, I look at and discuss some of these experiments under the heading democratic innovation. Although the popularity of these initiatives might be fueled by a crisis of representation, for the most part these are consultative bodies that do not challenge the centrality or role of elected representatives in democratic systems. In this chapter, I look at normative theories that propose sortition as either a better method than election for choosing legislators or as a necessary complement to elections in order to counter pathologies inherent in electoral democracy (Abizadeh 2021; Gastil and Wright 2019a; Guerrero 2014; Landemore 2020; Van Reybrouck 2016).

The defense of sortition begins with a criticism of electoral representation. That criticism has two sources. The first is a revisionist history of electoral democracy coupled with a normative deconstruction of elections that together suggest that elections were adopted and defended precisely because of their elitist tendencies. The second source is contemporary empirical evidence of what has been called the oligarchization of representative institutions.

Bernard Manin's 1997 book *The Principles of Representative Government* is a central text appealed to for the revisionist narrative, although he is not alone in making this assessment (Manin 1997). Manin points out that the founders of the new republics in America and France at the end of the seventeenth century were very clear in their opposition to democracy, which they associated with mob rule, the domination of the passions, and sortition. Up until this time, sortition or selection by lot was thought the core of democracy and election the heart of aristocracy or oligarchy (Manin 1997: 79, 134). This view goes all the way back to Aristotle and is reproduced in Montesquieu and other influential political theorists of the seventeenth and early eighteenth centuries. Election is a method of selection that seeks and then establishes distinctions. Voters look for people who stand out and are thought more gifted or more competent than the average person, and then election elevates them to a position of authority (Huq 2020: 32; Landemore 2020: 89; Manin 1997: 139). Underpinning the new seventeenth- and eighteenth-century enthusiasm for election over lot was the modern stress on the legitimizing role of consent. The rejection of sortition in favor of election reflects the fact that "this regime form has historically consisted in privileging the idea of people's *consent* to power over that of the people's exercise of power" (Landemore 2020: xiv). The ideal, very clearly articulated in Madison's defense of the new constitution in 1789, was to put the very best and the very brightest in positions of power to pursue reasonable and well-thought-out policies that served the public interest.[1] The fact that this elite was mostly drawn from a wealthy class was irrelevant, according to Madison and his fellow Federalists, as they argued that one need not be from a particular class in order to defend the interests of that class. But many democratic theorists challenge this view and argue that not only do representatives not look like ordinary citizens, but they also do not appear to be pursuing policy agendas in the interests of ordinary citizens (Guerrero 2014). This they back up with empirical evidence.

Although all liberal democracies guarantee an equal right to run for office, access to candidacy and election are significantly skewed along socio-economic, educational, and identity lines. This is particularly pronounced in the United States, where money plays such an oversized role in elections, but it is a fact across all democratic systems. The wealthy and already powerful are much more likely to run for and win office, which is indicative of a skewed candidate selection process (Bonica 2020; Carnes 2018). Popular culture is full of references to this skewing. Here is an excerpt from the comedian Chris Rock's *Saturday Night Live* monologue in October 2020: "We've agreed in the United States that we cannot have kings, yet we have dukes and duchesses running the Senate and Congress making decisions for poor people. That's right. [applause] Rich people making decisions for poor people. That's like your handsome friend giving you dating advice" (Rock 2020).

But is it true that the wealthy cannot look out for the interest of the less wealthy? There is a large and contested literature about how to measure the responsiveness of democratic institutions (Sabl 2015). Defenders of sortition often appeal to research that documents a large disconnect between the opinions and interests of lower- and middle-class constituents and the policy agendas, endorsements, and voting records of their elected representatives (Crouch 2004; Gilens 2012; Gilens and Page 2017; Hacker and Pierson 2011). Even more troubling, this research finds a strong correlation between business and financial interest lobbying and legislative policy agendas. Thus low- and middle-income citizens are doubly denied access to power, first, through skewed candidate selection and, second, through lack of influence over agenda setting.

When representatives fail to do their job and instead pursue the interests of an economic elite, then we should be able to throw the bums out of office and so create a system of accountability that incentivizes good representative behavior. But there is also some empirical evidence that suggests that policy agendas are very complicated, and elections are dominated by spin, framing, and misinformation, and all this is compounded by voter ignorance (Achen and Bartels 2016). Sometimes these accountability mechanisms work in egregious cases of a violation of public trust, and we throw the bum out. But very often that does not happen. So not only do these mechanisms of accountability not function the way they are supposed to, but elites also know that they do not function that way, so they know that there are ways to avoid being punished for pursuing policy agendas that favor the well-off rather than citizens in general.

How accurate is this assessment of the crisis of representation? This contains two questions. First, to what extent are existing representative institutions in fact oligarchic, measured along the three dimensions of candidacy selection, agenda setting, and responsiveness? And the second, slightly different question: to what extent do citizens feel like the system is rigged to benefit the rich and already powerful? The correct answer to both questions is "to some extent." But it makes a difference whether one thinks that the extent is so immense as to compromise any claim to democratic legitimacy on the part of electoral representative institutions or whether one thinks that oligarchic tendencies can be mitigated without doing away with elections all together.

There is a growing section of democratic theory that is convinced that competitive elections are a very poor instantiation of political equality as they inherently favor the wealthy, and elected representative assemblies are always on a slippery slope to oligarchy (Landemore 2020; McCormick 2006). This is not a new argument. The anti-Federalists had many of the same worries, and the American populist tradition of the late nineteenth century also made this argument. We are, however, seeing a new way to address it in the rise of sortition. Lottocracy has now entered our democratic lexicon to denote an alternative to electoral democracy.

Sortition, as I noted above, is selection by lot or random selection. It was used in Ancient Athens and (we think) other Greek democracies to choose executive or agenda-setting assemblies (Ober 2017). What features make it preferable to elections? There are three dimensions along which sortition is evaluated as superior to election. First, it is thought to be a better instantiation of political equality; second, it embodies a preferable ideal of representativeness; and, finally, it is epistemically superior in the sense that deliberation of such an assembly would be substantively better than that of an elected assembly and therefore have better outcomes.

"Lotteries express a strict principle of equality as well as a principle of impartiality between citizens. Random selection, unlike election, does not recognize distinctions between citizens because everyone has exactly the same chance of being chosen once they have entered into the lottery" (Landemore 2020: 90). The equal chance to hold office is a statistical equality that is justified by a deeper commitment to political equality. If we are committed to political equality, so the argument goes, then we should be committed to equalizing access to the exercise of power. Elections cannot do that not simply because of skewed candidacy selection, but because of the nature of competitive elections. With sortition there is no campaigning, no money, no parties, no celebrities, no robocalls, no fake news involved in the selection process. Even in political contexts with strict campaign regulation especially regarding money, it is not possible to create a perfectly level playing field. Good-looking people have an advantage in the election game. Is that really fair? Sortition is a perfectly level playing field. Given the state of electioneering in many democracies, this is an attractive prospect to some.

Replacing people's equal vote with a statistically equal chance to hold power is a radical move that requires an argument that connects the chosen representatives to the people (Warren 2008). In what sense does a citizens' assembly represent the people at large? The first and most obvious way is again statistically. Like a representative survey sample, a randomly selected assembly would reproduce a cross-section of the population. This is the idea of mirroring. The idea here is that legislators are "like me." There is some evidence that citizens at large favor citizens' assemblies and trust them because they do look like ordinary citizens. This trust is partly built on the thought that ordinary people are not subject to the same corrupting influences as elites, but also on the idea that they understand the trials and tribulations of the common person.

One common criticism of this idea of representation is why even have an assembly; why not simply use randomly sampled opinion polls to choose legislation? The answer, of course, is that members of the assembly deliberate. In fact, deliberation, or the epistemic dimension of citizens' assemblies, is their strongest selling point. Citizens' assemblies involve facilitated deliberation, meaning that it usually involves, first, an information stage where members hear from experts on a topic or issue and sometimes from stakeholders and civil society groups. Then, there is a deliberation phase where professional facilitators ensure that deliberative norms of civility and equality as well as epistemic norms of staying on topic and problem solving are maintained. There are four features of citizens' assembly deliberation that recommend this type of body: impartiality, diversity, equality, and track record. Participants are not members of parties, they do not represent groups, they are not beholden to a special constituency. All this means that they are free from partisanship and approach problem solving in the assembly from a place of impartiality. They are chosen at random and so the assembly will have a broad cross-section of ordinary people. Recalling the arguments we covered in chapter 7, many champions of sortition appeal to a diversity-trumps-ability intuition to argue that an elected assembly where, for example, more than half the members are drawn from the law profession will do a much poorer job at problem solving than a diverse cross-section of the population. Third, internal debate and deliberation is relatively non-hierarchical, meaning there is no seniority, no whips, no powerful committee sinecures, and so on. Finally, we have 30 years of experiments in citizens' assemblies and mini-publics to draw on as evidence that citizens do a good job at problem solving using evidence-driven argument (Curato et al. 2021; Fishkin 2009). But these initiatives have been consultative and not legislative. Are these arguments enough to justify replacing elections with sortition? The consensus in democratic theory is unsurprisingly no. Indeed, there is a rush to denounce lottocracy as a very dangerous trend in democratic theory. Here I look at three arguments against lottocracy.

One counterargument to the epistemic defense of sortition is the accusation that this is a form of technocracy. This might appear counterintuitive. Citizens' assemblies are popular precisely because many people feel that technocratic government is out of touch with how ordinary people live and feel. But if the biggest selling point of citizens' assemblies is that they get better answers to problems because they are not blinded by either partisan biases or the influence of money, then it would seem that their claim to rule is an epistemic one, just like technocrats. On this argument, we listen to them because they produce better policy, not because they are in some sense democratic. Here we can see that the claim to be representative and the claim to produce good outcomes are in tension. Significant and substantive deliberation within an assembly relying on expert informants and facilitators moves the resulting opinion away from what would be garnered in an opinion poll. But this also means that assembly members look less like ordinary citizens and more like experts as they deliberate. James Fishkin has argued that we need to think of deliberation in hypothetical terms (Fishkin 2009). The results of well-structured citizen deliberation represent the conclusions that ordinary citizens would have come to if they had had the same opportunity to deliberate. But we cannot take this logic too far, for example, to the point of suggesting that a randomly selected assembly produces the "will of the people." This is so first for purely technical reasons. They are not, nor can they ever be, perfectly random. Because they are voluntary, there will inevitably be an element of self-selection involved. Each group is different and has a different identity. Each deliberation is unique. This means there can be no strong claim that the outcomes of a citizens' assembly really are what everybody would decide if they had had the chance to deliberate. But even if this were not the case, claiming that a decision in which I took no part, not even voting for the people who are making the decision, was somehow my will is problematic (Lafont 2020). This introduces the second set of criticisms: citizenship loses its agential component.

Both voting and sortition instantiate political equality by recognizing "each citizen as equally entitled to render authoritative judgments as to how to organize and regulate all citizens' common life" (Wilson 2019: 49). But only voting calls on citizens to regularly exercise that judgment. Although under a purely sorted system, individual citizens might be encouraged to follow the deliberations and policy enactments of a lottocratic chamber, and these chambers would be mandated to engage in broad consultation, the lack of involvement in the selection process severely diminishes citizens' reasons to inform themselves or to connect their own political judgments to outcomes. This might make them less ready to exercise legislative power if called up to serve in a citizens' assembly. But there are more reasons to value voting than its instrumental worth as potential preparation for being selected to serve in a citizens' assembly. "One person, one vote" is a more robust recognition that each person's judgment counts equally in a democracy (Schwartzberg 2014: 111) than having an equal chance to be chosen to exercise judgment. Thus voting recognizes each citizen's agency in a way that sortition does not.

The final argument draws on some insights from minimalist theories of democracy but has non-minimalist implications. Minimalists suggest that democracy is stable because losers know that they will get another chance to be winners at the next set of elections. No such chance is available to losers in a lottocracy. This will lead, according to a minimalist logic, to growing frustration and dissatisfaction on the part of losers that will bleed into anti-system and violent interventions in order to have their positions heard. On this logic, a pure lottocracy will lead to civil war (Abizadeh 2021).

The impartiality envisioned in a sorted assembly is both a selling point for a randomly selected assembly as well as a reason why it would be inadequate (perhaps even disastrous) as the sole legislative chamber. Social groups need outlets to make claims and demand action. Social movements might still have a civil society and public sphere presence in the absence of elections, but their activity would have much less impact without parties and the electoral politics that can channel, aggregate, and articulate group interests via partisan agendas. Gastil and Wright, who endorse sortition as a method of choosing representatives in a second chamber, argue that "given the nature of power and inequality in contemporary societies, there are conflicts of interest that cannot be resolved simply through disinterested deliberation . . . Bargaining needs highly articulated expressions of interests with authorized representatives who can forge compromises" (Gastil and Wright 2019b: 33). This calls for parties and partisanship.

It is unclear what a public sphere would look like minus competitive electoral politics. Clearly, some communicative pathologies associated with competitive elections would disappear. But the potential for a type of generative public opinion and will formation would also, it seems to me, be diminished. The clash and competition of agendas, ideas, and positions are part of a process through which citizens come to have opinions and through which they come to understand their own interests. Partisanship, whether it is tied to a party or a cause, mobilizes and engages citizens in activities that get them thinking about politics, justice, and public issues. Can a democracy maintain the transformative potential of the public sphere as a place where new ideas emerge without regular elections and the contestation that comes with them? I think it is unlikely.

Before moving on to parties, there is one last observation to be made about the debate over sortition. The mounting criticism of the sortition turn (or against lottocracy) tends to target the minority of theorists who think that electoral democracy is unsalvageable, and we need to radically rethink democracy, including in ways that would do away with voting and elections (Lafont 2020). Critics say that the use of citizens' assemblies as integrated consultative mechanisms is fine but not as a replacement for elections. But the radical lottocrats are an easy target. Many critics fail to take seriously the much more interesting and reasonable proposals that agree with all the reasons why we cannot get rid of elections but argue that lottocratic institutions may be an important corrective to the oligarchic drift of electoral institutions. These proposals see citizens' assemblies as second chambers or integrated into assemblies that use multiple methods of selection (Abizadeh 2021; Gastil and Wright 2019b; Owen and Smith 2018). These suggestions seem a more interesting subject of debate.

Parties, partisans, and partisanship

Political parties have not been a traditional focus of normative democratic theory but a constant subject of interest for empirical political science. Why have parties been neglected until recently by normative theory? Since the ascendency of John Rawls and his type of ideal theorizing beginning in the 1970s, political philosophy has been dominated by the search for core principles rather than studying institutions (Waldron 2016). Justice, impartiality, neutrality, reasonableness, consensus, and the common good were the concepts at the center of political philosophy in the 1980s and 1990s, and political parties did not fit neatly into this narrative. In addition, many models of democracy – deliberative, participatory, agonistic, direct – were conceived as alternatives to the business-as-usual of electoral politics. This led to a focus on alternative sites of democratic participation – "social movements, civil society associations, deliberative experiments, spaces for local participatory government, and direct popular participation" (Muirhead and Rosenblum 2020: 96).

But the last 20 years or so has seen new interest in and defense of parties in normative democratic theory (Bonotti 2017; Invernizzi-Accetti and Wolkenstein 2017; Muirhead 2014; Rosenblum 2000, 2008; White and Ypi 2016). What accounts for this? Three things, I think. First, the interest in the normative dimension of parties is part of a larger trend in political philosophy swinging the pendulum back from the ideal theory alluded to above and toward empirically informed, institutionally anchored, and problem-driven political theory. The discussion of parties translates many of the abstract principles we reviewed in chapters 3, 4, and 5 into concrete institutional terms. Second is an empirically well-documented crisis of party democracy (Dalton and Wattenberg 2002; Mair 2013). Parties, like many institutions of representative democracy, have fallen on hard times. Sinking voter turnout is coupled with declines in party identification, membership, and respect, all of which indicate that citizens are not getting what they want from parties. Parties are either seen as all alike with no clear distinguishing policies or programs, or as focused so exclusively on gaining and maintaining power that they have lost touch with what citizens need and want. Normative theory has stepped in to remind us of what parties at their best can do and to argue that democracy is unthinkable without parties. This connects directly to the final reason for a newfound interest in parties: as a counterweight to the growing interest in and defense of sortition.

I will look at four dimensions of parties and party democracy that are getting attention. The first is a reassessment of partisanship and its positive contribution to democracy. Then there are three separate, but not mutually exclusive, views of the important function that parties play in democracy: to regulate rivalry, to create a linkage between citizens' interests and preferences and government, and as vehicles of public justification. Let me begin with partisanship.

Partisanship often has a negative connotation in popular discourse but also in some political philosophy. In popular discourses, it often means one-sided or biased and unwilling to compromise or listen to the other side. Many contemporary democratic theorists seek to rehabilitate partisanship and develop an ideal ethics of partisanship (Muirhead 2014; Rosenblum 2008; White and Ypi 2016). Partisanship can be broken down into four elements. First, it means that one has a cause, takes a side, or cares about something strongly. Thus one must be *for* something to be a partisan. This should be distinguished from polarization, which often means being simply against the other side, independent of the substantive content of their platform or position. So partisanship is tied to a cause, ideology, or substantive platform. It is difficult to imagine political mobilization and democratic participation without some degree of partisanship. This most basic understanding of partisanship and the first plank in its defense is used to question lottocratic ideals of politics without partisans and parties.

The second dimension of partisanship is that it mobilizes for a cause with others in a group. One is not a partisan alone or in the service of one's own individual preferences. A partisan takes up a cause with others in a party. A party joins people together and represents people with similar causes and interests. Partisans are *members* of parties. Group membership can have an educative function (schools of citizenship) that begins to encourage modern individuals to think in terms of group and collective interests.

A partisan mobilizes for a cause. The content of that cause is a set of policies or a political platform that is defended and campaigned for on the grounds that it is the best plan for the community to pursue. In other words, partisanship is about supporting an interpretation of the common good. This is the third plank in the picture of partisanship at its best. Partisanship according to its defenders is not about the pursuit of narrow sectoral interest. That is factionalism. The partisan claim, according to White and Ypi, is "to be adopting principles and aims that are *generalizable*, i.e., irreducible to the beliefs or interests of particular social groups" (White and Ypi 2016: 5). Partisans pursue the common good. Why do we need parties and partisans to pursue the common good? Because in modern democracies there will be disagreement about what the common good is. Thus, ideally, each party puts forward their sincere and committed view of policies that would make everybody better off. In party democracy, then, parties vie for partisans by articulating a picture of the common good. And in embracing elections and electoral turnover as the means of doing so, the partisan accepts that all political claims are contestable. Thus the final characteristic of partisans is that they accept pluralism and differences of opinion in matters of the common good. Partisans acknowledge "their partiality, that they do not and cannot speak for the whole" (Rosenblum 2008: 124).

To sum up: partisans have a cause that is a conception of the common good, pursue that cause with like-minded people in a party, and accept that their conception of the common good is contestable. This final picture of partisanship looks very different from what we see in the popular press as well as in the behavior of partisan actors on the political stage. Thus it is more of a critical yardstick to evaluate how our parties and partisans are failing to live up to the ideal than a description of contemporary partisan politics (Invernizzi-Accetti and Wolkenstein 2017). But it is also meant to suggest that, even if party politics look ugly, factional, and polarized now, this is not the essential or necessary core of party politics. Not everyone who is set on rehabilitating the normative desirability of party politics has such an idealized view of partisanship, but they do all see a positive function of parties and the partisans who join them. The function of parties is articulated in three ways. These are not mutually exclusive, and some theories endorse all three. Parties are an essential component of regulated rivalry, they serve as a linkage between opinions and interests of citizens and government action and legislation, and, finally, parties engage in public justification and in so doing they are an essential component in maintaining democratic legitimacy (Muirhead and Rosenblum 2020).

The first defense of parties starts from an acknowledgment of pluralism and disagreement. We have seen this before. But here the argument is not so much about how to come to a fair decision procedure among equals who disagree, but rather about how to avoid destructive conflict in a world of divergent and competing interests. Thus some defenses of parties, for example Russell Muirhead's and Nancy Rosenblum's, have more in common with some minimalist realist arguments than moral procedural arguments. The goal is to avoid violence and conflict. The goal is achieved through "regulated rivalry."

> Transforming pluralism into ongoing, managed, institutionalized conflict among parties is a hard-won and fragile historical development. The legitimacy of the other side to compete for power is acknowledged. Rotation in office entails a method of determining winners and acceptance of the results by losers, including the acceptance of the policies they oppose . . . Regulated party rivalry for office distinguishes party opposition from sedition, treason, conspiracy, rebellion, or civil war. (Muirhead and Rosenblum 2020: 100)

Some dislike for party politics rests on the inherent divisiveness of party competition. But Muirhead and Rosenblum suggest that all aspirations for unity are dangerous and problematic because such unity will always exclude some group who then might take up alternative means to have their vision come to power. What party democracy does, then, is to channel pluralism rather than let it descend into a literal battleground for power. The regulated rivalry view of parties puts forward a strong argument for why ideals of unity or impartiality will always face the challenge of pluralism and competing interests. But this view does not offer much help in confronting the crisis of party democracy. It points out the risks and dangers of channeling democratic politics away from parties but does not address the hollowing out of parties and citizens' dissatisfaction with party politics. The second way to conceive of the function of parties does address these questions more directly.

Parties perform the essential function "of linking society to the state, or more precisely of *mediating* the relationship between them in a way that allows political power to be exercised from the 'bottom up' as well as 'top down'" (Invernizzi-Accetti and Wolkenstein 2017: 97). The idea, then, is that parties absorb social grievances, claims, and demands and translate these into party platforms and public policy. These platforms are then presented to citizens at election times as competing responses to preferences and claims bubbling up from civil society. The linkage/responsiveness view of parties is the standard view of the function of parties that has dominated empirical political science for almost 50 years (Kirchheimer 1967; Sartori 1976). So, in what sense is this new? Many of the empirical claims were of the type "this is what parties do." With the crisis of parties, it appears that parties are either not doing this or doing a very poor job. In the context of failing linkage, mediation, and responsiveness, normative theory articulates why it is so important to revitalize the linkage and how these linkages are the backbone of any claim to self-government and democracy (Müller 2021). Thus they translate the descriptive theory into a normative register and connect it to normative ideas of value, legitimacy, and self-government. Many theories that stress linkage are Kelsenian proceduralist. Here they argue that under conditions of complexity, scale, and pluralism, only parties acting as "transmission belts" can approximate ideals of popular rule.

But the second thing that normative theory does is suggest ways to reverse the erosion of party support. One account of weakening linkage points to the move toward catch-all parties. In search of ever increasing their vote share, parties attempt to be all things to all people and end up being unable to appeal to anyone. Parties become empty shells. One answer to this is the development of intra-party democracy. The idea here is to open parties up to participation and more input from ordinary citizens, and this will undo alienation and create a more flexible responsive party structure (Invernizzi-Accetti and Wolkenstein 2017). More realist-minded theorists make the opposite argument: parties have strayed from the ideal of vehicles for the common good because they have been captured by the most radical elements of the base, and that capture has been facilitated by the democratization of parties (Rosenbluth and Shapiro 2018). Parties need more elite discipline to stay democratically functional. The American primary system, for example, is sometimes blamed for bringing Trump to power and sending the US Republican Party into a hard-right tailspin (Jacobs 2022). It is impossible for normative democratic theory to adjudicate this sort of difference of opinion. Political parties and the electoral, social, and cultural context in which they operate vary too much.

The mediation or linkage function of parties focuses on the way parties receive and are open to messages from civil society. The final function of parties looks more closely at the reverse direction of messaging. Here parties present and justify policies and legislative agendas to voters. This function is reimagined in terms of public justification and sometimes public reason. Parties, on this view, are important institutions contributing to "the process of public justification, that is, the process through which laws and policies are not merely implemented based on majoritarian decisions but also justified to all those who will be subject to them" (Bonotti 2022: 588). Recalling our discussion of mutual justification in chapter 3, one puzzle that we left unresolved was how to realistically scale up this ideal in modern mass democracies. Parties become the agents of public or mutual justification. Thus parties do not simply bundle interests and claims and translate them into legislative agendas. Parties also justify these agendas to a broader public. One might think that developing democratic theories that make parties the home of public justification and public reason pushes the debate about parties back onto an abstract level of ideal and principle. But we do have some informal expectations in the public sphere that political elites offer public reason. What would we think if the leader of a political party announced to the public: "I support this important piece of legislation because it will make me rich"? We would probably find this odd, foolish, and inappropriate (even if we think that it might be true). People usually do not talk like this in public, especially if they want to get reelected. There are certain expectations about what are, and what are not, appropriate reasons to support public policy. These expectations often vary from context to context. So, for example, what would we think if, in a private conversation, our neighbor said, "I think I will vote for X because those new tax policies will make me better off"? We still might not think that this was a particularly worthy reason, but it does not appear to be as inappropriate or as troubling as the representative saying it. We hold public actors, including party elite and spokespeople, to a higher standard, and I want to suggest that that standard has something to do with bringing forward reasons that are public in the sense of reasons for others and not just for me or people like me.

Our original disapproval of the representative who appealed to her own well-being as a reason for public policy is more than simply a recognition of political ineptitude. The rhetorical expectations that we place on our public figures reflect a deeper moral intuition. We generally think that our political leaders should seek forms of justification that are broadly inclusive. It is not the fact that the legislation benefited the party leader (or any particular individual, for that matter) that is at issue; it is using this fact as a justification that is the problem. Her own well-being might be a reason for her (as it was for the neighbor above), but, as a public figure, she ought to be offering justifications for us – that is, for the public. Public figures are under an obligation to justify policy and law to a public, and this calls for public sorts of reasons. This is to suggest that reading parties as agents of public reason is compatible with a realistic and grounded view of the function of parties.

Representatives and the constructivist turn

Almost every introduction to political science class has a section on what is a representative. And they almost always start with a standard set of definitions and distinctions. Focusing primarily on elected representatives, the class begins with the principal/agent distinction. The citizen or voter is the principal, and the representative is the agent. Getting a handle on how citizens are related to the people who actually pass the laws is the next topic on the agenda. Here the standard view of representation is trotted out: delegate and trustee. On the delegate model, representatives should follow the instructions given to them by the voters very closely. Agents are messengers passing on the directives and commands of the principal. The trustee model, most famously championed by Edmund Burke, points to a certain amount of independence on the part of representatives. Voters choose representatives that they trust to make good decisions. Thus the representative does not have instructions for every vote. And in some or perhaps many cases, the representative will use her judgment about what is the correct or proper way to vote on legislation. When or if the representative votes in a way that the constituent disagrees with, they try to elect someone else. It is difficult to imagine elected representatives as purely one or the other of these ideal types. Modern legislative agendas are too packed and busy to imagine that pure delegation would work. Pure trusteeship runs afoul of intuitive ideas of responsiveness.

This standard narrative is being challenged in two different ways in contemporary democratic theory. The first is the development of more complex and nuanced views of the different ways political representatives relate to voters. The second is more dramatic, and it involves questioning the principal/agent model underlying most ideas of political representation in democracy.

An important contribution to the first challenge was Jane Mansbridge's influential article "Rethinking Representation" (Mansbridge 2003, 2011; Rehfeld 2009, 2011), in which she offered a new typology to replace the delegate/trustee model. Mansbridge's typology introduced four categories of representation: promissory, anticipatory, gyroscopic, and surrogate. These identify four ways of understanding the accountability between the principal and agent and dispense with the dimension of binding versus non-binding that connected delegate and trustee. Promissory representation involves the promises that a representative makes regarding how she will act and vote. These promises can be specific votes on specific measures, but they could also be promises to be honest and always listen to her constituents. Making these promises creates a public and perhaps moral obligation between representative and voter. Anticipatory representation involves the representative looking forward to reelection time (or the voter looking back at the record during election time) and acting in such a way as to get or maintain the support of voters or to avoid punishment and sanction by losing electoral support. Anticipatory representation can lead to responsiveness, and, indeed, many models of electoral accountability rely on a retrospective model where voters evaluate the record and reward those who have done a good job or pursued courses of action that voters like. If this accountability mechanism is working, then it should create incentives for attentiveness and responsiveness. But there is also evidence (which I review in more detail below) that citizens are not always perceptive judges of performance or, more worrisome, are easily manipulated by questionable communicative strategies. This means that representatives are always anticipating the next election, and they construct narratives and sometimes misrepresent the record to better their chances of getting reelected. Thus, although they do contain normative standards of evaluation (did she keep her promises? did she do a good job?), both promissory and anticipatory representation can also be subject to distortion and manipulation.

The third category Mansbridge introduces she calls gyroscopic. Promissory and anticipatory principal/agent relationships both rely on an external mechanism – a promise or anticipation of electoral loss – to motivate the representatives to do their jobs. Therefore, both could countenance an instrumental relationship between principal and agent. Candidate A promises to do X to get elected or passes Y to stay elected. But how does candidate A feel about X or Y? In gyroscopic representation, candidates are internally motivated (imagine we each have an inner gyroscope directing our actions) to pursue public goals or a legislative agenda. Voters then choose representatives whose public goals and legislative priorities align with their own interests or identity and then withdraw support when there is no longer alignment. Gyroscopic representation is based more on trust than sanction. As Mansbridge notes, "Most actual representative–constituent relations mix elements of promissory, anticipatory, and gyroscopic relationships in greatly varying degrees, contingent on available degree of warranted trust" (Mansbridge 2020: 38).

Mansbridge's final conception is surrogate representation. Here there is no direct electoral link between principal and agent, but nevertheless a citizen feels represented by an official, or an official feels that they represent a group, or both. A classic and important case of surrogate representation can take place via descriptive representation. Descriptive representation happens when the experiences or background of a representative resembles that of citizens in an important way, for example, race, class, or gender (Phillips 1995; Williams 1998). A descriptively similar surrogate representative "can still give citizens the feeling, often warranted, of having a contact and an advocate on their behalf in the government who understands their backgrounds, perspectives, and interests. Citizens may have no power over their surrogate representatives but may contact them and see them correctly as advancing their collective interests in the legislature" (Mansbridge 2020: 38–9).

There has been an ongoing debate that further fine-tunes the different ways that representatives represent the principal (Rehfeld 2011; Wolkenstein and Wratil 2021). Although leaving the delegate/trustee distinction behind, this new direction in normative theories of representation is still wedded to the traditional view that representation primarily involves some principal–agent relationship and that this in turn means that democratic representation involves responsiveness. Responsiveness means that democratic governments ought to respond to, address, or listen to the grievances and claims of citizens. Democracy is not only by the people but for the people. A crude essentialist view of responsiveness says that governments should simply reflect or channel the opinions of citizens; legislative output should correlate to public opinion. Some empirical efforts to measure responsiveness do simply correlate public opinion to policy output. But no normative theory of democracy embraces a pure correlation view of responsiveness (Sabl 2015). So far, all the views we have looked at see the process of representation in a feedback loop where representatives or parties articulate claims that surface in civil society and then present them to the public, who then perhaps refine their views, and so on. Responsiveness is thus filtered through deliberation, justification, public debate, development of party platforms, and many other mechanisms that link the plural and often conflicting interests scattered throughout civil society to legislation. Often the meaning of ideal democratic responsiveness will involve improving, refining, and educating public opinion. But despite the embrace of ideas like loops, feedback, two-way processes, and interdependence, all these views believe the direction of the circle is or ought to be from the bottom up. Or, more precisely, democracy is working properly when institutions of government respond to the real concerns, interests, and claims of the people, whether those concerns have been articulated in a citizens' assembly, through a party platform, or in the legislative record of representatives. Thus citizens are still in some sense the principals, and the citizen-representatives, parties, or elected representatives are the agents. The final view I look at departs from this model.

The opening chapter of Lisa Disch's book defending a constructive view of representation is entitled "Responsiveness in Reverse." On this view, representatives do not respond to citizens and voters; citizens and voters respond to the narratives constructed by representatives. "Most people form opinions and political preferences based on the messages they receive from sources they trust – candidates, political parties, nongovernment organizations, advocacy groups, opinion shapers in the mass media or on social media, celebrities, and more" (Disch 2021: 1). Representatives mobilize and bring into political existence constituencies. "Political representation does not merely reflect social constituencies but participates in constituting them" (2021: 94). Disch's reversal of the standard view of responsiveness rests on combining a constructivist turn in representative theory inaugurated most clearly by Michael Saward with empirical data about political knowledge and preference formation (Saward 2010).

Saward is interested in thinking about representation beyond elected representatives. The mechanisms that make some into representatives and others into the represented in the political sphere are elections, but representation goes on in many different areas of life and society. Thinking about representation more broadly might help us to get at its core. Hannah Pitkin, in a treatment of representation that was considered authoritative for close to 30 years, famously formulated representation as *"re-presentation*, a making present again" or "making present in some sense of something which is nevertheless not present literally or in fact" (Pitkin 1967: 8–9). On this view, there is a presence that precedes and forms a substrate for the act of re-presenting: "the represented must be somehow logically prior; the representative must be responsive to him rather than the other way around" (Pitkin 1967: 140). Saward challenges this view by suggesting that when people or groups claim to represent some constituency, that constituency exists as a constituency only insofar as the claim is accepted. I could claim to speak for "Canadians who reside in the USA" and make that claim public, say, via social media and advocate on behalf of "Canadians who reside in the USA." It is an empirical fact that there are Canadians who reside in the USA, so my claim does not bring that category of people literally into existence, but "Canadians who reside in the USA" as a *constituency*, with collective interests to be pursued, is brought into existence by someone making the claim on their behalf. "Rather than speak and act for a constituency (represent in the typical sense), claims-making solicits a constituency to recognize itself in a claim and to support the person who made it" (Disch 2019: 7–8). Without representation – which is to say, without some people and groups making representative claims on behalf of some group – society is a swirling aggregate of multiple interests, identities, and grievances without political coherence. "Absent representation, there may be a population but there cannot be a people, constituency or group" (Disch 2019: 9).

Saward highlights the entrepreneurial function of representation and the possibility that the claim to represent a constituency might bring the constituency into being (Castiglione and Pollak 2019: 3). Disch connects this entrepreneurial idea of representation to empirical research on citizens' opinion formation to reverse the standard view of responsiveness. On a standard view of responsiveness, according to Disch, citizens are assumed to have preferences which they form in society prior to engaging in politics. They bring these preferences into the political arena, and then the democratic system responds to them. Empirical research on preference formation, however, tells a very different story. "Rather than form preferences prior to acts of representation, people shape their interests and demands in response to political communication that occurs over the course of the representative process" (Disch 2021: 16; see also Druckman 2014). A prime example is framing. Framing refers to the way a speaker or political communication more generally presents an issue or problem. A classic example is a study that compared framing a hate-group rally in terms of free speech or in terms of public safety. Opinion of the event varied dramatically depending on which frame was employed (Druckman 2014: 474). This suggests that preferences or opinions are deeply endogenous to the communicative context, meaning they are determined by that context. Endogeneity further complicates or perhaps even undermines claims of responsiveness.

To the feedback loops and interdependence suggested in more traditional views of representation, we now add the power of a political elite to shape the very preferences that they are supposed to be responding to.

What is the normative takeaway from the constructivist view of representation? One important question is, "What about manipulation?" (Talisse 2022). Manipulation not only reverses the responsiveness relationship, but it also denies the autonomy of citizens and makes them pawns of elite interests. This suggests that on a radical constructivist reading, most of what goes on in the political sphere and in the processes of preference formation is a form of manipulation. Disch prefers the term mobilization to manipulation. She is careful to note that elites might want to exploit framing and other communication strategies to create the constituencies they need to gain and stay in power, but it is in fact very difficult to do this successfully. "Manipulation is a false concern because politicians cannot script electoral cleavages however they please" (Disch 2019: 11). But the fact that successful manipulation is not that easy to pull off is not the same as saying it is a false concern. Observers of American democracy cannot but be amazed at the success of the completely fabricated "stop the steal" narrative to mobilize a constituency of active citizens.

It is hard to deny (and few people do deny) that the representative relationship plays a role in constituting the interests being represented (Warren 2019: 41). The question that Disch's constructivism raises is whether that endogeneity makes all talk about responsiveness and autonomy meaningless. Responsiveness speaks to a core pillar of normative democratic theory. On the one hand, most theory rejects a crude view of responsiveness, a view that equates it with a correlation of raw public opinion and legislative output, as being an undesirable as well as an implausible picture of the representative relationship (Sabl 2015). On the other hand, few want to give up entirely on the idea that good democratic government is supposed to respond to the real needs, interests, and concerns of citizens who ought to be treated as autonomous agents. This leads to the development of complex views of the feedback loops between citizens and representatives in which reflexivity and publicity function to expose the constructivist dimension of the relationship in such a way that it can be evaluated and justified if need be. For example, there are experiments that show that conversations and critical exchanges between citizens can weaken elite framing effects (Druckman and Nelson 2003). On a more normative dimension, Mansbridge has developed a recursive ideal of political representation where citizens play an active role in the process that constitutes the interests to be represented (Mansbridge 2019). This all suggests that the dividing line between constructivists and non-constructivists is on neither the question of endogeneity nor the recognition of the power that elite players have in how endogeneity plays out. The dividing line is often about assessing the power that reflexivity, publicity, and justification possess to include citizens in the process of construction. The more constructivists side with realist assessments of citizen competence, the less confidence they have that construction itself can be democratized.

Conclusion

One of the upshots of new theories of representation is to make the category of representative democracy less coherent as a self-contained alternative model to other forms or models of democracy. All imaginable democratic forms of governance involve multiple and complex representative claims and relationships. One sees more and more reference to the representative system rather than to representative government. "The network of people both elected and unelected who promote interests and respond to preferences can be thought of as a system of political representative" (Hutton Ferris 2022: 1; see also Mansbridge 2019; Rey 2020). This diversification of points of representation goes hand in hand with other trends we have followed in this book, for example, contestatory proceduralism covered in chapter 4 and dispersed popular sovereignty reviewed in the last chapter. Thinking about political representation as involving a complex system of relations also expands one's view beyond the elected representatives sitting in a national legislature. Using the idea of a system, one can then think about local and subnational representative relationships as well as supra-national and international representative relationships as interconnecting within a system. This has inspired interesting scholarship that integrates research about associations, NGOs, and global social movements into debates about democratic representation nicely captured in the title of Lara Montanaro's book *Who Elected Oxfam? A Democratic Defense of Self-Appointed Representatives* (Montanaro 2017).

10
Public Sphere

THE constructivist turn in theories of representation highlighted the central role of political communication in preference and identity formation. Political communication has two interdependent aspects. On the one hand, there is the crafting of the message, the frames chosen, the rhetoric used, and the audience targeted. This side of the equation involves the agents seeking to mobilize citizens and construct constituencies. On the other hand, there is the medium through which political communication circulates and disperses. In modern mass democracies, political communication is highly mediated. Newspapers, radio, and television have played a large role in connecting citizens and voters to representatives and government. Today, of course, all eyes are on the new digital landscape and the ways that it is changing the mediated public sphere. The diagnosis in both the popular press and scholarly research is that the digital revolution has been anything but good for democracy. "Today conventional wisdom holds that technologies have brought the world addictive devices, an omnipresent surveillance panopticon, racist algorithms, and disinformation machines that exacerbate polarization, threatening to destroy democracies from within" (Bernholz, Landemore, and Reich 2021: 3). In the relatively short time that digital political communication has come to dominate concern about the public sphere, there has been an explosion of research and interest in this topic.

I begin with an evaluation of the digital public sphere through the lens of deliberative democracy. Drawing on recent contributions to thinking about deliberative democracy in an age of social media, I outline the threats posed by this new media environment (Chambers 2021; Cohen and Fung 2021; Habermas 2022). This analysis begins with the centrality of the public sphere to a properly functioning democracy. Despite some alarming trends and evidence, the jury is still out on how bad the digital revolution and the "platformization" of the public sphere is for democracy. In the second section, I turn to democratic theorists who have taken the dive into technology and come away with (relatively) positive recommendations for making the internet more hospitable to truth and democracy (Forestal 2022; Landemore 2021). Finally, I look at the revival of interest in rhetoric in democracy. This too is an old topic going back to the ancient world. Now, however, the study of rhetoric can draw on modern science of opinion formation to open the black box of persuasion. But underlying much of the debate about rhetoric is the question of the relationship between autonomy and persuasion.

Deliberative democracy and the digital public sphere

Deliberative democracy is a broad research paradigm. Very generally, it can be described as a "talk-centric" rather than "vote-centric" view of democracy (Chambers 2003: 308) in which democracy is studied and evaluated "from the point of view of the quality of the processes through which individuals come to discuss, debate and mutually justify their respective stances before voting or taking other sorts of political action" (Scudder and White 2023: 12). This central normative core has been developed, studied, and theorized at what might be called two levels of democracy. On one level, we see the development and indeed proliferation of citizen deliberative initiatives. These concrete exercises in deliberative democracy bring citizens together in face-to-face designed settings with good information, trained moderators, and procedural norms that promote participant equality in the deliberative and decision-making process. Here deliberation is a practice structured within an institution. There are thousands of these initiatives across all democracies, and within non-democracies, with immense variation in design and function

(Curato et al. 2021). Their use and insertion into democratic systems is on the rise and, in many places, significantly addressing democratic deficit, or so I will argue in the next chapter. But this branch of deliberative democracy is not the topic of this part of the book. In deliberative mini-publics and citizens' assemblies there are no social media, no fake news, and no affective polarization, and many of the pathologies associated with post-truth are absent or mitigated. We can learn a great deal from these initiatives and translate some of it into the wild and open spaces of democracy writ large, but they do not add up to a democratic system, and it would be a mistake to think that deliberative democracy begins and ends with face-to-face citizens' deliberative initiatives (Neblo 2015; Scudder and White 2023).

The second branch of deliberative democracy seeks to develop a fuller theory of democracy that is applicable at the macro level. This fuller theory begins with a principle of democratic legitimacy and connects that principle to a systemic analysis of democracy. There are variations in the articulation of the principle of legitimacy (Cohen 1997b; Dryzek 2017; Habermas 1996; Mansbridge et al. 2012). But they all tie legitimacy to processes of inclusive reason giving where all affected have an equal right and opportunity to participate in collective opinion formation that is translated into action (or will) through, for example, elections.

But where exactly does "reason giving" go on in mass democracy? It is in translating the principle of deliberative legitimacy into the macro level that we see variation in theories. What is very rare to see (but what critics of deliberative democracy often claim to see) is the idea that this view of legitimacy translates into a utopian vision of democracy in which each and every citizen must engage in high-end deliberation about public matters. Applying the principle of legitimacy to the macro level involves looking at different parts of a full democratic system as playing different functions in instituting the ideal of legitimacy. The version that I investigate here is a two-track model of democracy introduced by Jürgen Habermas, a pivotal and influential figure in the field of deliberative democracy, and developed and applied to the digital public sphere in different ways by Joshua Cohen and Archon Fung, and myself. The two players here are the informal public sphere and the formal institutions of government, especially legislatures. Other models – for example, John Dryzek (2009), Bächtiger and Parkinson (2019), and Mansbridge and colleagues (2012) – all highlight different elements in the system and put less stress on the public sphere as the clearing house linking citizens to government.

The public sphere is a sphere of political communication that stands between civil society and the state. Communication is highly mediated and disaggregated and ranges along a vast multidimensional matrix that includes everyday talk, news, political speeches, editorials, advocacy campaigns, formal deliberation in parliamentary assemblies, and much more. The public sphere is also home to a growing number and variety of digital platforms. Public opinion takes shape via political communication in the public sphere When it works, the public sphere provides "a close-to-the ground, locally informed, dispersed arena for detecting problems, exploring them and bringing them to public view, suggesting solutions, and debating whether the problems are important and worth addressing" (Cohen and Fung 2021: 28; see also Habermas 2009: 155). Democracies function properly when they respond to and act on problems, concerns, and issues that confront real people in civil society. Democracies further the ideal of deliberative legitimacy to the extent that the process through which problems, topics, proposals, and solutions are raised, honed, and added to legislative agendas meets two conditions: that the process includes all those affected as equal participants, and that the process be governed by "the force of reason" (Habermas 2022: 150). Epistemic quality and equal participation are tightly linked in this picture of democracy (Chambers 2017).

In Habermas's version of the two-track model, there is some division of labor between inclusivity and epistemic quality. First, political communication is asymmetrical, with most citizens participating as audience members. In other words, most citizens are readers, viewers, listeners, and consumers of messages that one hopes become the subject of internal deliberation, reflection, informal everyday talk, and consideration (Goodin 2000). Second, not all ideas, claims, positions, and demands raised in the anarchic public sphere can be justifiably translated into a legislative agenda, and, in any case, all of them need clarification, articulation, and translation in order to make it onto an agenda. Therefore, the system must "filter," to use Habermas's word, the claims and demands by putting them through a feedback loop of public scrutiny and then ever more rigorous processes of justification (Habermas 2009: 159). As the political talk moves closer to the center, traditional rules of deliberation and arguing become more rigorous, and the conversation looks more and more like a deliberation (at least ideally). The more epistemically rigorous function of arguing and deliberating over clear policy options takes place higher up the system ladder. But, the content of deliberation – what gets deliberated – comes out of communicative processes that filter, clarify, and prioritize claims and narratives in the public sphere. When this is working well, the result is considered public opinion, that is, public opinion that has been shaped and constituted by an inclusive process of public debate and problem solving. This view does not deny many of the claims made by constructivist theories of representation. Citizens' political opinions and preferences are highly endogenous to the communication context in which they are formed. But it does deny that endogeneity must be a one-way process driven by elite agendas. Instead, the picture is of a democratic and critical form of endogeneity where, on the one hand, frames, manipulation, and mobilization tactics can be questioned, and, on the other hand, the raw material of the "deliberative" processes are real problems and concerns of citizens and not fabricated causes upon which to mobilize people.

The two-track theory of deliberative democracy is a highly stylized and ideal picture of the proper function of the public sphere. No real public sphere comes close, although we occasionally see glimpses of national debates that approximate some of the functional characteristics. Many conditions and prerequisites – from legal protection of speech and association to adequate levels of social equality – need to be in place to achieve even a minimum of functionality. But now I want to focus on media systems and the way that deliberative democratic theory is meeting the challenge of the digitalization of the public sphere.

The central issue is the way that new media sort, structure, and disseminate the information, topics, political news, and public statements that form the base material out of which people build their political opinions.

Technologically, a fundamental difference between the mass and digital era is the shift from broadcast (one-to-many) to networked (many-to-many) communication, with effectively zero marginal costs of information and communication. The digital infrastructure of the public sphere is defined by its distinctive flow of information in which there are (i) many more providers and distributors of content; (ii) people thus enjoy vastly greater choice among kinds and providers of content; and (iii) particular content can be directed (or targeted) by providers, advertisers, social media platforms companies, or other actors to particular users or groups of user. (Cohen and Fung 2021: 36)

This situation has a negative impact on both the epistemic and normative functions of the public sphere, which is to say, on the circulation of reasons and the inclusiveness of debate.

Networked communication leads to the demise of gatekeepers, who were never perfect and often leant on the side of the status quo or interests of the owners of media, but who nevertheless ensured some minimum standards of epistemic quality and political responsibility (Cohen and Fung 2021: 41; Habermas 2022: 160). The new media neither produce nor edit information; instead, they furnish platforms where anybody and everybody can connect to anybody and everybody and curate information using profit-oriented algorithms. There is a huge uptick in the amount of information accessible and a downtick in the quality of that information. This situation (and the fragmentation I discuss next) is then being exploited by bad actors to push political agendas via disinformation (Chambers and Kopstein 2022). Disinformation, manipulation, and propaganda are endemic to all democratic public spheres. There is concern that digitalization of communication, especially the outsized role of social media in the circulation of information, may exponentially increase the danger of falsehood. But part of the story here is not just that there are no gatekeepers, but also the creation of enclaves insulated from the types of debate and criticism that can expose falsehood. This leads to the second and in many ways more serious problem with the new digital landscape.

By far the most worrisome dimension of the digital public sphere is its centrifugal dynamic. "The boundless communication networks that spontaneously take shape around certain topics or individuals can spread centrifugally while simultaneously condensing into communication circuits that dogmatically seal themselves off *from each other*" (Habermas 2022: 160). The problem here is not that filter bubbles, digital enclaves, and fragmentation make it impossible to form a collective or common will. The deliberative ideal breaks with the tradition of the unified will of the people and aligns itself with the procedural view of the people discussed at the end of chapter 8. "The formation of opinion steered by mass media gives rise to a plurality of public opinions among the dispersed audience of citizens. These public opinions, which are compiled out of topics, contributions and information and thus assume a distinctive profile, compete over relevant issues, the correct policy goals and the best problem-solving strategies" (Habermas 2022: 151).

Communication in the public sphere is not directed toward consensus or producing a unified public will; it produces multiple and often conflicting opinions about a shared problem or salient concern. To the extent that the digital public sphere makes it impossible to have shared *topics* of conversation, it will be unable to perform its function as a clearing house for public opinion and will formation (Chambers and Kopstein 2022).

There is a paradox here. In one sense, the new digital public sphere is excessively inclusive, but it fails to create the conditions for that inclusivity to perform its democratic function, which is to have many voices contribute to the shaping of political agendas. Instead, users are increasingly siloed in enclaves talking to each other. But there is a further dimension of this situation that particularly worries Habermas. This has to do with the privatization of communication in the digital public sphere. Networked communication creates the opportunity for us all to be authors, not just readers. But as authors we are more like people writing personal letters that are massively and widely disseminated than self-conscious public figures contributing to a public debate. "Different standards apply to the composition of printed matter addressed to an anonymous reading public than to private correspondence" (Habermas 2022: 165). The digital public sphere becomes the place for sharing our private opinions about public matters and mostly with like-minded consumers. Here Habermas worries that citizens will no longer see the public sphere as the (potential) place of inclusive public debate over shared problems. This, he suggests, would be a radical and democratically unfortunate transformation of the public sphere.

Habermas and Cohen and Fung offer a diagnosis of the dangers of the new digital landscape for deliberative opinion formation. Epistemically, the worry is threefold: first, citizens will lose access to trustworthy sources of facts and information upon which to build considered opinions; second, citizens will become skeptical and distrustful of all sources of facts and information, including trustworthy ones; and, finally, citizens will believe that fellow citizens have lost access to trustworthy sources of fact and information and so lose trust in democracy. But the second normative dimension is more serious. Here the overarching worry is about fragmentation, privatization, and the migration of political communication into closed enclaves. Under these conditions, inclusiveness loses its democratic force as a means for all those affected by a decision to take part in the making of the decision. Political communication becomes millions upon billions of personal letters sent to friends or to the whole world in a virtual and boundless messaging universe.

How accurate is this diagnosis? Most people entering the debate about how the digital revolution impacts democracy admit that it is early days in this revolution and so often use the future conditional tense. Like with the climate crisis, there is a lot of "this will happen if we do not act." The worries about the transformation of the public sphere have fueled an astonishing and unprecedented explosion of institutes, centers, programs, think tanks, NGOs, academic studies, and research devoted to assessing and studying the new digital landscape across all domains, from the humanities to the hardest of hard sciences. Money and resources have poured in from public and private sources to support work and research in this area. The flood of research and study has been paralleled by an equally constant stream of discussion and reflection in the popular press, as well as endless public commissions and congressional committees disturbed by post-truth and the black box of algorithmic curation. Much of the scrutiny in the popular press and governmental investigations has taken aim at rapacious platforms and the Big Tech moguls who run them as the primary villains in this narrative. Despite its massive market share, Facebook is the platform everyone loves to hate and revelations about shenanigans, double standards, and ethics violations are popular in the press. Big Tech exposés and whistle-blowing are now a journalistic genre in their own right. Furthermore, survey after survey shows citizens across the ideological spectrum and indeed across the globe are concerned with the ways that social media have undermined trust in information (Rainie, Keeter, and Perrin 2019).

The intense public scrutiny and broad knowledge mobilization generated by widespread concern about the impact of digital communication on the functioning of our democratic systems is beginning to underpin and inform three areas of reform: citizen competence navigating the internet, platform self-regulation, and governments' commitment to sensible public regulation. Parliaments and legislatures in all liberal democracies have the regulation of the digital public sphere on their agendas. It is impossible to tell how effective that regulation will be in protecting and strengthening the democratic functions of public debate. We are at the very beginning of this transformation. But what does seem clear is that there is very wide agreement that we are facing a challenge. This, it seems to me, is indirect evidence that our public spheres can still host a broad and inclusive debate about a shared topic of concern.

Technological affordances

According to the Merriam-Webster *Dictionary*, an affordance is "the quality or property of an object that defines its possible uses or makes clear how it can or should be used." Affordance has moved into the common vocabulary of democratic theory that looks at how we can use the internet to enhance democracy. One significant characteristic of the affordances debate is the growing technical sophistication of theorists who offer a more fine-grained analysis of the digital public sphere than, for example, Habermas or Cohen and Fung.

At first glance, Jennifer Forestal's development of "democratic affordances" seems to move in the opposite direction of Habermas and Cohen and Fung. The deliberative democrats focus on the creation or maintenance of interconnected and inclusive public debates that can or ought to inform responsive and publicly justified central legislation. Following the tradition of Alexis de Tocqueville and John Dewey, Forestal is interested in the creation of distinct and bounded communities that can offer members the goods of recognition, bonding, and growth.

She identifies with a participatory tradition of democratic theory that emphasizes grassroots community building and civil association membership rather than the public opinion formation that feeds into formal institutions of voting (Forestal 2022: 7). Although offering different foci, these two approaches are not at odds, however. The public sphere stands between civil society and the state. The deliberative democrats discussed above are interested in looking at relations between the public sphere and the state. Forestal asks us not to forget the civil society side of that equation. The citizens who process political messages in the public sphere have become the citizens that they are via their interactions and engagements in civil society. Those interactions and engagements are migrating to online platforms at a fast rate.

Forestal asks what kind of communities have we, are we, and could we build in virtual civil society? Whereas the deliberative democrats offer a broad and sweeping diagnosis of the full impact of the digital revolution on democratic opinion and will formation, Forestal compares different platforms to assess their relative success and potential in fostering democratic affordances, of which she identifies three: recognition, attachment, and experimentalism (Forestal 2022: 4). Civic engagement via community requires that we recognize ourselves and others as part of a community. Here the unbounded nature of, for example, Facebook makes it impossible to acquire this type of recognition and so, by extension, to build the types of connections that can undergird a healthy democracy. Members also need to form meaningful attachments to the community itself in order for that space to become a democracy-building space. Twitter's mass of shifting followers and followed and endlessly morphing hashtags fails to have the durability that could sustain this type of attachment. Forestal argues that in the case of Facebook and Twitter, "the threat to democratic politics is not simply in the content users disseminate on the platforms. It is rather in the ways these spaces facilitate (or not, as the case may be) the community ties upon which democracy depends" (Forestal 2022: 5). Finally, digital communities need to be flexible and willing to grow, learn, and improve their communities. The last affordance strikes me as both the most important and in some ways the most challenging. As I argue below, it suggests that to be good virtual citizens we need to learn to be amateur software engineers or at least to be software literate in order to see how various software design choices structure the communities to which we belong.

Is there any hope for democratic affordances? Somewhat surprisingly, the new internet role model is Wikipedia, which many people now tout as a success story of crowdsourcing and community building. Forestal also mentions Reddit's subreddits as having community-building potential in relation to the behemoths Facebook and Twitter.

Forestal is focused on the potential to build durable community ties within online spaces, but she directs our gaze more generally toward thinking about platform design from a democratic point of view. Others, not working from a participatory framework, have looked at other affordances. For example, Alfred Moore has looked at the question of how identity rules – for example, is one required to give one's real name – on various types of platforms affect the quality of the "speech" (Moore 2018). This research debunks the idea that anonymity has been an across-the-board epistemic and normative disaster for online communication because it shields "speakers" from accountability and so encourages offensive garbage. But the story is more complicated than this, and Moore and his colleagues have been able to connect fine-grained design choices made by platforms in user profiles to the quality of contributions to debate (Moore et al. 2021).

New platforms are being launched almost daily, many of which are seeking to build new types of community and interaction. Like social movements in real civil society, we are seeing the growth of creative internet designs that aim to empower users over owners by, for example, insisting on participatory governance rather than centralized moderation (Rajendra-Nicolucci and Zuckerman 2021). Democratic theorists are proposing, designing, and testing digital spaces to enhance forms of democratic participation, some examples of which I discuss in the next chapter under the heading democratic innovation (Gastil and Broghammer 2021; Neblo,

Esterling, and Lazer 2018). There is a growing enthusiasm for innovative uses of e-voting to bring more citizens into the democratic process (Landemore 2021). And out on the edge are radical visons of Web3 powered by blockchain technology that would in effect bring full decentralization and user control to the internet (Smith and Hall 2022).

This is not the place (and I am not the person) to draw up a score card on the thousands of digital spaces open to us or the development of new spaces. And, in any case, by the time this book sees the light of day, the landscape will already have changed. But there is a great deal of internet activism and design creativity pushing back against the domination of Big Tech, and a lot of this has to do with a new generation of activists and theorists who are mastering the political implications of digital design. This brings us back to democratic theory. Forestal reminds us that the internet is a built environment. The concept of the public sphere relies on a spatial metaphor, of course, but Forestal draws on urban design, architecture, environmental psychology, and the work of democratic space theorists such as Margaret Kohn and Bonnie Honig for inspiration in fleshing out the space metaphor (Honig 2017; Kohn 2003, 2004). Reminiscent of the birth of the public sphere in the coffeehouses and debating salons of the seventeenth and eighteenth centuries, Forestal asks us to think about the ways the spaces we occupy in our virtual world are constructed and what sorts of activities and interactions they facilitate. To do this, we need to become internet literate. By this, I do not mean that we need to be able to tell fake news from real information. We need to acquire a better understanding of software as well as network design. Perhaps we do not need to become architects, interior designers, or contractors to be able to choose a house we would like to live in, a classroom that would be conducive to teaching and learning, a space that would work for a political meeting, or the cafe where we will listen in on political conversations. But we do need to understand the way spaces – including and perhaps especially digital spaces – work or do not work for various purposes, and that involves digging deeper than the immediate interface and understanding how the design and algorithms are curating information, sorting users, and creating relations between people.

There is one final area of digital technology that I will mention here but discuss in more detail in the next chapter. This is how the digital age has transformed and supercharged mobilization (Tufekci 2017). From the 2019 democracy protests in Hong Kong to the 2020 Black Lives Matter marches, the size, speed, and coordination of these movement protests is unimaginable without new communication technology. Mobilization afforded by internet communication of course can be used by anti-democratic forces just as much as pro-democratic forces. The 2017 white supremacist rally in Charlottesville, Virginia, or the January 6, 2021 assault on the Capitol building in Washington, DC are equally unimaginable without the internet. But cellphone journalism has been a more powerful weapon for movements intent on exposing real injustice than for those fabricating false histories. We are living in an era of deep fakes and misinformation, but the images of George Floyd pinned to the ground as his life ebbed away and of the insurrectionists in combat gear climbing the walls of Congress have been powerful catalysts that have been hard to deny, despite efforts to spin and misdirect. But, again, the internet is a double-edged sword for mobilization. And authoritarian forces have been quick to master effective techniques to undermine the democratic functions of the public sphere (Chambers and Kopstein 2022).

Rhetoric

In 2011, Bryan Garsten wrote an influential essay charting and analyzing what he called the rhetorical revival in political theory (Garsten 2011). That revival is still in full swing if the 36 chapters of the 2022 *Oxford Handbook of Rhetoric and Political Theory* is anything to go on (Gaonkar and Topper 2022). Garsten explains the renewed interest in rhetoric as both consonant with and a critical rejoinder to the rise of deliberative democracy beginning in the 1990s. It is consonant in that scholars both of rhetoric and of deliberative democracy are interested in speech, communication, discourse, and persuasion and place these elements at the center of democratic politics. Many theoretical treatments of rhetoric criticized deliberative democracy, however, especially what was seen as a problematic rationalism at the center of this tradition. Rawls's ideal of public reason and Habermas's ideal speech situation seemed to suggest that citizens and representatives ought to talk and debate about politics as if they were either impartial constitutional judges or participating in a philosophy seminar. Many scholars of rhetoric sought to criticize and correct this view (Garsten 2006; Remer 1999; Young 2000). The thrust of these early critiques of deliberative democracy was to point out that the exclusion of passion, emotion, eloquence, and audience from the normative study of political communication was as implausible as it was undesirable. In the intervening years since the first contributions to this critical exchange, deliberative democracy has taken many of the criticisms to heart. Nevertheless, there are still points of disagreement. But, rather than a dividing line between views of communication in which rhetoric is absent versus present, now the divide is between how one understands the rhetorical dimension of public and political speech.

Rhetoric is a difficult term to define. For now, I will leave it at the very abstract level of referring to the nature of persuasion. In democratic theory, the study of rhetoric takes place on several levels. On one level is the study of what people are saying, how they are saying it, and what effect that has on democracy. A second level looks at methods and tools of persuasion, for example framing and priming. A third level of analysis touches on deeper questions of agency, autonomy, and judgment. Let me take a moment to briefly flesh out and offer examples of these lines of scholarship.

A fruitful and illuminating way to study rhetoric is through analyzing particular rhetorics, for example, fascist rhetoric (Connolly 2017), the rhetoric of white nationalism (Kelly 2020), Trump's rhetoric (Stuckey 2020), the rhetoric of self-ownership (Shanks 2019), comedy as rhetoric (Lambek 2022), populist rhetoric (Laclau 2005), plebiscitary rhetoric (Chambers 2009), trust-building rhetoric (Allen 2004), bridging rhetoric (Dryzek 2010), or the political rhetoric of W. E. B. Du Bois (Rogers 2012) to name just a few in this large category. This list does not do justice to the richness and variety in this area of democratic theory. These studies often describe and unpack the substantive content of the rhetorics employed in our public spheres, the style or form of the rhetoric, the general strategy of persuasion, and the ways that these rhetorics contribute to or undermine democracy. Furthermore, they are informed by sometimes radically different philosophical traditions that shape and determine the analysis of the type of rhetoric under inspection.

Strategies of persuasion connect to our discussion of framing, priming, and crafting speech in the public sphere. This angle on the politics of rhetoric within democracies often has a substantial empirical and descriptive component to it. Deva Woodly, for example, asks what can account for the relatively rapid shift in American public opinion regarding marriage equality (Woodly 2018). The speed with which this came about suggests that a generational turnover cannot explain changing opinions. How and in what sense were hundreds of thousands of citizens persuaded to support marriage equality? The picture of persuasion that she paints stresses the role and function of frames rather than, say, reasons in political discourse. She shows that changing public opinion was not a shift from negative attitudes toward gay marriage to positive attitudes toward gay marriage. The underlying value orientation did not change. What changed was the frame. Rather than thinking that the question of gay marriage was a question about one's personal beliefs and values about marriage, the frame shifted to one about fairness and equal access to family life. Social movement activists worked over a 10-year period to shift this frame to bring about the persuasion effect. Woodly's study uncovers and exposes how frames work in a particular instance. It also highlights that persuasion often works over time and in the background. Framing is a central theme in political communication. Any interest or concern with persuasion and political rhetoric needs to focus on framing. As Calvert and Warren point out, "frames are necessarily prior to opinion-formation on an issue or policy: they enable people to understand the problem and form preferences" (Calvert and Warren 2014: 206).

The next level of analysis returns us to the themes articulated by Garsten in 2011. Here the question of persuasion touches on deeper questions of agency, autonomy, and judgment, and on what rhetoric *is* and how it works. All the studies listed above that take up particular rhetorics have either an explicit or implicit view of what rhetoric is and how it works. Although there are a number of traditions drawn from in this debate, I focus on the ongoing tension between deliberative democracy and revivalism.

Habermas's communication theory has been very influential in deliberative democratic theory. That view employed a stark contrast between "the unforced force of the better argument" motivating action and the use of threat or bribery to wring compliance out of people (Habermas 1996: 306). It asks us to imagine agreeing to a proposition or a collective course of action because one was genuinely persuaded by the arguments in support of the proposition or course of action versus going along with the proposition or course of action out of fear or benefit. Thus deliberative democracy does try to think about what types of speech might be conducive to the ideal of autonomy at the center of Habermas's famous phrase. But more empirical and realistic theory of the last 20 years understands that real-world communication falls in a messy space between the counterfactual ideal of the unforced force of the better argument and a gun to one's head, or, more appropriately perhaps, brainwashing or hoodwinking. Deliberative theories of rhetoric focus, on the one hand, on the dichotomy of autonomy and manipulation and, on the other hand, on the way types and modes of rhetoric carry and communicate reasons and arguments. Here one sees many deliberative democracy theorists embracing the legitimate and unavoidable introduction of emotion, feelings, tropes, hyperbole, and many other rhetorical strategies, as well the necessity of shaping one's message to fit the audience.

John Dryzek, for example, is interested in strategies that might further progressive climate change policy (Dryzek and Lo 2015). The question motivating Dryzek and Lo's study is how to persuade climate deniers and get them behind sensible policy agendas. As a deliberative democrat, Dryzek is ultimately interested in policy backed by the best reasons endorsed through an inclusive process. But he admits that hitting people over the head with evidence and argument will often not budge them off their position and sometimes leads to the entrenchment of those opinions. So he endorses adopting rhetorical strategies that seek some overlap and common ground with climate deniers. This is, of course, a sensible strategy and does not undermine the underlying rationality of policy developments. But, as Garsten notes, on this view, rhetoric is a tool that can be used in the service of reason and so is separable from it (Garsten 2011: 164).

Thus in deliberative democracy there is perhaps a tendency to see rhetoric as packaging. Deliberative democrats concede that politics does not proceed through the exchange of raw reasons, although it can be analytically reconstructed to get at the underlying reasons. Politics proceeds through the packaging, framing, and communication of reasons. In politics and in real public spheres, there is no escape from rhetoric. A systems approach to deliberative democracy has been especially conducive to the entrance of rhetoric into the analysis of political communication.

Rhetoric revivalists draw inspiration and insight from ancient traditions of rhetoric, especially Aristotle and Cicero (Abizadeh 2002; Allen 2004; Garsten 2006; Goodman 2021; Remer 2017; Yack 2006). This group, while tied more closely to the history of political theory than many of the traditions I have been canvasing, nevertheless almost always plumbs that history for insight into contemporary democracy and the analysis of political communication in the here and now. Deliberative democracy is often the foil against which these theories build their alternative view. "In recent years, rhetoric revivalists have worked to correct what they see as a misguided view of an earlier generation of deliberatively oriented theorists who treat rhetoric as a deficient or inherently suspect form of communication" (Goodman and Ballacci forthcoming: 8). The problem with trying to sum up this criticism is that deliberative democracy is a moving and scattered target, and many contributors have moved away from earlier neo-Kantian rationalism (Chambers 2022). Some attempts to maintain a sharp critical contrast with deliberative democracy and revivalism often fail to do justice to the deliberative tradition. I attempt to reconstruct revivalism here without paying too much attention to its analysis and interpretation of the deliberative tradition. To be fair, though, although the contrast between revivalism and deliberative democracy is simply less stark now than it was 15 years ago at the launch of the rhetoric revival when Rawls's ideal of public reason was ubiquitous, there are still important differences of emphasis and approach. The most significant differences are, first, that revivalists analyze political communication through the asymmetrical categories of orator and audience and, second, they resist attempts to separate form and content (packaging and reason giving). But, as with the distinction between deliberative democracy and agonism, the difference between deliberative democracy and revivalism is not about condemning types of speech, for example unruly exuberant speech or emotionally charged speech. Both deliberative democrats and revivalists might see some (but not all) unruly speech as important contributions to a public sphere and political communication, but deliberative democrats and revivalists offer different analyses of why some forms of unruly speech enhance democracy.

The category of the audience is central to revivalists. If we stay with rhetoric as persuasion, then rhetoric must be directed at or appeal to an audience. This brings in a deeply contextualist element to public speech. Rarely can one find an effective one-size-fits-all persuasion strategy "(s)ince persuasion requires adjusting not only the substance but also the form of one's argument to one's audience" (Garsten 2006: 189). Audience is not entirely absent even in early versions of public reason and deliberative democracy. Rawls we will recall defines public justification as justification "addressed to others" (Rawls 2005: 465). But Rawls thought this required stepping back to seek arguments so general as to be acceptable to all, or to a generalized other, to use Seyla Benhabib's formulation, while revivalists argue that addressing arguments to others requires stepping in and becoming intensely acquainted with the particular concrete other one is addressing (Benhabib 1992). While adjusting what one says to one's audience might appear strategic, revivalists point out that speaking to an audience and really thinking through their concerns and interests is a form of recognition and respect that is absent in less contextually tailored understandings of political speech. Furthermore, attentiveness to the audience can lead to the inclusion of marginalized groups, which might have been left behind by mainstream forms of speech (Young 2000). Speaking in the idiom of place and people can promote political equality and inclusion (Allen 2004).

In addition to unpacking what it means to address an audience, the revivalist tradition is also interested in what it means to be a good orator. Aristotle's tripartite model of *logos*, *pathos*, and *ethos* has been influential in this regard (Garsten 2006; Yack 2006).

In addition to a good argument (*logos*), effective persuasion must move and motivate an audience to follow the speaker (*pathos*), and the speaker can only do that if she is trusted (*ethos*). Early contributions to the rhetoric revival were interested in the rehabilitation of emotion and character as a counterpoint to deliberative democracy but especially disembodied public reason theory. These critics stressed that there is no reasoning and judgment without affect and the engagement of emotion (Abizadeh 2007) and that political communication is mediated through an elite that has a near monopoly on public speech (Yack 2006).

Cicero also offers a fertile source to think through the role and place of the orator in the public sphere (Goodman 2021; Kapust and Schwarze 2016; Remer 2017). Goodman argues that Cicero understood that creating that special relationship between orator and audience where words can have a seismic effect on an audience involves risk. By opening themselves to the persuasive power of words, the audience risks "having its convictions called into question and transformed" (Goodman 2021: 15). For speakers, rhetorical bids for attention and uptake can be rejected, ignored, or rebuked. In making those bids, the orator exposes himself to the audience's judgment; being open to those bids exposes the audience to the transformative force of words. Goodman calls this the rhetorical bargain and argues that it can create a political relationship between elite speakers and mass listeners that avoids domination via mutual burden sharing. Goodman suggests that the loss of eloquence, or what he calls "words on fire," has significant repercussions for democracy. Those repercussions are the loss of the transformative power of words. Waning eloquence signals a risk-averse elite who fall back on "algorithmic rhetoric . . . that is certain to be approved before it is uttered" (Goodman 2021: 18). This is rhetoric that is *done to* an audience, not *done with* an audience. Goodman, while resisting a Kantian notion of individual autonomy (as do all revivalists), does embrace an ideal of audience autonomy inherent in the idea of mutual risk in the speaker–audience relationship. Algorithmic rhetoric effaces audience autonomy and so can become an exercise of domination.

While both deliberative democrats and revivalists are interested in identifying public speech that promotes reflection in an audience, for revivalists and theorists influenced by Hannah Arendt

(1954) and others, the language of judgment replaces the language of reason giving (Garsten 2006; Goodman 2021; Rogers 2012; Zerilli 2016). Judgment is a slippery concept that I cannot fully unpack here. Let me mention two characteristics of judgment that are often stressed by revivalists. First, while clearly cognitive and involving reflection, good judgment is often not tied to any strong epistemic claims of "truth tracking" or "correct" answers. Rather than an audience finding a reason for, say, progressive climate policy persuasive, engendering good judgment about climate justice in an audience involves inspiring or motivating a certain disposition of cognitive openness, receptivity, and reflection. Melvin Rogers, in an extended study of the rhetorical power of W. E. B. Du Bois to move white readers, writes that "the success of Du Bois's narrative depends not on impartial judgment, but rather on the partiality of the reader. When he seeks to persuade his readers he meets them where they stand; he addresses their existing bundles of commitments, values, and norms with the hope of expanding their horizons" (Rogers 2012: 200). Second, judgment involves reason and emotion working together; indeed, even the phrase "working together" is problematic as it implies two separate things yoked together. Brain science might suggest that calculation and feeling happen in different parts of the brain, but judgment occurs when the whole person is *moved* (often by moving words having been addressed *to* them) to take a reflective position on a question. There can be no separation between form and content in judgment. Rhetoric on this view then is not packaging; it is not the style in which detachable content is delivered. Rhetoric is the medium of politics.

Conclusion

Debate in democratic theory about the public sphere is characterized by continuity and change. On the one hand, rhetoric is one of the oldest topics of democratic theory, standing as it does at the center of Plato's critique of democracy. We are still trying to understand persuasion, identify demagogues, and reconcile (or not) truth and power. On the other hand, new media technologies make our public sphere almost unrecognizable from just 15 years ago. This may be signaling a new structural transformation of the public sphere. Furthermore, modern science is telling us more and more about how opinions are formed, and minds changed via mediated messages and political communication. This science is being drawn on by democratic theorists to develop sophisticated pictures of the effects of political communication on public opinion. But the very same science also can be used by elites to craft messages that push the right buttons rather than instigate reflection. Until we get a regulative and normative handle on the new digital communicative technologies, these will also be abused and exploited by elites seeking to manipulate, push propaganda, and undermine the trustworthy sources of truth in the quest for power. Who controls information and communication and for what purposes have always been essential questions in democratic theory. The digital revolution has made the answer even more complicated and difficult to find.

11
Innovation and Disobedience

IN this chapter, I discuss democratic innovation and civil disobedience. At first sight, this might seem like an unlikely pairing of topics. Democratic innovation literature is full of critical optimism and energy regarding the possibility of improving democracies. Theorizing about protest and civil disobedience often involves thinking through the place of anger, disappointment, and, sometimes, desperation in our failing democracies. But there are a number of points of contact between these two literatures. First, both bodies of theory connect to practitioners and activists in a way that we do not often see in democratic theory. Democratic innovation is all about designing, testing, and implementing new institutions. Many of the theorists involved in this debate are also practitioners in the field setting up real-world initiatives (Neblo, Esterling, and Lazer 2018; Smith 2009). And this literature has a real-world, non-academic audience looking for normative and theoretical guidance as they build innovative venues of citizen participation. Something similar can be said about the relationship between civil disobedience studies and activism. Alexander Livingston describes the new wave of civil disobedience theory as "drawing theoretical insights from protest movements themselves" that result in "mutual entanglement in a mediated process of co-constitutions" between activist practices and scholarly discourse (Çidam et al. 2020: 540, 541).

The second common feature between these two research areas is that both study bottom-up citizen participation in democracy. The democratic innovation field in normative theory is primarily interested in ways to bring citizens into the democratic process and not in all possible improvements to democratic procedures. Civil disobedience is also of course a bottom-up political action, and although some would question whether it is best understood as a form of democratic participation, it is nevertheless about citizens taking the political initiative and not elites. This leads to a third dimension that links the two fields. Social movements that have traditionally used protest and civil disobedience as avenues to push their agendas are now also looking toward democratic innovations as potential allies in furthering their causes. Extinction Rebellion, for example, a global environmental movement that advocates nonviolent civil disobedience, has endorsed using citizens' climate assemblies and indeed has demanded that these institutions be given more power in the fight for climate survival (Extinction Rebellion 2019).

The final common theme between these two areas of normative democratic theory is perhaps more a reflection of my framing of these two debates, especially civil disobedience, than of how the theorists themselves see the work. Both democratic innovation and civil disobedience are future oriented, and, I might go so far as to say, have an underlying logic of hope – not optimism, but hope – to them. This is most clear in democratic innovation theory, some of which explicitly claims that it is about designing institutions that are future oriented, for example, by including future generations as "participants" (Smith 2021; MacKenzie 2021). Hope also seems to be the backdrop for protest and disobedience, however. My Habermasian instincts say, why put one's life on the line in the streets of Tehran or Los Angeles if there is no hope. One answer is that acts of protest and disobedience are sometimes expressive (White and Farr 2012). They say "We are mad as hell and want everyone to know it" but with no expectation that anything will come of it except reclaiming one's own self-respect (Livingston 2021). But my reading of the democratic theory of civil disobedience points in a different direction. Far from giving up on the possibility of salutary effects of protest and disobedience, theory has retreated from the high moralism of Rawls, where it was about an individual's personal fidelity to principles, and toward a strongly instrumental focus on what works and why. This is especially clear in the debate about whether civil disobedience is to be understood as a form of persuasion or a form of coercion. The civil disobedience discourse has moved away from romanticizing civil disobedience to a much more hardheaded picture of direct action under conditions of injustice. While, on the one hand, this contemporary direction of civil disobedience theory starts from a much grimmer assessment of contemporary conditions than did liberalism – and perhaps even than great figures of the civil rights movement – on the other hand, it produces theory that can more adequately and realistically answer the question "What is civil disobedience good for?" An instrumental approach must be concerned with the ends and this, it seems to me, means it must be concerned with bringing about some better future state of affairs.

Democratic innovation

Democratic innovation has become a thriving subfield within democratic theory. One sure-fire way to know that a research question is reaching the level of a subfield is the presence of sustained debates about definitions and boundaries as well as the appearance of handbooks on the subject and the establishment of an American Political Science Association-recognized group – all of which is going on in democratic innovation studies. The field of democratic innovation is roughly divided into case studies of actual on-the-ground innovations and debates about the theory of democratic innovation. So let me start with the theoretical debates and then move to some examples of innovation.

The questions animating the theoretical debate are, first, what is democratic innovation and then, second, what counts as innovation according to this definition? The question "What counts as democratic innovation?" has led to several typologies of innovation (Elstub and Escobar 2019; Smith 2009; Hendricks 2021). The final question on the theoretical agenda is what criteria we should use to evaluate the success, failure, or contribution of democratic innovation to a democratic system.

On the question of definition, almost everyone starts with Graham Smith's definition put forward in his influential 2009 book *Democratic Innovations: Designing Institutions for Citizen Participation*. Indeed, some think that this book launched the democratic innovation discourse (Elstub and Escobar 2019). Democratic innovations are "institutions that have been specifically designed to increase and deepen citizen participation in the political decision-making process" (Smith 2009: 1). Elstub and Escobar offer a slightly more expansive definition but with a similar thrust: "democratic innovations are processes or institutions that are new to a policy issue, policy role, or level of governance, and developed to reimagine and deepen the role of citizens in governance process by increasing opportunities for participation, deliberation and influence" (Elstub and Escobar 2019: 11).

Some definitions leave out the participatory and citizen-focused dimensions of innovation and simply stress ideas to improve democracy (Newton 2012), but these are exceptions and often reflect more empirically oriented scholarship. The democratic innovation discourse in normative theory has been heavily influenced by participatory or deliberative democratic theory, hence its citizen-centered character.

The opposite of innovation is stagnation. Much of the democratic innovation literature either explicitly or implicitly contrasts innovation to the stagnation of traditional institutions of democratic participation, especially elections, but also unimaginative or pro forma consultation mechanisms, for example, focus groups, that fail to empower citizens. But democratic innovation theory usually does not come with deep or detailed criticism of existing institutions and instead points to the "public disillusionment" with these institutions as the reason to think hard about alternatives (Smith 2009). This disillusionment is not about democracy per se but about present institutions, practices, and elites. Here we see the assumption that falling trust in democratic institutions is fueled, on the one hand, by actual bad behavior, weak responsiveness, and poor performance but also, on the other hand, by a public that is raising the bar of what they want and expect from democratic institutions. Thus democratic innovation studies are not usually about designing institutions that will reverse apathy and withdrawal. Rather, they are about designing institutions that will meet citizens' (quite often sophisticated) demands for better democracy. Smith quotes the empirical political scientist and public opinion scholar Russel Dalton in this respect: "Even though contemporary publics express decreasing confidence in democratic politicians, parties, and parliaments, these sentiments have not carried over to the democratic principles and goals of these regimes. Most people remain committed to the democratic ideal; if anything these sentiments have apparently strengthened as satisfaction with actual democratic politics has decreased" (Dalton 2004: 47; Smith 2009: 4).

All definitions of democratic innovation stress citizens' input as well as institutional design. Categories of types of democratic innovations vary slightly across the literature, but there is a great deal of overlap as well. The deliberative mini-public (DMP) is always one category and probably the institution that is getting the most attention and use (Curato et al. 2021). Although there is a lot of variety in design features and uses across and within democratic systems, two features are defining elements of all DMPs. The first is a random selection of participants, and the second is facilitated deliberation. Because DMPs are quite small – rarely more than 150 people – a pure random sample would never get a good cross-section of the population, and therefore the selection process is often stratified. Stratification ensures that relevant groups are represented. This in turn requires thinking through what the relevant groups are. For example, in the British Columbia Citizens' Assembly, it was important to have Indigenous peoples represented. In some DMPs in Latin America that address housing issues, stratification insures the representation of the poor. Gender is almost always a necessary line of stratification.

The other defining feature is facilitated deliberation. The actual nuts and bolts of deliberation – plenary versus breakout rooms, what sort of instructions are given to participants, how and by whom information is circulated – varies a great deal (Curato et al. 2021). But a common format involves three phases beginning with education where participants learn from neutral or impartial informants (experts) about the topic under discussion. The second phase involves hearing from stakeholders or civil society organizations. The final stage is deliberation. Many DMPs, and certainly the larger ones, end in a vote.

Although there is considerable variation among DMPs, they are highly structured and so exhibit a clear family resemblance to each other. This is contrasted to a category sometimes referred to as popular assembly, where participation is made up of self-selected citizens, and deliberation is often less structured and facilitated. This category is very broad and includes such things as New England town hall meetings, participatory budgeting, and community policing initiatives. Collaborative governance is also a category used to capture the dimension of citizens participating with elected or other types of state representatives to problem-solve and shape policy. The contrast between random selection of DMPs and the self-selection of popular assemblies and collaborative governance has been much discussed. Many people see self-selection as a problem because it means the overrepresentation of certain types of citizens. Images of the cranky retiree with a NIMBY (Not In My Back Yard) mentality come to mind. Champions of self-selection respond with several arguments. First, all selection processes involve self-selection. Sortition can never be perfectly random because it is voluntary and not everyone wants to spend time in these assemblies. Voting also involves self-selection as not everybody shows up at the polls. Second, empirical evidence suggests that different groups are overrepresented in different types of open assemblies and that overrepresentation is not always pernicious (Curato et al. 2021). The "type" of person who shows up to open meetings is often a civic type who cares about public issues (Landemore 2020). This is exactly who you want to come to the meeting and articulate the citizens' point of view. Third, there is also evidence, especially in experiments of participatory budgeting, that if properly organized and mobilized by activists on the ground, underrepresented citizens will come to the meetings and make contributions.

The next category is direct legislation or citizen initiatives. Referendums, plebiscites, and initiatives are on the rise across all democracies, although different institutional jurisdictions make it more or less difficult to implement or add these forms of popular votes. Along with this rise, one sees a theoretically rich debate in democratic theory about the design and integration of popular vote processes into democratic systems (el-Wakil and McKay 2020). Within the democratic innovation literature, usually only bottom-up citizen-initiated popular vote processes are considered as interesting cases of innovation. Although always included in the list of democratic innovations, these initiatives garner less interest than DMPs and popular assemblies. One reason for this is that in some places, for example the United States, bottom-up initiatives can be easily captured by corporate and elite interests. Another reason is that, although direct forms of citizen participation, initiatives are a form of aggregative participation, and there is more interest in the way citizens can make substantive contributions to decision making. Where one does see a lot of interest is in coupling DMPs with referendums and initiatives. In these cases, DMPs are used to either formulate the question that goes to a referendum or as sources of impartial information in initiative processes (Gastil and Knobloch 2020). In one of the most touted uses of a DMP, Ireland successfully amended its constitution using an innovative process that joined a citizens' assembly with a referendum (Farrell et al. 2020).

The final category in innovation literature is e-democracy or digital participation. Some of the innovations here are about thinking of ways to enhance existing forms of participation through digital interventions. For example, Michael Neblo and his co-authors have developed a very promising model for constituency town hall meetings with elected representatives in an effort to enhance the relationship between representatives and voters (Neblo, Esterling, and Lazer 2018). Also promising has been the crowdsourcing for widespread citizen input into various policy documents. This was one pillar of the Icelandic constitutional process, for example (Landemore 2015). Finally, there are proposals for designing e-voting tools that would allow for an immense amount of flexibility with what one can do with one's vote and how votes get counted. These designs often target the phenomenon of wasted votes and are intended to enhance a sense of efficacy in voting (Ford 2021).

The focus of democratic innovation literature is on institutional design that enhances and empowers citizens in the decision-making process. This emphasis means that some things get left out. Democratic innovation in firms, workplaces, and market models does not have much uptake in this literature (Malleson 2014). A second area of innovation that is left out due to the weight placed on institutions of decision making are grassroots-level informal civil society initiatives to improve the foundations of democracy (Hendriks, Ercan, and Boswell 2020).

Innovation and Disobedience 205

The final topic touching on the theory of democratic innovation is about the criteria one should use to evaluate these initiatives. There is a consensus that early on in the enthusiasm for democratic innovation, there was an overemphasis on internal standards of evaluation and input legitimacy (Pogrebinschi and Ryan 2018). Both participatory democracy and deliberative democracy have been very involved in the democratic innovation debates, and this led to a focus on the participatory experience or the quality and structure of the deliberation within institutions. More recently, the evaluative frameworks have expanded to include important dimensions of efficacy and integration within the broader democratic system. As Frank Hendriks puts it, now we see an interest in input, throughput, *and* output (Hendriks 2021). Input values include such things as inclusion, equal input, popular control, and effective participation. Throughput values are deliberative process, enlightened understanding, transparency, and openness. Output values include efficiency, consequentiality, resilience, and integration. Different studies use different combinations of these or similar values to measure success and failure.

Let me return briefly to DMPs, arguably the most successful democratic innovation to date. There is a huge variety of types, sizes, uses, and designs in this category, but the exemplar that is garnering the most interest is the citizens' assembly. A citizens' assembly is a relatively large DMP that is mandated to discuss and come to a decision about a question of public policy. Democratic theory began to take an interest in citizens' assemblies after the pioneering establishment of the British Columbia Citizens' Assembly in 2004 (Warren and Pearse 2008). As we saw in chapter 9, Hélène Landemore defends these as potential all-purpose assemblies that could replace elected assemblies. One argument for their appropriateness as all-purpose assemblies is that a diversity of outlooks and perspectives is especially epistemically useful when a group will have to solve a broad variety of questions. But a more common argument in favor of integrating citizens' assemblies into democratic systems is that they are particularly good at solving a certain type of problem. These are problems where the partisanship of elected representatives hinders their ability to solve the problem adequately. The British Columbia Citizens' Assembly was tasked with discussing and proposing electoral reform which would then go to a referendum. The logic here was that elected officials are not in a good position to make this decision because of their stakeholder status. Other possible uses are redistricting, as well as oversight functions and corruption and ethics boards. Which type of problems citizens' assemblies are good at solving then has become a central theme in innovation debates.

One type of problem that has gained a lot of interest and traction is the idea that citizens' assemblies are especially well suited to problem solving on policy that has an extended temporal dimension. This is to say that they are good at making decisions for the future, and the evidence for this is in the proliferation of citizens' climate assemblies. Denmark, France, Germany, Ireland, Scotland, United Kingdom, Austria, Luxembourg, and Spain have all either completed such an initiative or are in the process of doing so (Boswell, Dean, and Smith 2022). The assemblies are an eye-opener on the relationship of democracy to policy questions like climate change. For the most part, the recommendations of these assemblies are far more progressive, climate friendly, future-oriented, and sensitive to imminent climate disaster than those of elected assemblies. This suggests that slow action on climate policy cannot be placed entirely at the feet of democratic publics. What is it about citizens' assemblies that makes them good for deliberations on climate policy? Electoral democracy, it is argued, suffers from myopia – the tendency toward short-term thinking in democratic decision making (Mackenzie 2021; Smith 2021). Causes of myopia are various, but at the top of the list are electoral cycles and short-term profit margins. Political and economic elites have few incentives to propose long-term policy or to take the interests and concerns of future generations (who do not vote or pay for gas and heating) into consideration in policy design. Citizens' assemblies face neither of these pressures on their deliberation. There is a further consideration that contributes to future-oriented policy in citizens' assemblies that is also perhaps their Achilles' heel. These assemblies are all consultative. They make recommendations. This might mean that deliberation can be more ambitious and less constrained. This can be good because even if some of the recommendations are not immediately implementable or the goals, say for zero emissions, are too ambitious, these assemblies move the topic-of-debate needle in the right direction. There is evidence that the general public trusts the conclusions of citizens' assemblies more than they do elected assemblies (Pow 2021). Also, as recommenders and not binding decision makers, citizens' assemblies have avoided the sort of hard lobbying and attempts at capture that would surely go on if they gained more power. But as merely consultative, the recommendations sometimes disappear into the committee systems of legislative assemblies with some public lip service but not much action. Input and throughput are good. But we are still waiting for the output. Nevertheless, citizens' climate assemblies are and will continue to play an important role in speeding up responses to climate insecurity.

Civil disobedience and protests

The contemporary interest in the democratic theory of protest stems from many of the same trends that we have discussed throughout the book (Celikates 2016; Delmas 2018; Livingston 2020; Pineda 2021; Scheuerman 2018). First there is the widespread dissatisfaction with normal channels of political participation, the glaring failures of democratically elected governments to even acknowledge the severity of many social problems, and a trend toward global democratic backsliding that has seen autocracies doubling down on repression. "Long relegated to the margins of political philosophy as the object of an exhaustive debate in the 1970s, recent waves of protest around the globe have returned civil disobedience to the center of political theory and practice" (Livingston 2019: 591). The 2010s have been dubbed the decade of protest (Çidam et al. 2020). The Black Lives Matter movement, launched in 2013, and the 2020 summer of protest in the wake of George Floyd's murder – the largest protest event in the history of the United States – have been particularly central to the new wave of civil disobedience theory.

Second, there is a critical rethinking of the views that dominated the post-civil rights discourse up until the end of the twentieth century. Like many of the developments I have been following in this book, this involves pushing back on Rawls's ideal theory and the way that civil disobedience was construed within that framework and replacing it with a more realistic view of protest and the politics of power. This reevaluation of and response to past debates includes rethinking and radicalizing the tradition of nonviolent civil disobedience that goes back to Thoreau, Gandhi, and Martin Luther King Jr. The radicalization is not simply about offering new interpretations of these canonical figures; it is also about exposing how the mythologizing of nonviolent civil disobedience has been used ideologically to in fact suppress and tame protest.

Finally, much of the democratic theory of protest follows the trend that we have been tracing that develops dispersed and contestatory ideals of democracy that displace elections as the core institutional feature of democratic theory. This third trend tends to rethink the role and function of protest and civil disobedience from an occasional remedial and unfortunate corrective in an otherwise well-functioning system to a full and permanent, if also episodic, expression of democratic sovereignty.

Protest versus civil disobedience raises somewhat different questions for democratic theory. All democratic theory includes the protection of protest and assembly as an important civil liberty and form of political participation and expression. Variations in democratic theory have to do with what role or function protest plays in a democratic system. Deliberative democracy, for example, will tend to think about protest (as well as civil disobedience) as contributing to public debate and discourse by getting topics on the agenda, including excluded voices, or educating the public about an issue (Mansbridge et al. 2012; Smith 2012). Protest itself may not look very deliberative and may involve various levels of disruption and incivility, but the justification is always tied back to furthering and strengthening the underlying ideal of deliberative legitimacy. More radical democrats that I discuss below might take a tougher line and see protest as a necessarily disruptive force that employs threats and coercion (not persuasion and reason giving) to push back against a recalcitrant system. While civil disobedience is often included in these democratic function debates, it raises additional questions of the limits to legitimate protests. Civil disobedience involves breaking the law and transgressing public norms. Black Lives Matter protests have been generally peaceful but also included stone throwing, vandalism, and looting, as well as unruly behavior and speech that does not comport with the traditional picture of *civil* disobedience. Civil disobedience calls for another layer of justification, as well as a discussion about limits. Protest as a form of sanctioned political participation and expression takes place within the constituted order and is often compared to voting. Civil disobedience is at the other end of the spectrum and involves stepping out of the constituted order and as such is often compared to revolution and insurrection.

Because civil disobedience involves breaking the law, debate about its meaning and justification often strays from democratic theory into legal and moral theory about obligation to obey the law. In what follows, however, I stay as much as possible within the framework of democratic theory to discuss the issues and avoid some of the intricacies of the philosophical debate. Following William Scheuerman, I take civil disobedience to be an essentially contested concept, meaning both that there is an unresolvable plurality of definitions and also that we should not worry too much about that fact (Scheuerman 2021). The question that concerns me is: What functions do civil disobedience and protest play in a democracy? I begin with a radical democratic answer to this question. In the second part of this section, I discuss a trend toward a realist answer to this question.

I begin with a discussion of radical democracy because, as we will see, disobedience has a special role to play in that view of democracy. What is radical democracy? This is a difficult question as the meaning of radical democracy is quite elastic, and the term is invoked by many theorists who often do not have a great deal in common. Habermas, for example, in *Between Facts and Norms*, claimed to be outlining a theory of radical democracy, and in 2004 Joshua Cohen and Archon Fung defended deliberative democracy as a form of radical democracy (Cohen and Fung 2004; Habermas 1996). My brief discussion of dispersed popular sovereignty in chapter 8, as well the two-track model of democracy in chapter 10, did not suggest radicalness, however, if by radical we mean a politics of revolutionary transformation or opposition. In particular, the central institutions of constitutional democracy – elections, parliaments, state bureaucracies, constitutions, and the courts – remain intact but with a call to be more receptive to citizens' claims and considered opinions. Today, few would call deliberative democracy radical. That name is used for theories influenced by a generation of postmodern and Marxist theory that includes Chantal Mouffe, Ernesto Laclau, Étienne Balibar, Jacques Rancière, William Connolly, James Tully, and many more. There is a great deal of variety and depth to these thinkers to which I am unable to do justice here. But let me see if I can articulate some very general overarching themes in their views of democracy. To do this, it might be helpful to go back to what Habermas meant by radical democracy because there is a connection.

By radical democracy, Habermas meant a foundational principle of popular sovereignty. There are no external sources of authority, legitimacy, or justification beyond the people. Democratic government is self-constituting. Democracy in a sense goes all the way down. But Habermas added something to this picture. "The rule of law cannot be maintained without radical democracy" (Habermas 1996: xlii). Modern law needs justification, and the old sources of justification (God, King, Nature, Natural Law) are no longer available. Democracy becomes the source of justification of the law. But the rule of law is also the precondition of democracy. The people are the source of all authority and justification only if the people can act in a way that maintains their freedom and equality. Thus Habermas makes constitutions, including the way that constitutions structure institutions of representative government, the precondition upon which democracy has its constituting power. Habermas's co-original thesis, which serves to balance democracy and constitutional constraint, tames and circumscribes the radical self-constituting power of democracy but without postulating an external justificatory authority outside democracy itself.

Radical democrats start from the same idea of the self-constituting power of democracy and denial of external foundations or justifications of that power. They dispense with the other half of the equation, however, namely, the part that insists only people acting within a set of institutionalized rights and established procedures can be said to wield the self-constituting power. Instead, radical democrats suggest, in one way or another, that the existing institutions of representative government, including some dimensions of constitutional rights, cannot be said to bind and limit democracy because democracy *really* goes all the way down. This is a radical view. No institution can claim to be settled. Constituent power is ever present, ever active, ever the final word.

Two features stand out in the radical view of democracy. The first is the claim to continual and present constituent power vested in democratic actors. In the radical democratic theory associated with hegemony, as we saw in chapter 8, that constituent power is vested in a constructed collective agent – the people (Laclau 2005; Mouffe 2018). But more common in radical democracy is a rejection of the populist framing in favor of a radically plural framing of constituent power that itself can always be contested. This suggests that constituent power is exercised in fragmented, episodic, partial acts remaking democratic orders and not in large acts of constitution making.

The second important feature is the idea that democracy stands in an antagonistic relationship to all settled and stable orders. Democracy does not aim to bring about an ideal form or regime; instead, it is an essentially destabilizing force pitted against what Robert Michels at the beginning of the twentieth century famously called "the iron law of oligarchy" (Michels 1962). All organizations, including ones committed to democracy, inevitably rely on, and therefore cede power to, an elite. As Rancière puts it, democracy is "the public activity that counteracts the tendency of every State to monopolize and depoliticize the public sphere. Every state is oligarchic" (Rancière 2005: 71). Étienne Balibar echoes this view by defining democracy as "a process of permanent anti-oligarchic 'insurrection' rather than a stable regime" (Balibar 2008: 522). Democracy "is not an established reality or a constitution in the material sense of the term, but also not a mere ideal: it is rather a permanent struggle for its own democratization and against its own reversal into oligarchy and monopoly of power" (Balibar 2008: 528). Democracy is a destabilizing force that involves permanent struggle or permanent "insurgency." This second feature introduces an ambivalent normativity to radical democracy. In the version that Rancière endorses, democracy is a permanent struggle because "every state is oligarchic." But one might want to embrace radical democracy because all states within our neoliberal capitalist context are more or less oligarchic. This second reading of the source of oligarchy opens the door to the possibility that there are modes of collective organization that might not be oligarchic or at least might be less so.

This view of democracy is obviously contestatory. But we have seen a number of democratic theories claim that title which do not go quite as far as to suggest that democracy is a form of permanent popular insurgency that serves as a bottom-up counterweight to the inevitable top-down logic of the state. For radical democrats, either because of the nature of states in general or because of the nature of liberal democratic states in the twenty-first century, contestation, resistance, dissent, and insurgency are the core elements of democracy in action. From this view, then, it becomes clear that protest and civil disobedience are an important expression of democratic politics.

I want to turn to how Robin Celikates places civil disobedience in this frame and how he juxtaposes it to a liberal understanding of civil disobedience. In the liberal view, civil disobedience is justified when there has been a violation of rights or fundamental principles of justice (Kaufman 2021; Rawls 1971). Civil disobedience is a response and corrective to unfortunate failures of the constitutional order to live up to internal standards of justice. In this picture, democracy itself is often the source of this failure:

> Civil disobedience is justified because a just constitutional regime will require a democratic form of government, and democratically elected legislatures will predictably enact at least some unjust legislation. When the legislation enacted is sufficiently unjust – when it violates fundamental rights or liberties – the injustice outweighs the duty to obey unjust law that is usually effective under a nearly just constitution. (Kaufman 2021: 103)

Radical democrats take issue with this view on many fronts. First, on the question of justification of civil disobedience, radical democrats are suspicious of the claim that philosophy can lay out clear justificatory criteria for civil disobedience. Justification itself is subject to contestatory democratic debate and arguments (Celikates 2021: 138). Second, and more important, is that radical democrats, to the extent that they do justify civil disobedience or propose justifications for debate, justify it in terms of democracy rather than rights, and this in turn broadens the grounds for disobedience. "The main radical democratic claim is that civil disobedience is legitimate not as constraint on, but rather as an expression of, a democratic practice of collective self-determination. It opens up possibilities of contestation and participation for citizens and other subjects where and when regular institutional channels for articulating their claims are blocked or ineffective" (Celikates 2021: 139). On this view, civil disobedience is an "episodic, informal, and extra-institutional or anti-institutional form of political action" that serves as an expression "of a democratic practice of collective self-determination" (Celikates 2016: 41).

For radical democrats, civil disobedience does not get triggered by aberrant rights violations but is a legitimate response to a wide variety of failures of democratic states, from failures to address climate crisis to persistent and growing economic inequality. Radical democrats reject the Rawlsian view of civil disobedience, which is developed against the backdrop of an imagined ideally just political order. For Rawlsians, civil disobedience has a remedial function made sadly necessary by misbehaving majorities but which one could imagine never needing to have recourse to in the ideal state. For radical democrats, disobedience is not remedial, or never purely so. As an expression of self-determination, it is generative and transformative and the conduit through which citizens can exercise constituent power. For example, protest and disobedience undertaken by migrants and undocumented residents challenge and expand our view of the agent of constituent power and enlarge our idea of the source of legitimate democratic action.

If the justification of civil disobedience is anchored in the constituent power of citizens vis-à-vis all constituted orders and institutions, then what limits are placed on the means and ends of acts of civil disobedience? Celikates insists that civil disobedience must be distinguished from revolution or full insurrection. He interprets the "civil" of civil disobedience not as a call for civility but as suggesting that it is action undertaken by citizens in a political arena and not, for example, a type of military intervention or extra-political strike force. Thus, despite being an exercise of constituent power, disobedience undertaken by *citizens* is still in some sense within the constituted order or at least is not seeking to destroy or completely overthrow that order. "In acting as citizens, they acknowledge some kind of bond with their adversaries, which goes hand in hand with certain forms of self-limitation and self-restraint" (Celikates 2021: 134). But drawing the line is difficult. Every act of civil disobedience is contextually situated, calling for different types and levels of tactics and actions.

Celikates joins many other contemporary theorists of civil disobedience, not all of whom embrace radical democracy, in rethinking what limits ought to be placed on direct action by claiming that it must be civil (Delmas 2018). More particularly, there is a deep interrogation of the tradition that, to use Scheuerman's words, sees "nonviolence as a *sine qua non* of civil disobedience" (Çidam et al. 2020: 519). First, contemporary theory broadens the repertoire of acts of civil disobedience beyond spiritual passivism and admits that "violent" is a difficult standard to measure at the margins. Although there is variation about where the line is to be drawn, there is also a consensus that "being civil . . . does not require disobedience be strictly *nonviolent*, only *less violent*" (Livingston 2021: 254). But the debate about nonviolence does not primarily focus on tallying up tactics on one side or the other of the violence/nonviolence line. Does smashing a window fall in or out of the repertoire? These are context-specific calls that are evaluated on a scale of proportionality, often with some line between property and persons. The debate about nonviolence often takes up questions of the ideological function of the call for nonviolence. New theory in civil disobedience often sets itself against an interpretation of nonviolence as suggesting that action be primarily symbolic and communicative rather than physical and confrontational. But the rethinking of nonviolence also leads to a questioning of the liberal appropriation and interpretation of the civil disobedience tradition. Martin Luther King Jr and the civil rights movement are a particular focus in this debate.

A generation of liberal scholars read King's defense of civil disobedience as, on the one hand, primarily about laying the grounds for legitimate law breaking and, on the other hand, about tactics that would appeal to the moral conscience of the white majority.

All the qualities that made King a revered figure in liberal circles are being reassessed in a time that sees how little headway the civil rights movement has made against white supremacy and structural racism. This re-reading often does not involve rejecting King as a false role model for struggle, but instead involves both articulating why dominant interpretations of King have functioned to suppress and domesticate resistance, as well as offering a new interpretation of nonviolence (Delmas 2018; Livingston 2020). The theme of this new direction is to question the idea that the civil in civil disobedience is supposed to circumscribe law breaking by understanding it as part of a strategy of persuasion.

Juliet Hooker revisits the civil rights-era civil disobedience tradition in light of, or rather under the glare of, unaddressed police violence against black people that suggests that, for many Americans, black lives do not matter. She questions the romanticization of nonviolence, which sees that the function and purpose of turning the other cheek was to activate white conscience through exemplary acts of sacrifice. "The common assumption that black sacrifice will induce shame among white citizens, which will in turn produce a re-orientation to racial justice, is thus predicated on a particular account of white psychology that fails to take the effects of racialized solidarity into account" (Hooker 2016: 460). Here Hooker takes an instrumental view and asks, first, if the sort of sacrifice connected to nonviolence is actually effective and, second, how could it possibility be considered fair or reasonable to ask black citizens to undertake such an asymmetrical sacrifice when they have been the "perpetual losers in US democracy" (Hooker 2016: 449). Others have revisited the civil rights era to suggest that King's (and Gandhi's) tactics were more realistic than has been thought and less reliant on an idealized idea of an appeal to moral consciences (Livingston 2020; Mantena 2012). Still others have suggested that the mythologizing of nonviolence is an ideological move intended to blunt the force of resistance (Delmas 2018).

One way to understand some of the new thinking about civil disobedience is to see it as a debate between understanding civil disobedience as a form of persuasion or as a form of coercion. For many, the pendulum has swung away from thinking about civil disobedience as primarily a way to persuade fellow citizens to take notice of injustice. Civil disobedience is instead about disruption and cost (Hayward 2017). Things change not because the majority or those in power have a moment of epiphany and shame. Change happens in order to get things back to normal or to reassert some level of stability. Livingston calls this the "coercive turn" in civil disobedience theory and suggests that it coincides with the growing embrace of more realist views of politics and democracy (Livingston 2021). Rather than seeing civil disobedience as a symbolic expression of dissent, that is, as a form of communication, the coercive turn in theories sees civil disobedience as an exercise of disruption, that is, as a flexing of a power potential on the part of dissenters.

Embracing the coercive dimension of disobedience does not require one to reject the persuasion dimension altogether. Indeed, it often rests on questioning the sharp dichotomy between persuasion and coercion articulated in the ideal of the unforced force of the better argument. Coercive tactics can be used to force power holders to come to the table and so open the possibility of persuasion. Livingston notes King's tactics involved "learning to use the tools of coercion as tools of persuasion." For example, "the campaign of mass withdrawal from riding busses leveraged economic costs on bus companies, provoked violent disruption, and ultimately mobilized the coercive power of the federal government with the Supreme Court striking down segregation on city buses" (Livingston 2020: 860). The realist perspective leans toward forcing an outcome rather than forcing a conversation to happen. Here, "The purpose of direct action is to impose harm" (Livingston 2021: 261). But Livingston notes that realist logic also places significant limits on action. If the object is change (and not the expression of rage or the overthrow of the system), then consideration about how violent action might elicit backlash or entrenchment must be part of the calculation. And that calculation inevitably leads back to some idea of civility or self-limitation. Both realist logic, as well as deliberative logic, suggests that effective and normatively limited disobedience needs to find a middle position between disruption and civility: "Disobedience, particularly the disruptive kind championed by the coercive turn, escalates conflict. It deepens animosities, hardens identities, and triggers reactive counterforce. Civility, by contrast, entails respect, keeping identities fluid, and limiting reaction by seeking understanding" (Livingston 2021: 267).

Conclusion

I opened this chapter by suggesting that there were several points of interesting comparison between democratic innovation and civil disobedience. But there are also some tensions. The radical democratic reading of civil disobedience has an anti-institutional dimension to it that sets it apart from other contestatory theories of democracy. With contestatory proceduralism as well as democratic pluralism, we saw a view of democracy in which citizens access and exercise "ruling" or popular control via multiple entry points. To be sure, many of these sites work against each other, as when majorities lean in one direction and protest leans in another. But the counterbalancing is exactly what the system is supposed to be doing. On these views, democratic innovations become part of the repertoire and one more point of access into the democratic system. Radical democrats privilege unstructured informal extra-institutional action over institutionalized action. Thus it is difficult to see how radical democratic theory could envision protest and citizens' assemblies as working together collaboratively or even being different but equally legitimate ways to exercise democratic agency. Erin Pineda worries, for example, that radical democracy focuses too much on the insurgent event and not enough on building the social movements that underpin and sustain direct action. She worries about "elevating protest, disobedience and demonstration – as a mode of expression, petition or disruption – as the hallmark of radicalism or privileged means of social change, severing it from less visible, longer-term processes that enable people to build and sustain power" (Çidam et al. 2020: 536).

12
Conclusion

THIS book could have, perhaps should have, been twice as long as it is. There is more to say on each topic covered, and I did not cover all the interesting, new, and innovative trends and arguments in contemporary democratic theory. When people talk about democracy, they sometimes mean broadly the type of society we live in. There are many wonderful and insightful theoretical and normative reflections about the state of our democracies in this expansive sense that I have not explored (for example, Calhoun, Gaonkar, and Taylor 2022). Two framing issues have circumscribed this survey of contemporary democratic theory. The first is taking democracy as a way in which we govern ourselves, therefore focusing on the institutions of ruling. The second is reading democratic theory as a response to twenty-first-century challenges and problems. These two themes are interconnected, as much of what can be counted as evidence of crisis, or at least ill health, is tied to decaying and poorly functioning institutions of governance (Runciman 2018). This focus has made the topic manageable but also, I believe, reflects a real trend in contemporary democratic theory toward unpacking both the intrinsic and instrumental value of institutions. Asking what ails our democratic societies more generally is always an important question and it has stood in the background of my investigation. However, conceptions of, problems with, and threats to popular *rule* have determined the specific lines of exploration in this book.

The overarching theme of this book then has been the ways that democratic theory is responding to real-world threats to,

Conclusion

and erosion of, democracy. The two primary threats come from authoritarianism and oligarchization. The former poses both an internal and external threat. Full-on authoritarianism involves the exclusion of citizens from participating or having a meaningful say in political decisions or the selection of those who make the decisions. At the extreme, this means denying citizens voting and other basic rights of political participation, such as equal opportunity to run for office and free speech to discuss political matters. Authoritarianism is the opposite of democracy. Authoritarian threats internal to democracy involve tendencies and trends that diminish the means, opportunities, and efficacy of citizens' democratic input and participation while frequently staying within the bounds of electoral democracy. Some of these trends are driven by populist movements that seek to strengthen executive power in the name of the people and undermine institutional and cultural protection of opposition and minority voices. Although voter suppression and some election irregularities are part of internal authoritarian threats, the basic institutions of regular elections are usually not directly dismantled. Thus internal authoritarian threats are creeping incremental trends, the severity or danger of which is a contested question. Is vilifying one's opposition a sign of an authoritarian tendency that seeks to close down free public debate or is it simply negative campaigning and part of electoral democracy? Only a handful of democratic regimes have found themselves relatively far down the slippery slope to authoritarianism. But this type of backsliding has fueled or perhaps reinvigorated a debate about what it means for the people to rule themselves.

The external authoritarian threat is less direct. It resides in the possibility that full-on authoritarian regimes or autocracies might begin to perform better than democracies on some basic outcome measures. Less dramatically, the real-world policy challenges of the twenty-first century have put performance and outcome on the normative democratic theory agenda in a way not seen before. This in turn has elicited strong counterarguments that defend democracy on intrinsic moral grounds. Both these trends in democratic theory reflect an insecurity about performance. Questions about performance are not likely to lead established democracies to throw in the democratic towel, but they might erode commitment to some democratic norms and impede democratization in already weak or unstable democracies. Democratization across the globe depends on democracy being "viewed both as the global standard of political legitimacy and as the best system for achieving the kind of prosperity and effective governance that almost all countries seek" (Plattner 2015: 7). At the end of the twentieth century, both these views of democracy had a strong purchase. Almost a quarter of the way into the twenty-first century, democracy's reputation, as both the only standard of legitimacy as well as the best road to prosperity, is severely tarnished.

The threat of oligarchy also has an internal and external dimension. Oligarchy is rule by the few rather than the many, in the interest of the few rather than the many. Democracy is rule by the many in the interest of all. As a generic threat, oligarchy points to the problems of responsiveness, alienation, and representation. Authoritarianism raises the danger that democratic government is no longer *by* the people; oligarchy involves the risk that democratic government is no longer *for* the people. Government is out of touch, unresponsive, and fails to represent the interests, concerns, and needs of ordinary citizens. This threat has generated a lot of rethinking about what government for the people might look like in institutional terms. When one drills down a little deeper into the threat of oligarchy, the most common specification of the oligarchic few is along economic lines, the rule of the rich.

Since the first democracy in ancient Athens, the democratic regime type has always had to face struggles between the rich and the poor, and all normative democratic theory has either implicitly or explicitly assumed that democracy requires some basic floor of social justice to remain stable. What is new is the intense focus on the ways that electoral democracy can change, and perhaps has already in some cases morphed, into plutocracy or rule by the rich. This concern for money in politics is not a narrow concern for campaign finance laws (a concern that is primarily focused on the United States) but rather a concern for the ways growing economic inequality feeds destructive polarization and division, which are in turn exploited and supercharged by elites to drive political campaigns. Also important is the worry that technocratic questions of economic regulation both overwhelm democratic agendas and skew those agendas toward creating favorable conditions for wealth accumulation. The shorthand slogan version of this worry is that while democratic government is nominally by the 99%, its policies are for the 1%; it is responsive to the few rather than to the many. Externally, the worry is that global economic forces have a large role to play in setting democratic agendas.

The worry about oligarchization is a populist worry in the sense that it warns against the way that elites can and do dominate a democracy. And this worry has generated a lot of theorizing about how we can shore up our institutions to reduce that threat. Paradoxically, although contemporary democratic theory is generally very ill disposed toward populist political parties and the ways that those parties are warping democratic regimes, there is a clear populist sentiment running through a great deal of contemporary democratic theory that can be seen in the worry about oligarchization.

Where I do not see a threat to democracy is in citizen apathy, ignorance, or incompetence. The fundamental capabilities, both psychological and cognitive, of citizens have not changed between the good times of democratic boom and the bad times of democratic decline. This suggests, and a great deal of contemporary democratic theory supports this, that rising citizen-level pathologies, for example, affective and destructive polarization, are the product of political and contingent forces often driven by elite agendas. Citizens in general will never acquire high levels of political knowledge. But it is not clear that the knowledge base of a high-school civics teacher is what citizens need to make minimally sensible decisions or think about their interests and needs. Citizens do appear to be somewhat fed up with democratic institutions. Rising disillusionment with democratic institutions, however, can be the product of rising democratic expectations rather than sinking esteem for democracy itself. People across the globe still want democracy. The survey data are clear on this. Citizen disenchantment is not a threat to democracy; it is a demand that democracies do better.

My focus on regime-type threats of authoritarianism and oligarchy prioritizes the question of who rules, how they rule, and the vertical relationship between citizens and the state. This emphasis has perhaps crowded out a concern for a more citizen-level perspective and horizontal relations between citizens. Democratic theory in the 1990s and early 2000s was preoccupied with multiculturalism, recognition, and the democratic potential of social movements to inaugurate a new era of democratic governance that took difference, diversity, identity, and minority status seriously (Carens 2000; Kymlicka 1995; Levi 2000; Markell 2003; Taylor 1994; Tully 1995; Williams 1998). From the vantage point of difference, diversity, and identity, threats to democracy often involve a failure of citizens to see each other or treat each other with respect and dignity. The term "multiculturalism," denoting a particular model of integration that rejects assimilation in favor of protecting and respecting the distinctiveness of cultures, has a diminished presence in democratic theory today. "Recognition" – meaning an affirmation of and respect for particular identities – as a term of art is also less pervasive in democratic theory than it once was. But this does not reflect a diminished interest in questions of integration or identity. Identity politics are the new battle lines in culture wars between right and left across all democracies, from concerns about Islamophobia in integrating immigrants to gender-neutral bathrooms. And inclusion is a word that is ubiquitous in democratic theory today. There is a continued and intense interest in democratic theory to investigate the history and practices of exclusion along with the means and methods of inclusion. Also, following a trend I have identified in this book, the means and methods of inclusion often involve a contestatory and dispersed ideal of democratic rule. The Black Lives Matter movement, for example, has generated intense study of the movement's function, role, goals, and impact on democracy in America, as well as on the political identity of African Americans (Hooker 2016; Lebron 2022; Woodly 2021). Some of the main areas animating contemporary theory are gender identity, colonial legacies of immigration practices and border regimes, indigenous subjugation by settler colonial regimes, and persistent and pernicious racism. I have not been able to take up these themes in this book in the detail that they deserve. This is partly due to the fact that many of these are situated and contextually specific studies, exposing and excavating the historical record of exclusion and its present-day consequences. I have focused on more general discussions of democratic theory. Briefly taking up the example of race in America, I want to insist, however, that the reason for this absence is mundane and not methodological. I have simply not been able to discuss all democratic theory, but this is not because I think that certain types of historically situated critical theory are not normative theory.

The last 25 years have seen a most remarkable explosion of scholarship on race, especially in the American context, as well as investigations into the continued and persistent failing of democratic societies to put racism and race-based exclusion behind them. A number of theorists have set out to expose deep and pervasive injustice and immorality at the heart of democratic regimes but especially American democracy (Anker 2022; Hanchard 2018; Olson 2004). I have not set aside space to discuss these critical genealogical studies of American democracy. One reason for this might have been the claim that these theories are not normative theories in a narrow sense of seeking out and de- or reconstructing moral principles that undergird the idea of democracy but are instead historically informed criticism of actually existing democracies. According to this argument (which we briefly encountered in the introduction), normative theory studies, analyzes, and justifies the moral or normative core of the idea and/or ideal of democracy (an example would be Christiano 2004), and historical and genealogy studies expose and catalogue the violent origins and development of historically situated democracies (an example would be Olson 2004). I am not happy with this stark distinction between normative and critical theory. Baked into this distinction is the unstated assumption that the evils of our historical democracies are contingent, empirical, and thus corrigible compared to the principles of democracy that stand unharmed and unaffected by the travesties of history. This is something democratic theory should not assume but rather investigate. The historically informed indictment of democracies often goes very deep, even if few critical theorists go so far as to reject any and all ideas of democracy. Central and exemplary in this regard is the work of Charles Mills, who exposed the deep connection between the history of the social contract tradition, in which free and equal persons agree to fair and just institutions, and the unstated racial contract that excluded people of color from being considered those persons (Mills 1999). The racial contract did not simply accompany the social contract as some contingent historical fact to be eventually overcome; the racial contract was an essential component in the very conceptualization of the normative core of the contract tradition. This study then asks theorists and philosophers to interrogate not simply the historical record to see if we have been living up to our ideals but the philosophical record as well to see where our ideals have aided and abetted immoral practices. Despite very radical and damning analyses of both the historical record of democracies and mainstream theories of democracy, however, few critics dismiss democracy or even democratic ideals of political equality as such.

Racism and white supremacy (or Islamophobia, xenophobia, anti-Semitism, misogyny, transphobia – I could go on as the list is unfortunately very long) are surely as serious a threat to democracy as authoritarianism and oligarchy. But they are not entirely separate sorts of threats. Although often having deep roots in history, culture, and society, identity-based animus can also be a political weapon for authoritarians interested in stoking division and polarization. Above I noted that successful authoritarian regimes pose an indirect threat to democracy by suggesting that political equality and stable prosperity might not always go together. But there is a way that authoritarian regimes (or authoritarian actors within democracies) pose a more direct threat. There is very strong evidence, for example, that Russian interference in democratic elections both in the United States and in Europe between 2016 and 2020 involved using social media to exacerbate existing cleavages, drive debate to the extreme, and heighten racial and ethnic tensions between groups (Barnes and Goldman 2021). In Europe, this often involved pushing stories about immigrant misbehavior, and in the US case it involved pushing stories surrounding racial violence and division. Elite failures to disavow white supremacy or the employment of tropes about the threat of Islamic terrorists trying to cross our borders are strategies to mobilize constituencies but they are also strategies friendly to authoritarianism. Division, cleavage, and in-group/out-group animus are destabilizing forces in democracies and make the compromises necessary for effective democratic governance less likely. Democracies can thrive under conditions of pluralism and disagreement, but they fail under conditions of hatred and intolerance. The enemies of democracy know this very well.

Conclusion

Democracy is facing hard times. But those hard times have produced good and interesting democratic theory. Does this bode well for the future of democracy? It is not uncommon to conclude overviews of democratic theory such as this one with next steps into the future. At the end of the twentieth century, those next steps were often thought to lead in a transnational direction toward global democracy (Cunningham 2002; Held 1987). I do not finish the book with the promise of global democracy, and I have neglected the topic of transnational democracy almost altogether. This is not because there is nothing interesting to say about global governance. The field is large, active, and producing thought-provoking scholarship (Archibugi, Koenig-Archibugi, and Marchetti 2012; Cabrera 2020; Kuyper 2014). It is again because the twin focus of crisis and democratic rule has guided my narrative. Global democracy is not in crisis because it is still primarily aspirational. The aspiration for global democracy is premised to some extent on the continued health and growth of democracy within nation-states. Furthermore, new realities of the twenty-first century have also had subtle effects on the global democracy debate. Although there is still a great deal of interesting scholarship and research about the possibility of expanding democracy beyond the nation-state, a certain level of energy and optimism that characterized the late twentieth-century era of democratization has seeped out of this debate. Models of world government and/or cosmopolitan governance have less traction in an intellectual environment that leans toward the realistic and feasible rather than the ideal and principled. Global democracy debates have seen an analogous turn away from halcyon days of ideal theory and high moral principle (Erman and Kuyper 2020). Furthermore, crisis and erosion of democracy at the national level have encouraged more problem-driven democratic theory. Feasibility and realism, as well as crisis and erosion, have pushed the pendulum back toward achievable goals and getting our domestic homes in order before projecting a new democratic world order.

But these shifts have not meant the abandonment of questions of democracy beyond the nation-state. For one thing, even though internal problems of sinking trust and backsliding distract from supra-national aspirations for democratic governance, it is still the case that the world is becoming ever more interconnected and integrated (Scholte 2005). The global web of interdependence, legal regulation, international organizations, communication, and cooperation grows denser every year. This proliferation and intensification of law, regulation, and organizations is driven by the need to solve coordination problems at the supra-state level. As the scale and scope of international organization, regulation, and legal structure continues to expand, this affects, sometimes gradually but frequently dramatically, the real lives of individual citizens as well as the power and sovereignty of democratic peoples to *self*-govern. Therefore, questions of accountability and the problem of the democratic deficit of international governance structures are pressing concerns for reasons internal to national democracies (Dellmuth et al. 2022). But as I noted above, global democratization is premised on the continued health and viability of democracy at the nation-state level, and this has led me to prioritize national democratic orders at the expense of transnational democracy.

So what is the future of democracy? I do not know. I feel more confident commenting on the future of democratic theory at least in the near term. Democracy under threat and perhaps in decline has and will continue to produce engaged, interesting, problem-driven, democratic theory. Most serious democratic theorists have not thrown in the towel and declared democracy in a terminal stage of decline. The volume, quality, and care of emerging democratic theory, especially among younger scholars, is evidence that there is still energy and, if not optimism, at least some hope that the patient can be revived. Twenty-first-century democratic theory is not Hegel's owl of Minerva that flies at dusk "when a shape of life has grown old." The scholarship is future oriented and motivated to some extent by the persistent and global desire for democracy.

Let me end with an anecdote. Donald Trump's election to the US presidency in 2016 was cause for a great deal of alarm and despondency among democracy boosters including, perhaps especially, among intellectuals and scholars who write and research about democracy. How could this happen in the oldest and most stable democracy in the world? Early predictions of the dire consequences of that election for the health of democracy if anything were too modest, as no one would have thought that a sitting president would countenance or at least do very little to try to stop attempts to violently overturn national election results. But I want to point to a very small ripple effect that tells a slightly different story. After Trump's election, the number of undergraduates signing up to major in political science in my home department significantly increased. I have no survey data or strong evidence to correlate Trump's win with increased numbers of majors, but it does make a certain amount of sense. Students wanted to know what all the fuss was about. They wanted to understand and get explanations for what they were being told was a momentous political event. Threats to democracy created interest in democracy, at least in my neck of the woods. It is certainly the case that the more common response to the election was to harden partisan polarized divides on both sides rather than motivate knowledge acquisition. But still, political crisis can have the effect of knowledge mobilization, not to mention political mobilization. I allude to this small observed effect in my department as a metaphor for democratic theory in times of crisis. Democratic crisis is spurring on a lot of excellent democratic theory. The field of democratic studies, both normative and empirical, is booming. Students and the general public are on high alert and want to know and understand what's going on and how to fix it. Democratic theory is rising to the occasion.

Notes

Chapter 2 Justifying Democracy

1 Aristotle also talks about true friendship as having intrinsic value but acknowledges that some friendships can have instrumental value as well.

Chapter 3 Equality

1 Rawls's "burdens of judgment" argument did not need to assume any unreasonable or non-reasonable elements in human cognition such as self-interest, cognitive bias, or prejudice. Christiano by comparison does appeal to contemporary cognitive science to claim that disagreement is unavoidable and ubiquitous. Rawls suggests that even at our very best and under the best of conditions, we will still disagree. Nevertheless, Christiano's is a "burdens of judgment" argument.
2 I borrow this term from Christina Lafont (2020).
3 A fourth option is that we give up on a collective course of action and just do what we want. This anarchist option is swiftly dismissed (Waldron 1999: 108).

Chapter 4 Freedom

1 Cristina Lafont's recent book lays out very nicely the way court contestation instantiates political equality. Democracy

> requires institutions to be in place such that citizens can contest any laws and policies that they cannot reasonably accept by asking that either proper reasons be offered for them or that they be changed. To the extent that such institutions are available to all citizens, even

to those who happen to find themselves in the minority, they can see themselves as equal members of a collective political project of self-government. (2020: 16–17)

Chapter 5 Instrumentalism 1: Realism

1 I want to thank Samuel Bagg for this formulation.

Chapter 6 Instrumentalism 2: Performance Skeptics

1 In all four areas, there is a massive amount of literature and research. I cite only some classic examples.

Chapter 7 Instrumentalism 3: Epistemic Democracy

1 Aristotle is often cited as the first to articulate this as a political principle (Aristotle 1984: III, 10, 1281a11).
2 Joshua Cohen first introduced the concept of epistemic democracy in the 1986 essay "An Epistemic Conception of Democracy." In that essay he insisted that "an independent standard of correct decisions" was indeed a defining feature of such an approach (Cohen 1986: 34). But the debate has moved on and it is not clear that Cohen himself still embraces this view of democracy (Schwartzberg 2015: 189).
3 Rousseau has famously said that individuals voting in the general will should not communicate. This has been interpreted as an appeal to something like the CJT independence condition (Grofman and Feld 1988). But what this passage means and whether Rousseau was really saying "no deliberation" versus "no creating voting cartels" is hotly debated.
4 David Estlund offered some early defenses of CJT especially with regard to a narrow interpretation of independence. But in his later work (Estlund 2008), he criticizes using CJT to defend epistemic democracy.
5 There is a lively debate about whether the math underpinning DTA is any good. See Thompson 2014 for a no, and Kuehn 2017 for a yes, and Sakai 2020 and Vasić 2022 for overviews. I will not weigh in on this question but note that even if the math is not airtight, the diversity argument still has legs.
6 There is no mathematical proof attached to this theorem, however.

Chapter 8 Populism and the People

1 The "people" can be traced back to the Ancient world of Athens and Rome, but popular sovereignty is a distinctively modern idea arising in the sixteenth and seventeenth centuries (Canovan 2005).

Chapter 9 Representation

1 Madison argued that the advantage of a republic over a democracy consisted "in the substitution of Representatives, whose enlightened views and virtuous sentiments render them superior to local prejudices, and to schemes of injustice" (Wooton 2003: 173).

References

Abizadeh, Arash. 2002. "The Passions of the Wise: *Phronêsis*, Rhetoric, and Aristotle's Passionate Practical Deliberation." *Review of Metaphysics* 56: 267–96.
Abizadeh, Arash. 2007. "On the Philosophy/Rhetoric Binaries: Or is Habermasian Discourses Motivationally Impotent?" *Philosophy and Social Criticism* 33(4): 445–72.
Abizadeh, Arash. 2008. "Democratic Theory and Border Coercion: No Right to Unilaterally Control Your Own Borders." *Political Theory* 36(1): 37–65.
Abizadeh, Arash. 2021. "Representation, Bicameralism, Political Equality, and Sortition: Reconstituting the Second Chamber as a Randomly Selected Assembly." *Perspectives on Politics* 19(3): 791–806.
Abts, Koen and Rummens, Stefan. 2007. "Populism and Democracy." *Political Studies* 55(2): 405–24.
Achen, Christopher H. and Bartels, Larry M. 2016. *Democracy for Realists: Why Elections Do Not Produce Responsive Government*. Princeton: Princeton University Press.
Allen, Danielle. 2004. *Talking to Strangers: Anxieties of Citizenship since Brown v. Board of Education*. Chicago: University of Chicago Press.
Anderson, Elizabeth. 1999. "What is the Point of Equality?" *Ethics* 109: 287–337.
Anderson, Elizabeth. 2006. "The Epistemology of Democracy." *Episteme* 3(1–2): 8–22.
Anderson, Elizabeth. 2009. "Democracy: Instrumental and Non-Instrumental Value," in Thomas Christiano and John Christman (eds), *Contemporary Debates in Political Philosophy*. Cambridge: Wiley-Blackwell, 213–27.

Anderson, Elizabeth. 2018. "An Epistemic Defense of Democracy: David Estlund's *Democratic Authority.*" *Episteme* 5(1): 129–39.
Anker, Elisabeth R. 2022. *Ugly Freedoms.* Durham: Duke University Press.
Arato, Andrew and Cohen, Jean. 2022. *Populism and Civil Society: The Challenge to Constitutional Democracy.* Oxford: Oxford University Press.
Archibugi, Daniel, Koenig-Archibugi, Matthias, and Marchetti, Raffaele (eds). 2012. *Global Democracy: Normative and Empirical Perspectives.* Cambridge: Cambridge University Press.
Arendt, Hannah. 1954. "Truth and Politics," in *Between Past and Future: Eight Exercises in Political Thought.* London: Penguin Books, 227–64.
Aristotle. 1984. *The Politics*, trans. Carnes Lord. Chicago: University of Chicago Press.
Arlen, Gordon and Rossi, Enzo. 2021. "Must Realists Be Pessimists About Democracy? Responding to Epistemic and Oligarchic Challenges." *Moral Philosophy and Politics* 8(1): 27–49.
Arneson, Richard J. 2003. "Defending the Purely Instrumental Account of Democratic Legitimacy." *Journal of Political Philosophy* 11(1): 122–32.
Arneson, Richard J. 2004. "Democracy is Not Intrinsically Just," in Keith Dowding and Robert E. Goodin (eds), *Justice and Democracy: Essays for Brian Barry.* Cambridge: Cambridge University Press, 40–58.
Arrow, Kenneth J. 2012. *Social Choice and Individual Values.* New Haven: Yale University Press.
Bächtiger, André, Dryzek, John, Mansbridge, Jane, and Warren, Mark. 2018. *The Oxford Handbook of Deliberative Democracy.* Oxford: Oxford University Press.
Bächtiger, André and Parkinson, John. 2019. *Mapping and Measuring Deliberation: Towards a New Deliberative Quality.* Oxford: Oxford University Press.
Bagg, Samuel. 2022. "Sortition as Anti-Corruption: Popular Oversight against Elite Capture." *American Journal of Political Science.* https://doi.org/10.1111/ajps.12704
Bagg, Samuel (forthcoming). *The Dispersion of Power: A Critical Realist Theory of Democracy.* Oxford: Oxford University Press.
Bai, Tongdong. 2019. *Against Political Equality: The Confucian Case.* Princeton: Princeton University Press.
Balibar, Étienne. 2008. "Historical Dilemmas of Democracy and Their Contemporary Relevance for Citizenship." *Rethinking Marxism* 20(4): 522–38.

Barnes, Julian E. and Goldman, Adam. 2021. "Russia Trying to Stoke US Racial Tensions Before Election, Officials Say." *New York Times.* March 16. Retrieved at https://www.nytimes.com/2020/03/10/us/politics/russian-interference-race.html

Bartels, Larry M. 2003. "Democracy with Attitudes," in Michael B. MacKuen and George Rabinowitz (eds), *Electoral Democracy*. Ann Arbor: University of Michigan Press, 48–82.

Bartels, Larry M. 2023. *Democracy Erodes from the Top: Leaders, Citizens, and the Challenge of Populism in Europe*. Princeton: Princeton University Press.

Beitz, Charles. 1989. *Political Equality: An Essay in Democratic Theory*. Princeton: Princeton University Press.

Bell, Daniel A. 2015. *The China Model: Political Meritocracy and the Limits of Democracy*. Princeton: Princeton University Press.

Bellamy, Richard. 2007. *Political Constitutionalism*. Cambridge: Cambridge University Press.

Benhabib, Seyla. 1992. *The Generalized and the Concrete Other: The Kohlberg–Gilligan Controversy in Moral Theory*. New York: Routledge.

Bernholz, Lucy, Landemore, Hélène, and Reich, Rob. 2021. "Introduction," in Lucy Bernholz, Hélène Landemore, and Rob Reich (eds), *Digital Technology and Democratic Theory*. Chicago: Chicago University Press, 1–22.

Bickerton, Christopher and Invernizzi-Accetti, Carlo. 2017. "Populism and Technocracy: Opposites or Complements." *Critical Review of International Social and Political Philosophy* 20(2): 186–206.

Bird, Colin. 2019. *An Introduction to Political Philosophy*. Cambridge: Cambridge University Press.

Boettcher, James. 2020. "Deliberative Democracy, Diversity, and Restraint." *Res Publica* 26: 215–35.

Bonica, Adam. 2020. "Why Are There so Many Lawyers in Congress?" *Legislative Studies Quarterly* 45: 253–89.

Bonotti, Matteo. 2017. *Partisanship and Political Liberalism in Diverse Societies*. Oxford: Oxford University Press.

Bonotti, Matteo. 2022. "Party Linkage, Public Justification and Mixed Electoral Systems." *Political Studies* 70(3): 586–602.

Boswell, John, Dean, Rikki, and Smith, Graham. 2022. "Integrating Citizen Deliberation into Climate Governance: Lessons on Robust Design from Six Climate Assemblies." *Public Administration*: 1–19. https://doi.org/10.1111/padm.12883

Bradsher, Keith and Myers, Steven Lee. 2021. "Ahead of Biden's Democracy Summit, China Says: We're Also a Democracy." *New*

York Times, December 7. https://www.nytimes.com/2021/12/07/world/asia/china-biden-democracy-summit.html
Brennan, Jason. 2016. *Against Democracy*. Princeton: Princeton University Press.
Brennan, Jason and Landemore, Hélène. 2022. *Debating Democracy. Do We Need More or Less?* Oxford: Oxford University Press
Brighouse, Harry. 1996. "Egalitarianism and the Equal Availability of Political Influence." *Journal of Political Philosophy* 4(2): 118–41.
Cabrera, Luis. 2020. *The Humble Cosmopolitan: Rights, Diversity, and Trans-state Democracy*. Oxford: Oxford University Press.
Calhoun, Craig, Gaonkar, Dilip Parameshwar, and Taylor, Charles. 2022. *Degenerations of Democracy*. Cambridge, MA: Harvard University Press
Calvert, Aubin and Warren, Mark E. 2014. "Deliberative Democracy and Framing Effects: Why Frames are a Problem and How Deliberative Mini-publics Might Overcome Them," in K. Grönlund, A. Bächtiger, and M. Setälä (eds), *Deliberative Mini-Publics: Involving Citizens in the Democratic Process*. Colchester: ECPR Press, 203–24.
Campbell, Tom. 2011. "Review of *The Constitution of Equality*." *Australian Journal of Philosophy* 89: 169–71.
Canovan, Margaret. 1999. "Trust the People! Populism and the Two Faces of Democracy." *Political Studies* 47(1): 2–16.
Canovan, Margaret. 2005. *The People*. Cambridge: Polity Press.
Caplan, Bryan. 2007. *The Myth of the Rational Voter: Why Democracies Choose Bad Policies*. Princeton: Princeton University Press.
Carens, Joseph. 2000. *Culture, Citizenship, and Community: A Contextual Exploration of Justice as Evenhandedness*. Oxford: Oxford University Press.
Carnes, Nicholas. 2018. *The Cash Ceiling: Why the Rich Run for Office – And What We Can Do About It*. Princeton: Princeton University Press.
Castiglione, Dario and Pollak, Johannes. 2019. "Introduction," in Dario Castiglione and Johannes Pollak (eds), *Creating Political Presence: The New Politics of Democratic Representation*. Chicago: Chicago University Press, 1–15.
Celikates, Robin. 2016. "Rethinking Civil Disobedience as a Practice of Contestation – Beyond the Liberal Paradigm." *Constellations* 23(1): 37–45.
Celikates, Robin. 2021. "Radical Democratic Disobedience," in William E. Scheuerman (ed.), *The Cambridge Companion to Civil Disobedience*. Cambridge: Cambridge University Press, 128–51.
Chambers, Simone. 2003. "Deliberative Democracy Theory." *Annual Review of Political Science* 6: 307–26.

Chambers, Simone. 2009. "Rhetoric and the Public Sphere: Has Deliberative Democracy Abandoned Mass Democracy?" *Political Theory* 37 (3): 323–50.
Chambers, Simone. 2010. "Theories of Political Justification." *Philosophy Compass* 5(1): 893–903.
Chambers, Simone. 2017. "Balancing Epistemic Quality and Equal Participation in a Systems Approach to Deliberative Democracy." *Social Epistemology* 31(3): 266–76.
Chambers, Simone. 2019. "Democracy and Constitutional Reform: Deliberative versus Populist Constitutionalism." *Philosophy and Social Criticism* 45: 1116–31.
Chambers, Simone. 2021. "Truth, Deliberative Democracy and the Virtues of Accuracy: Is Fake News Destroying the Public Sphere?" *Political Studies* 69(2021): 147–63.
Chambers, Simone. 2022. "An Ethics of Public Political Deliberation: The Case of Rhetoric," in Dilip Gaonkar and Keith Topper (eds), *The Oxford Handbook of Rhetoric and Political Theory*. Oxford: Oxford University Press.
Chambers, Simone and Kopstein, Jeffrey. 2022. "Wrecking the Public Sphere: The New Authoritarian Attack on Pluralism and Truth." *Constellations* https://DOI: 10.1111/1467-8675.12620
Chapman, Emilee. 2022. *Election Day: How We Vote and What It Means for Democracy*. Princeton: Princeton University Press.
Christensen, Johan, Holst, Cathrine, and Molander, Anders. 2022. *Expertise, Policy-Making and Democracy: Leave It to the Experts?* New York: Routledge.
Christiano, Thomas. 1996. *The Rule of the Many: Fundamental Issues in Democratic Theory*. Boulder: Westview Press.
Christiano, Thomas. 2004. "The Authority of Democracy." *Journal of Political Philosophy* 12(3): 266–90.
Christiano, Thomas. 2008. *The Constitution of Equality: Democratic Authority and its Limits*. Oxford: Oxford University Press.
Christiano, Thomas and Bajaj, Sameer. 2022. "Democracy," in Edward N. Zalta (ed.), *The Stanford Encyclopedia of Philosophy* (Spring). https://plato.stanford.edu/archives/spr2022/entries/democracy/
Çidam, Çiğem, Scheuerman, Williams E., Delmas, Candice, Pineda, Erin R., Celikates, Robin, and Livingston, Alexander. 2020. "Theorizing the Politics of Protest: Contemporary Debates in Civil Disobedience." *Contemporary Political Theory* 19: 513–46.
Cohen, Joshua. 1986. "An Epistemic Conception of Democracy." *Ethics* 97: 6–38.
Cohen, Joshua. 1997a. "Procedure and Substance in Deliberative

Democracy," in James Bohman and William Rheg (eds), *Deliberative Democracy: Essays on Reason and Politics*. Cambridge: MIT Press, 407–37.

Cohen, Joshua. 1997b. "Deliberation and Democratic Legitimacy," in James Bohman and William Rehg (eds), *Deliberative Democracy*. Cambridge, MA: MIT Press, 67–91.

Cohen, Joshua. 2010. *Rousseau: A Free Community of Equals*. Oxford: Oxford University Press.

Cohen, Joshua and Fung, Archon. 2004. "Radical Democracy." *Swiss Journal of Political Science* 10(4): 23–34.

Cohen, Joshua and Fung, Archon. 2021. "Democracy and the Digital Public Sphere," in Lucy Bernholz, Hélène Landemore, and Rob Reich (eds), *Digital Technology and Democratic Theory*. Chicago: Chicago University Press, 23–61.

Cole, Matthew. 2022. "What is Wrong with Technocracy?" *Boston Review*, August 22. https://www.bostonreview.net/articles/whats-wrong-with-technocracy/

Connaughton, Aidan, Kent, Nicholas, and Schumacher, Shannon. 2020. "How People Around the World See Democracy in 8 Charts." *Pew Research Center*, February 27, 2020. How people around the world see democracy in 8 charts | Pew Research Center.

Connolly, William. 2017. "Trump, the Working Class, and Fascist Rhetoric." *Theory and Event* 20(1): 23–37.

Converse, Philip E. 2000. "Assessing the Capacity of Mass Electorates." *Annual Review of Political Science* 55: 269–80.

Crouch, Colin. 2004. *Post-Democracy*. Cambridge: Polity Press.

Cunningham, Frank. 2002. *Theories of Democracy: A Critical Introduction*. New York: Routledge.

Curato, Nicole, Farrell, David M., Geissel, Brigitte, et al. 2021. *Deliberative Mini-Publics: Core Design Features*. Bristol: Bristol University Press.

Dahl, Robert. 1989. *Democracy and Its Critics*. New Haven: Yale University Press.

Dalton, Russell J. 2004. *Democratic Challenges, Democratic Choices: The Erosion of Political Support in Advanced Industrial Democracies*. Oxford: Oxford University Press.

Dalton, Russell J. and Wattenberg, Martin P. (eds). 2002. *Parties without Partisans*. Oxford: Oxford University Press.

de la Torre, Carlos. 2019. "Global Populism Histories, Trajectories, Problems, and Challenges," in Carlos de la Torre (ed.), *Routledge Handbook of Global Populism*. New York: Routledge Publishing, 1–27.

Delli Carpini, Michael X. and Keeter, Scott. 1996. *What Americans*

Know about Politics and Why it Matters. New Haven: Yale University Press.
Dellmuth, Lisa, Scholte, Jan Aart, Tallberg, Jonas, and Verhaegen, Soetkin. 2022. *Citizens, Elites, and the Legitimacy of Global Governance*. Oxford: Oxford University Press.
Delmas, Candice. 2018. *A Duty to Resist: When Disobedience Should Be Uncivil*. Oxford: Oxford University Press.
Dewey, John. 1954. *The Public and Its Problems*. Chicago: Swallow Press.
Diamond, Larry. 2015. *In Search of Democracy*. New York: Routledge.
Disch, Lisa. 2011. "Towards a Mobilization Conception of Democratic Representation." *American Political Science Review* 105: 100–14.
Disch, Lisa. 2019. "Introduction: The End of Representative Politics?" in Lisa Disch, Mathijs van de Sande, and Nadia Urbinati (eds), *The Constructivist Turn in Political Representation*. Edinburgh: Edinburgh University Press, 1–18.
Disch, Lisa. 2021. *Making Constituencies: Representation as Mobilization in Mass Democracy*. Chicago: University of Chicago Press.
Druckman, James N. 2014. "Pathologies of Studying Public Opinion, Political Communication, and Democratic Responsiveness." *Political Communication* 31: 467–92.
Druckman, James N. and Nelson, K. R. 2003. "Framing and Deliberation: How Citizen's Conversations Limit Elite Influence." *American Journal of Political Science* 47: 729–45.
Dryzek, John. 2009. "Democratization as Deliberative Capacity Building." *Comparative Political Studies* 42(11): 1379–1402.
Dryzek, John. 2010. "Rhetoric in Democracy: A Systemic Appreciation." *Political Theory* 38(3): 319–39.
Dryzek, John. 2017. "The Forum, the System, and the Polity: Three Varieties of Democratic Theory." *Political Theory* 45(5): 610–36.
Dryzek, John and Lo, Alex Y. 2015. "Reason and Rhetoric in Climate Communication." *Environmental Politics* 24(1): 1–16.
Dworkin, Ronald. 1987. "What is Equality? Part 4: Political Equality." *University of San Francisco Law Review* 22: 1–30.
Economist. 2022. "A New Low for Global Democracy." *The Economist*, February 9, 2022. https://www.economist.com/graphic-de tail/2022/02/09/a-new-low-for-global-democracy?utm_medium=cpc .adword.pd&utm_source=google&ppccampaignID=17210591673& ppcadID=&utm_campaign=a.22brand_pmax&utm_content=conver sion.direct-response.anonymous&gclid=EAIaIQobChMIjceF6pHH -gIVBA6tBh1n0gCgEAAYAiAAEgIm-vD_BwE&gclsrc=aw.ds
Eisgruber, Christopher. 2001. *Constitutional Self-Government*. Cambridge, MA: Harvard University Press.

Elliott, Kevin. 2018. "Review of Jason Brennan *Against Democracy.*" *Contemporary Political Theory* 17: 94–7.
Elliott, Kevin J. 2019. "Democracy and the Epistemic Limits of Markets." *Critical Review* 31(1): 1–25.
Elliott, Kevin J. 2023. *Democracy for Busy People.* Chicago: University of Chicago Press.
Elstub, Stephen and Escobar, Oliver. 2019. "Defining and Topologizing Democratic Innovation," in Stephen Elstub and Oliver Escobar (eds), *Handbook of Democratic Innovation and Governance.* Cheltenham: Edward Elgar Publishing, 11–31.
Elstub, Stephen and McLaverty, Peter. 2014. *Deliberative Democracy: Issues and Cases.* Edinburgh: Edinburgh University Press.
el-Wakil, Alice and McKay, Spencer. 2020. "Disentangling Referendums and Direct Democracy: A Defence of Systems Approach to Popular Vote Processes." *Representation* 56(4): 449–66.
Erman, Eva and Kuyper, Jonathan W. 2020. "Global Democracy and Feasibility." *Critical Review of International and Social Political Philosophy* 23(3): 311–31.
Estlund, David M. 1994. "Opinion Leaders, Independence, and the Condorcet's Jury Theorem." *Theory and Decision* 36(2): 131–62.
Estlund, David M. 2008. *Democratic Authority: A Philosophical Framework.* Princeton: Princeton University Press.
Estlund, David M., Waldron, Jeremy, Grofman, Bernard, and Feld, Scott L. 1989. "Democratic Theory and the Public Interest: Condorcet and Rousseau Revisited." *American Political Science Review* 83(4): 1317–40.
Extinction Rebellion. 2019. "The Extinction Rebellion Guide to Citizens' Assemblies," 25 June. https://extinctionrebellion.uk/wp-content/uploads/2019/06/The-Extinction-Rebellion-Guide-to-Citizens-Assemblies-Version-1.1-25-June-2019.pdf
Farrell, David, Suiter, Jane, Cunningham, Kevin, and Harris, Clodagh. 2020. "When Mini-Publics and Maxi-Publics Coincide: Ireland's National Debate on Abortion." *Representation* 59(2): 1–19. https://www.tandfonline.com/doi/full/10.1080/00344893.2020.1804441
Farrell, Henry, Mercier, Hugo, and Schwartzberg, Melissa. 2023. "Analytic Democratic Theory: A Microfoundational Approach." *American Political Science Review* 117(2): 767–72.
Festenstein, Matthew. 2019. "Does Dewey Have an 'Epistemic Argument' for Democracy?" *Contemporary Pragmatism* 16: 217–41.
Fischer, Frank. 2009. *Democracy and Expertise.* Oxford: Oxford University Press.
Fishkin, James. 2009. *When the People Speak: Deliberative Democracy and Public Consultation.* Oxford: Oxford University Press.

Fleuss, Dannica. 2021. *Radical Proceduralism: Democracy from Philosophical Principles to Political Institutions.* Bingley: Emerald Publishing.
Ford, Bryan. 2021. "Technologizing Democracy or Democratizing Technology? A Layered-Architecture Perspective on Potentials and Challenges," in Lucy Bernholz, Hélène Landemore, and Rob Reich (eds), *Digital Technology and Democratic Theory.* Chicago: Chicago University Press, 274–308.
Forestal, Jennifer. 2022. *Designing for Democracy: How to Build Community in Digital Environments.* Oxford: Oxford University Press.
Freeman, Samuel. 1994. "Political Liberalism and the Possibility of a Just Democratic Constitution." *Chicago-Kent Law Review* 69(3): 619–68.
Fukuyama, Francis. 1992. *The End of History and the Last Man.* New York: Free Press.
Fung, Archon and Gray, Sean W. D. (eds) (forthcoming). *Empowering All-Affected Interests: Foundations for 21st Century Democracy?*
Gaonkar, Dilip and Topper, Keith (eds). 2022. *The Oxford Handbook of Rhetoric and Political Theory.* Oxford: Oxford University Press.
Garsten, Bryan. 2006. *Saving Persuasion: A Defense of Rhetoric and Judgment.* Cambridge: Harvard University Press.
Garsten, Bryan. 2011. "The Rhetoric Revival in Political Theory." *Annual Review of Political Science* 14: 159–80.
Gastil, John and Broghammer, Michael. 2021. "Linking Theories of Motivation, Game Mechanics, and Public Deliberation to Design an Online System of Participatory Budgeting." *Political Studies* 69(1): 7–25.
Gastil, John and Knobloch, Katherine R. 2020. *Hope for Democracy: How Citizens Can Bring Reason Back into Politics.* Oxford: Oxford University Press.
Gastil, John and Wright, Erik Olin (eds). 2019a. *Legislature by Lot: Transformative Design for Deliberative Governance.* London: Verso.
Gastil, John and Wright, Erik Olin. 2019b. "Legislature by Lot: Envisioning Sortition within a Bicameral System," in John Gastil and Erik Olin Wright (eds), *Legislature by Lot: Transformative Design for Deliberative Governance.* London: Verso, 3–38.
Gilens, Martin. 2012. *Affluence and Influence: Economic Inequality and Political Power in America.* Princeton: Princeton University Press.
Gilens, Martin and Page, Benjamin. 2017. *Democracy in America? What Has Gone Wrong and What We Can Do About It.* Chicago: University of Chicago Press.
Goodin, Robert E. 2000. "Democratic Deliberation Within." *Philosophy and Public Affairs* 29(1): 81–109.

Goodin, Robert E. 2017. "The Epistemic Benefits of Deliberative Democracy." *Policy Sciences* 50: 351–66.
Goodin, Robert E. and List, Christian. 2001. "Epistemic Democracy: Generalizing the Condorcet Jury Theorem." *Journal of Political Philosophy* 3: 277–306.
Goodin, Robert E. and Spiekermann, Kai. 2018. *An Epistemic Theory of Democracy*. Oxford: Oxford University Press.
Goodman, Rob. 2021. *Words on Fire: Eloquence and Its Conditions*. Cambridge: Cambridge University Press.
Goodman, Rob and Ballacci, Giuseppe (forthcoming). "Introduction," in Giuseppe Ballacci and Rob Goodman (eds), *Populism, Demagoguery, and Rhetoric in Historical Perspective*. Oxford: Oxford University Press.
Green, Jeffrey Edward. 2016. *The Shadow of Unfairness: A Plebeian Theory of Liberal Democracy*. Oxford: Oxford University Press.
Griffin, Christopher. 2003. "Debate: Democracy as a Non-Instrumentally Just Procedure." *Journal of Political Philosophy* 11(1): 111–21.
Grofman, Bernard and Feld, Scott L. 1988. "Rousseau's General Will: A Condorcetian Perspective." *American Political Science Review* 82(2): 567–76.
Guerrero, Alexander A. 2014. "Against Elections: The Lottocratic Alternative." *Philosophy and Public Affairs* 42(2): 135–78.
Geuss, Raymond. 2008. *Philosophy and Real Politics*. Princeton: Princeton University Press.
Gunn, Paul. 2019. "Against Epistocracy." *Critical Review* 31(1): 26–82.
Gutmann, Amy and Thompson, Dennis. 1996. *Democracy and Disagreement*. Cambridge, MA: Harvard University Press.
Habermas, Jürgen. 1996. *Between Facts and Norms: Contributions to a Discourse Theory of Law and Democracy*, trans. William Rheg. Cambridge, MA: MIT Press.
Habermas, Jürgen. 2009. "Political Communication in Media Society: Does Democracy Still have an Epistemic Dimension? The Impact of Normative Theory on Empirical Research," in Jürgen Habermas, *Europe: The Faltering Project*. Cambridge: Polity Press, 138–83.
Habermas, Jürgen. 2022. "Reflections and Hypotheses on a Further Structural Transformation of the Political Public Sphere." *Theory, Culture & Society* 39(4): 145–71.
Hacker, Jacob S. and Pierson, Paul. 2011. *Winner Take-All Politics: How Washington Made the Rich Richer – and Turned its Back on the Middle Class*. New York: Simon and Schuster.
Hacker, Jacob S. and Pierson, Paul. 2020. *Let them Eat Tweets: How the Right Rules in an Age of Extreme Inequality*. New York: Liveright.

References

Hamid, Shadi. 2022. *The Problem of Democracy: America, the Middle East, and the Rise and Fall of an Idea*. Oxford: Oxford University Press.

Hanchard, Michael G. 2018. *The Specter of Race: How Discrimination Haunts Western Democracies*. Princeton: Princeton University Press.

Hanson, Stephen E. and Kopstein, Jeffrey S. 2022. "Understanding the Global Patrimonial Wave." *Perspectives on Politics* 20(1): 237–49.

Hayward, Clarissa Rile. 2017. "Responsibility and Ignorance: On Dismantling Structural Injustices." *Journal of Politics* 79(2): 396–408.

He, Baogang, Tin-bor Hui, Victoria, Jenco, Leigh, et al. 2016. "What Exactly Is 'The Chinese Ideal?' A Discussion of Daniel A. Bell's *The China Model: Political Meritocracy and the Limits of Democracy*." *Perspectives on Politics* 14(1): 147–61.

He, Baogang and Warren, Mark E. 2020. "Can Meritocracy Replace Democracy? A Conceptual Framework." *Philosophy and Social Criticism* 46(9): 1093–112.

Held, David. 1987. *Models of Democracy*. Palo Alto: Stanford University Press.

Hendriks, Carolyn M., Ercan, Selen A., and Boswell, John. 2020. *Mending Democracy: Democratic Repair in Disconnected Times*. Oxford: Oxford University Press.

Hendriks, Frank. 2021. "Key Values for Democratic Governance Innovation: Two Traditions and a Synthesis." *Public Administration* 100(4): 803–20.

Holst, Cathrine and Molander, Anders. 2020. "Epistemic Worries about Economic Expertise," in Jozef Bátora and John R. Erik Fossum (eds), *Towards a Segmented European Political Order: The European Union's Post-Crisis Conundrum*. Abingdon: Routledge, 72–92.

Hong, Lu and Page, Scott E. 2004. "Groups of Diverse Problem Solvers Can Outperform Groups of High-Ability Problem Solvers." *Proceedings of the National Academy of Sciences* 101(46): 16385–9.

Honig, Bonnie. 1993. *Political Theory and the Displacement of Politics*. Ithaca: Cornell University Press.

Honig, Bonnie. 2017. *Public Things: Democracy in Disrepair*. New York: Fordham University Press.

Hooker, Juliette. 2016. "Black Lives Matter and the Paradoxes of US Black Politics: From Democratic Sacrifice to Democratic Repair." *Political Theory* 44(4): 448–69.

Huq, Aziz Z. 2020. "Failing Democracy," in Melissa Schwartzberg and Daniel Viehoff (eds), *Democratic Failure: Nomos LXIII*. New York: New York University Press, 11–49.

Hutton Ferris, Daniel. 2022. "Centripetal Representation." *American*

Journal of Political Science. https://onlinelibrary.wiley.com/doi/full/10.1111/ajps.12726

Ingham, Sean. 2012. "Disagreement and Epistemic Arguments for Democracy." *Politics, Philosophy & Economics* 12(2): 136–55.

Ingham, Sean. 2019. *Rule by Multiple Majorities: A New Theory of Popular Control.* Cambridge: Cambridge University Press.

Ingham, Sean. 2022. "Representative Democracy and Social Equality." *American Political Science Review* 116(2): 689–701.

Ingham, Sean and Wiens, David. 2021. "Demographic Objections to Epistocracy: A Generalization." *Philosophy and Public Affairs* 49(4): 323–49.

Invernizzi-Accetti, Carlo. 2017. "Does Democratic Theory Need Epistemic Standards: Grounds for a Purely Procedural Defense of Majority Rule." *Democratic Theory* 4(2): 3–26.

Invernizzi-Accetti, Carlo and Oskian, Giulia. 2022. "What is a Consultative Referendum? The Democratic Legitimacy of Popular Consultations." *Perspectives on Politics* 20(1): 123–38.

Invernizzi-Accetti, Carlo and Wolkenstein, Fabio. 2017. "The Crisis of Party Democracy, Cognitive Mobilization, and the Case for Making Parties More Deliberative." *American Political Science Review* 111(1): 97–109.

Iyengar, Shanto, Sood, Gaurav, and Lelkes, Yphtach. 2012. "Affect, Not Ideology: A Social Identity Perspective on Polarization." *Public Opinion Quarterly* 76(3): 405–31.

Jacobs, Lawrence R. 2022. *Democracy under Fire: Donald Trump and the Breaking of American History.* Oxford: Oxford University Press.

Jacobs, Lawrence R. and Shapiro, Robert Y. 2000. *Politicians Don't Pander: Political Manipulation and the Loss of Democratic Responsiveness.* Chicago: University of Chicago Press.

Jones, Garret. 2020. *10% Less Democracy: Why You Should Trust Elites a Little More and the Masses a Little Less.* Stanford: Stanford University Press.

Kahneman, Daniel, Slovic, Paul, and Tversky, Amos (eds). 1982. *Judgment under Uncertainty: Heuristics and Biases.* New York: Cambridge University Press.

Kaltwasser, Cristóbal Rovira, Taggart, Paul, Ochoa Espejo, Pauline, and Ostiguy, Pierre. 2017. "Populism: An Overview of the Concept and the State of the Art," in Cristóbal Rovira Kaltwasser, Paul Taggart, Pauline Ochoa Espejo, and Pierre Ostiguy (eds), *Oxford Handbook of Populism.* Oxford: Oxford University Press, 1–24.

Kapust, Daniel J. and Schwarze, Michelle A. 2016. "The Rhetoric of

Sincerity: Cicero and Smith on Propriety and Poetical Context." *American Political Science Review* 110(1): 100–11.
Kaufman, Alexander. 2021. "Liberalism: John Rawls and Ronald Dworkin," in William E. Scheuerman (ed.), *The Cambridge Companion to Civil Disobedience*. Cambridge: Cambridge University Press, 80–104.
Kelly, Casey Ryan. 2020. "Donald J. Trump and the Rhetoric of White Ambivalence." *Rhetoric and Public Affairs* 23(2): 195–224.
Kelsen, Hans. 1955. "Foundations of Democracy." *Ethics* 66(1): 1–101.
Kelsen, Hans. 2013. *The Essence and Value of Democracy*. New York: Rowman & Littlefield.
Kirchheimer, Otto. 1967. "The Transformation of the Western European Party System," in Joseph La Palombara and Myron Weiner (eds), *Political Parties and Political Development*. Princeton: Princeton University Press, 177–200.
Kirshner, Alexander S. 2022. *Legitimate Opposition*. New Haven: Yale University Press.
Knight, Jack and Johnson, James. 2011. *The Priority of Democracy: Political Consequences of Pragmatism*. Princeton: Princeton University Press.
Knight, Jack, Landemore, Hélène, Urbinati, Nadia, and Viehoff, Daniel. 2016. "Roundtable on Epistemic Democracy and its Critics." *Critical Review* 28(2): 137–70.
Kohn, Margaret. 2003. *Radical Space: Building the House of the People*. Ithaca: Cornell University Press.
Kohn, Margaret. 2004. *Brave New Neighborhoods: The Privatization of Public Space*. Cambridge: Routledge.
Kolodny, Niko. 2014a. "Rule Over None I: What Justifies Democracy." *Philosophy and Public Affairs* 42(3): 195–229.
Kolodny, Niko. 2014b. "Rule Over None II: Social Equality and the Justification of Democracy." *Philosophy & Public Affairs* 42(4): 287–336.
Kolodny, Niko. 2023. *The Pecking Order: Social Hierarchy as a Philosophical Problem*. Cambridge: Cambridge University Press.
Korsgaard, Christine. 1996. "Two Distinctions in Goodness," in *Creating the Kingdom of Ends*. Cambridge: Cambridge University Press, 249–74.
Kuehn, Daniel. 2017. "Diversity, Ability, and Democracy: A Note on Thompson's Challenge to Hong and Page." *Critical Review* 29(1): 72–87.
Kuyper, Jonathan W. 2014. "Global Democratization and International

Regime Complexity." *European Journal of International Relations* 20(3): 620–46.
Kymlicka, William. 1995. *Multicultural Citizenship: A Liberal Theory of Minority Rights*. Oxford: Oxford University Press.
Laclau, Ernesto. 2005. *On Populist Reason*. London: Verso.
Lafont, Cristina. 2020. *Democracy without Shortcuts: A Participatory Conception of Deliberative Democracy*. Oxford: Oxford University Press.
Lambek, Simon. 2022. "Comedy as Dissonant Rhetoric." *Philosophy & Social Criticism* 0(0) https://doi.org/10.1177/01914537221079677
Landemore, Hélène. 2012. *Democratic Reason: Politics, Collective Intelligence, and the Rule of the Many*. Princeton: Princeton University Press.
Landemore, Hélène. 2013. "Deliberation, Cognitive Diversity, and Democratic Inclusiveness: An Epistemic Argument for the Random Selection of Representatives." *Synthese* 190: 1209–31.
Landemore, Hélène. 2015. "Inclusive Constitution-Making: The Iceland Experiment." *Journal of Political Philosophy* 23(2): 166–91.
Landemore, Hélène. 2016. "Roundtable on Epistemic Democracy and Its Critics." *Critical Review* 28(2): 137–70.
Landemore, Hélène. 2020. *Open Democracy: Reinventing Popular Rule for the Twenty-First Century*. Princeton: Princeton University Press.
Landemore, Hélène. 2021. "Open Democracy and Digital Technologies," in Lucy Bernholz, Hélène Landemore, and Rob Reich (eds), *Digital Technology and Democratic Theory*. Chicago: Chicago University Press, 62–89.
Lebron, Christopher J. 2022. *The Making of "Black Lives Matter": A Brief History of an Idea*, 2nd edn. Oxford: Oxford University Press.
Lefort, Claude. 1988. *Democracy and Political Theory*. Minneapolis: University of Minnesota Press.
Lenard, Patti Tamara. 2021. "Unintentional Residence and the Right to Vote." *Journal of Applied Philosophy*, April 27. https://onlinelibrary.wiley.com/doi/full/10.1111/japp.12513
Levi, Jacob T. 2000. *Multiculturalism of Fear*. Oxford: Oxford University Press.
List, Christian and Goodin, Robert E. 2001. "Epistemic Democracy: Generalizing the Condorcet Jury Theorem." *Journal of Political Philosophy* 9(3): 277–306.
Livingston, Alexander. 2017. "Between Means and Ends: Reconstructing Coercion in Dewey's Democratic Theory." *American Political Science Review* 111(3): 522–34.
Livingston, Alexander. 2019. "Against Civil Disobedience: On Candice

Delmas' *A Duty to Resist: When Disobedience Should Be Uncivil.*" *Res Publica* 25(4): 591–97.
Livingston, Alexander. 2020. "'Tough Love': The Political Theology of Civil Disobedience." *Perspectives on Politics* 18(3): 851–66.
Livingston, Alexander. 2021. "Nonviolence and the Coercive Turn," in William E. Scheuerman (ed.), *The Cambridge Companion to Civil Disobedience.* Cambridge: Cambridge University Press, 254–79.
Lodge, Milton and Taber, Charles S. *The Rationalizing Voter.* New York: Cambridge University Press.
Lopez-Guerra, Claudio. 2011. *Democracy and Disenfranchisement: The Morality of Electoral Exclusion.* Oxford: Oxford University Press.
Lupia, Arthur and McCubbins, Matthew D. 1998. *The Democratic Dilemma: Can Citizens Learn What They Need to Know?* Cambridge: Cambridge University Press.
Luskin, Robert C. 1987. "Measuring Political Sophistication." *American Journal of Political Science* 31(4): 856–99.
MacGilvray, Eric. 2014. "Democratic Doubts: Pragmatism and the Epistemic Defense of Democracy." *Journal of Political Philosophy* 22(1): 105–23.
MacKenzie, Michael. 2021. *Future Publics: Democracy, Deliberation, and Future-Regarding Collective Action.* New York: Oxford University Press.
Mackie, Gerry. 2003. *Democracy Defended.* Cambridge: Cambridge University Press.
Mackie, Gerry. 2012. "Rational Ignorance and Beyond," in Hélène Landemore and Jon Elster (eds), *Collective Wisdom: Principles and Mechanisms.* Cambridge: Cambridge University Press, 290–318.
Mair, Peter. 2013. *Ruling the Void: The Hollowing of Western Democracy.* London: Verso.
Malleson, Tom. 2014. *After Occupy: Economic Democracy for the 21st Century.* New York: Oxford University Press.
Manin, Bernard. 1997. *The Principles of Representative Government.* Cambridge: Cambridge University Press.
Mansbridge, Jane. 2003. "Rethinking Representation." *American Political Science Review* 97(4): 515–28.
Mansbridge, Jane. 2011. "Clarifying the Concept of Representation." *American Political Science Review* 105(3): 621–30.
Mansbridge, Jane. 2019. "Recursive Representation," in Dario Castiglione and Johannes Pollak (eds), *Creating Political Presence: The New Politics of Democratic Representation.* Chicago: Chicago University Press, 298–338.
Mansbridge, Jane. 2020. "The Evolution of Political Representation

in Liberal Democracies: Concepts and Practices," in Robert Rohrschneider and Jacques Thomassen (eds), *The Oxford Handbook of Political Representation in Liberal Democracies*. Oxford: Oxford University Press, 16–54.

Mansbridge, Jane, Bohman, James, Chambers, Simone, et al. 2012. "A Systemic Approach to Deliberative Democracy," in John Parkinson and Jane Mansbridge (eds), *Deliberative Systems*. Cambridge: Cambridge University Press, 1–26.

Mansbridge, Jane and Macedo, Stephen. 2019. "Populism and Democracy." *Annual Review of Law and Social Science* 15: 59–77.

Mantena, Karuna. 2012. "Another Realism: The Politics of Gandhian Non-violence." *American Poltical Science Review* 106(2): 455–70.

Markell, Patchen. 2003. *Bound by Recognition*. Princeton: Princeton University Press.

Mason, Lilliana. 2018. "Ideologies without Issues: The Polarizing Consequences of Ideological Identities." *Public Opinion Quarterly* 82: 280–301.

Matthijs, Matthias and Blyth, Mark. 2018. "When is it Rational to Learn the Wrong Lessons? Technocratic Authority, Social Leaning, and Euro Fragility." *American Political Science Review* 16(1): 110–26.

McCormick, John P. 2006. "Contain the Wealthy and Patrol the Magistrates: Restoring Elite Accountability to Popular Government." *American Political Science Review* 100: 147–63.

McCormick, John. 2011. *Machiavellian Democracy*. Cambridge: Cambridge University Press.

McCormick, John P. 2019. "The New Ochlophobia? Populism, Majority Rule and Prospects for Democratic Republicanism," in Yiftah Elazar and Geneviève Rousselière (eds), *Republicanism and the Future of Democracy*. Cambridge, Cambridge University Press, 130–51.

McQueen, Alison. 2018. *Political Realism in Apocalyptic Times*. Cambridge: Cambridge University Press.

Medearis, John. 2015. *Why Democracy is Oppositional*. Cambridge, MA: Harvard University Press.

Michels, Robert. 1962. *Political Parties: A Sociological Study of the Oligarchical Tendencies of Modern Democracy*, trans. Eden and Cedar Paul. New York: The Free Press.

Mills, Charles W. 1999. *The Racial Contract*. Ithaca: Cornell University Press.

Mittiga, Ross. 2022. "Political Legitimacy, Authoritarianism, and Climate Change." *American Political Science Review* 116(3): 998–1011.

Mizak, Cheryl. 2008. "A Culture of Justification: The Pragmatist's Epistemic Argument for Democracy." *Episteme* 5(1): 94–105.

Montanaro, Lara. 2017. *Who Elected Oxfam? A Democratic Defense of Self-Appointed Representatives.* Cambridge: Cambridge University Press.

Moore, Alfred. 2017. *Critical Elitism, Deliberation, Democracy, and the Problem of Expertise.* Cambridge: Cambridge University Press.

Moore, Alfred. 2018. "Anonymity, Pseudonymity, and Deliberation: Why Not Everything Should Be Connected." *Journal of Political Philosophy* 26(2): 169–92.

Moore, Alfred, Fredheim, Rolf, Wyss, Dominik, and Beste, Simon. 2021. "Deliberation and Identity Rules: The Effect of Anonymity, Pseudonyms and Real-Name Requirements on the Cognitive Complexity of Online News Comments." *Political Studies* 69(1): 45–65.

Morgan, Edmund Sears. 1989. *Inventing the People.* New York: Norton.

Mouffe, Chantal. 2008. "The 'End of Politics' and the Challenge of Right-wing Populism," in Francisco Panizza (ed.), *Populism and the Mirror of Democracy.* London: Verso, 50–71.

Mouffe, Chantal. 2018. *For a Left Populism.* London: Verso.

Mounk, Yascha. 2018. *The People vs. Democracy: Why Our Freedom Is in Danger and How to Save It.* Cambridge: Cambridge University Press.

Mudde, Cas and Kaltwasser, Cristóbal Rovira. 2012. "Populism: Corrective and Threat to Democracy," in Cas Mudde and Cristóbal Rovira Kaltwasser (eds), *Populism in Europe and Americas: Threat or Corrective for Democracy?* Cambridge: Cambridge University Press, 205–22.

Muirhead, Russell. 2014. *The Promise of Party in a Polarized Age.* Cambridge, MA: Harvard University Press.

Muirhead, Russell and Rosenblum, Nancy. 2020. "The Political Theory of Parties and Partisanship: Catching Up." *Annual Review of Political Science* 23: 95–110.

Müller, Jan-Werner. 2016. *What is Populism?* Philadelphia: University of Pennsylvania Press.

Müller, Jan-Werner. 2017. "Populism and Constitutionalism," in Cristóbal Rovira Kaltwasser, Paul Taggart, Paulina Ochoa Espejo, and Pierre Ostiguy (eds), *The Oxford Handbook of Populism.* Oxford: Oxford University Press, 590–606.

Müller, Jan-Werner. 2021. *Democracy Rules.* New York: Farrar, Straus and Giroux.

Mulligan, Thomas. 2018. "Plural Voting for the Twenty-first Century." *Philosophical Quarterly* 60: 286–306.

Mulvad, Andreas Møller and Stahl, Rune Møller. 2019. "Civilizing Left Populism: Towards a Theory of Plebian Democracy." *Constellations* 26: 591–606.

Neblo, Michael A. 2015. *Deliberative Democracy Between Theory and Practice*. Cambridge: Cambridge University Press.
Neblo, Michael, Esterling, Kevin M., and Lazer, David M. J. 2018. *Politics with the People: Building a Directly Representative Democracy*. Cambridge: Cambridge University Press.
Newton, Kenneth. 2012. "Curing the Democratic Malaise with Democratic Innovations," in Brigitte Geissel and Kenneth Newton (eds), *Evaluating Democratic Innovations: Curing the Democratic Malaise?* London: Routledge.
Nichols, Tom. 2017. *The Death of Expertise: The Campaign against Established Knowledge and Why it Matters*. Oxford: Oxford University Press.
Niesen, Peter. 2021. "Truth-tracing versus Truth-tracking: Lafont, Landemore and Epistemic Democracy." *Philosophy and Social Criticism* 47(1): 31–4.
Ober, Josiah. 2017. *Demopolis: Democracy before Liberalism in Theory and Practice*. Cambridge: Cambridge University Press.
Ochoa Espejo, Paulina. 2017. "Populism and the Idea of the People," in Cristóbal Rovira Kaltwasser, Paul Taggart, Paulina Ochoa Espejo, and Pierre Ostiguy (eds), *Oxford Handbook of Populism*. Oxford, Oxford University Press, 607–27.
Olson, Joel. 2004. *The Abolition of White Democracy*. Minneapolis: University of Minnesota Press.
Olson, Kevin. 2017. *Imagined Sovereignties: The Power of the People and Other Myths of the Modern Age*. Cambridge: Cambridge University Press.
Owen, David and Smith, Graham. 2018. "Sortition, Rotation, and Mandate: Conditions for Political Equality and Deliberative Reasoning." *Politics and Society* 46(3): 419–34.
Page, Scott E. 2007. *The Difference: How the Power of Diversity Creates Better Groups, Firms, Schools, and Societies*. Princeton: Princeton University Press.
Pamuk, Zeynep. 2021. *Politics and Expertise: How to Use Science in a Democratic Society*. Princeton: Princeton University Press.
Peruzzotti, Enrique. 2019. "Laclau's Theory of Populism," in Carlos de la Torre (ed.), *Routledge Handbook of Global Populism*. New York: Routledge Publishing, 31–43.
Peter, Fabienne. 2009. *Democratic Legitimacy*. New York: Routledge.
Peter, Fabienne. 2013. "The Procedural Epistemic Value of Deliberation." *Synthese* 190: 1253–66.
Pettit, Phillip. 2012. *On the People's Terms: A Republican Theory and Model of Democracy*. Cambridge: Cambridge University Press.

Phillips, Anne. 1995. *The Politics of Presence*. Oxford: Oxford University Press.
Pineda, Erin. 2021. *Seeing Like an Activist: Civil Disobedience and the Civil Rights Movement*. Oxford: Oxford University Press.
Pitkin, Hanna F. 1967. *The Concept of Representation*. Berkeley: University of California Press.
Plattner, Marc F. 2015. "Introduction," in Larry Diamond and Marc F. Plattner (eds), *Democracy in Decline*. Baltimore: Johns Hopkins University Press, 3–24.
Pogrebinschi, Thamy and Ryan, Matt. 2018. "Moving Beyond Input Legitimacy: When Do Democratic Innovations Affect Policy Making?" *European Journal of Political Research* 57(1): 135–52.
Pow, James. 2021. "Mini-publics and the Wider Publics: The Perceived Legitimacy of Randomly Selected Citizen Representatives." *Representation*. https://www.tandfonline.com/doi/full/10.1080/00344893.2021.1880470
Przeworski, Adam. 1999. "Minimalist Conception of Democracy: A Defense," in Ian Shapiro and Casiano Hacker-Cordón (eds), *Democracy's Value*. Cambridge: Cambridge University Press, 23–55.
Przeworski, Adam. 2019. *Crises of Democracy*. Cambridge: Cambridge University Press.
Quong, Jonathan. 2010. *Liberalism without Perfection*. Oxford: Oxford University Press.
Rainie, Lee, Keeter, Scott, and Perrin, Andrew. 2019. "Trust and Distrust in America." *Pew Research Center*. https://www.pewresearch.org/politics/2019/07/22/americans-struggles-with-truth-accuracy-and-accountability/
Rajendra-Nicolucci, Chand and Zuckerman, Ethan. 2021. "An Illustrated Guide to Social Media." Knight First Amendment Institute at Columbia University. https://knightcolumbia.org/blog/an-illustrated-field-guide-to-social-media
Rancière, Jacques. 2005. *Hatred of Democracy*. London: Verso
Rawls, John. 1971. *A Theory of Justice*. Cambridge: Harvard University Press.
Rawls, John. 2005. *Political Liberalism*, expanded edn. New York: Columbia University Press.
Raz, Joseph. 1990. "Facing Diversity: The Case for Epistemic Abstinence." *Philosophy and Public Affairs* 19(1): 3–46.
Rehfeld, Andrew. 2009. "Representation Rethought: On Trustees, Delegates, and Gyroscopes in the Study of Political Representation and Democracy." *American Political Science Review* 103(2): 214–30.

Rehfeld, Andrew. 2011. "The Concepts of Representation." *American Political Science Review* 105(3): 631–41.
Remer, Gary. 1999. "Political Oratory and Conversation: Cicero versus Deliberative Democracy." *Political Theory* 27(1): 39–64.
Remer, Gary. 2017. *Ethics and the Orator: The Ciceronian Tradition of Political Morality*. Chicago: University of Chicago Press.
Rey, Felipe. 2020. "The Representative System." *Critical Review of International Social and Political Philosophy*, 1–24.
Riker, William H. 1988. *Liberalism against Populism: A Confrontation between the Theory of Democracy and the Theory of Social Choice*. Prospect Heights: Waveland Press.
Rock, Chris. 2020. SNL Transcripts Tonight. *Saturday Night Live*, Season 46, episode 1, October 14. https://snltranscripts.jt.org/2020/chris-rock-stand-up-monologue.phtml
Rogers, Melvin L. 2012. "The People, Rhetoric, and Affects: On the Political Force of Du Bois's *The Souls of Black Folk*." *American Political Science Review* 106(1): 188–203.
Rosanvallon, Pierre. 2008. *Counter-Democracy: Politics in an Age of Distrust*, trans. Arthur Goldhammer. Cambridge: Harvard University Press.
Rosanvallon, Pierre. 2021. *The Populist Century: History, Theory, Critique*, trans. Catherine Porter. Cambridge: Polity Press.
Rosenblum, Nancy. 2000. "Political Parties as Membership Groups." *Columbia Law Review* 100(3): 813–44.
Rosenblum, Nancy. 2008. *On the Side of the Angels: An Appreciation of Parties and Partisanship*. Princeton: Princeton University Press.
Rosenbluth, Frances McCall and Shapiro, Ian. 2018. *Responsible Parties: Saving Democracy from Itself*. New Haven: Yale University Press.
Rossi, Enzo and Sleat, Matt. 2014. "Realism in Normative Theory." *Philosophy Compass* 9/10: 689–701.
Rostbøll, Christian F. 2015a. "Non-domination and Democratic Legitimacy." *Critical Review of International Social and Political Philosophy* 18(1): 424–39.
Rostbøll, Christian F. 2015b. "The Non-Instrumental Value of Democracy: The Freedom Argument." *Constellations* 22(2): 267–78.
Rostbøll, Christian F. 2020. "Democracy as a Good in Itself: Three Kinds of Non-Instrumental Justification," in Ester Herlin-Karnell and Matthias Klatt (eds), *Constitutionalism Justified: Rainer Forst in Discourse*. Oxford: Oxford University Press, 236–63.
Rostbøll, Christian F. 2023. *Democratic Respect: Populism, Resentment, and the Struggle for Recognition*. Cambridge: Cambridge University Press.

Rousseau, Jean-Jacques. 1987. *On the Social Contract*. Indianapolis: Hackett Publishing.

Rummens, Stefan. 2017. "Populism as a Threat to Liberal Democracy," in Cristóbal Rovira Kaltwasser, Paul Taggart, Paulina Ochoa Espejo, and Pierre Ostiguy (eds), *The Oxford Handbook of Populism*. Oxford: Oxford University Press, 554–70.

Runciman, David. 2017. *The Confidence Trap*. Princeton: Princeton University Press.

Runciman, David. 2018. *How Democracy Ends*. New York: Basic Books.

Sabl, Andrew. 2015. "Two Cultures of Democratic Theory: Responsiveness, Democratic Quality, and the Empirical–Normative Divide." *Perspectives on Politics* 13(2): 345–65.

Saffon, Maria Paula and Urbinati, Nadia. 2013. "Procedural Democracy: The Bulwark of Equal Freedom." *Political Theory* 41(3): 441–81.

Sakai, Ryota. 2020. "Mathematical Models and Robustness Analysis in Epistemic Democracy: A Systematic Review of Diversity Trumps Ability Theorem Models." *Philosophy of Social Sciences* 50(3): 195–214.

Sánchez-Cuenca, Ignacio. 2017. "From a Deficit of Democracy to a Technocratic Order: The Postcrisis Debate on Europe." *Annual Review of Political Science* 20(3): 351–69.

Sartori, Giovanni. 1976. *Parties and Party Systems: A Framework for Analysis*. Cambridge: Cambridge University Press.

Saward, Michael. 2010. *The Representative Claim*. Oxford: Oxford University Press.

Saward, Michael. 2021. *Democratic Design*. Oxford: Oxford University Press.

Scheuerman, William E. 2018. *Civil Disobedience*. Cambridge: Polity Press.

Scheuerman, William E. 2021. "Introduction: Why, Once Again, Civil Disobedience?" in William E. Scheuerman (ed.), *The Cambridge Companion to Civil Disobedience*. Cambridge: Cambridge University Press, 1–25.

Scholte, Jan Aart. 2005. *Globalization: A Critical Introduction*. London: Red Globe Press.

Schumpeter, Joseph. 1942. *Capitalism, Socialism and Democracy*. New York, Harper Perennial.

Schupmann, Benjamin A. 2022. "Hans Kelsen's Political Theology: Science, Pantheism, and Democracy." *Austrian Journal of Political Science* 52(3): 42–51.

Schwartzberg, Melissa. 2014. *Counting the Many: The Origins of Supermajority Rule*. Cambridge: Cambridge University Press.

Schwartzberg, Melissa. 2015. "Epistemic Democracy and its Challenges." *Annual Review of Political Science* 18: 187–203.

Schwartzman, Micah. 2011. "The Sincerity of Public Reason." *Journal of Political Philosophy* 19: 375–98.

Scudder, Mary F. and White, Stephen K. 2023. *The Two Faces of Democracy: Decentering Agonism and Deliberation*. Oxford: Oxford University Press.

Shanks, Torrey. 2019. "The Rhetoric of Self-ownership." *Political Theory* 47(3): 311–37.

Shapiro, Ian. 2016. *Politics against Domination*. Cambridge, MA: Harvard University Press.

Shaw, Tamsin. 2017. "Invisible Manipulators of Your Mind." *New York Review of Books*, April 20. https://www.nybooks.com/articles/2017/04/20/kahneman-tversky-invisible-mind-manipulators/

Shearman, David and Smith, Joseph Wayne. 2007. *The Climate Change Challenge and the Failure of Democracy*. Westport: Greenwood Publishing Group.

Sides, John. 2021. "Response to Michael Patrick Lynch's 'Truth as a Democratic Value,'" in Melissa Schwartzberg and Philip Kitcher (eds), *Truth and Evidence Nomos LXIV*. New York: New York University Press, 35–48.

Sintomer, Yves. 2018. "From Deliberative to Radical Democracy? Sortition and Politics in the Twenty-first Century." *Politics and Society* 46(3): 337–57.

Sleat, Matt. 2018. "Introduction: Politics Recovered – on the Revival of Realism in Contemporary Theory," in Matt Sleat (ed.), *Politics Recovered: Realist Thought and Practice*. New York: Columbia University Press, 1–25.

Smith, Graham. 2009. *Democratic Innovations: Designing Institutions for Citizen Participation*. Cambridge: Cambridge University Press.

Smith, Graham. 2021. *Can Democracy Safeguard the Future?* Cambridge: Polity Press.

Smith, Porter and Hall, Andrew. 2022. "Toppling the Internet's Accidental Monarchs: How to Design web3 Platform Governance." October 21 blog post *a16zcrypto*. https://a16zcrypto.com/content/article/toppling-the-internets-accidental-monarchs-how-to-design-web3-platform-governance/

Smith, William. 2012. *Civil Disobedience and Deliberative Democracy*. New York: Routledge.

Somin, Ilya. 2013. *Democracy and Political Ignorance*. Palo Alto: Stanford University Press.
Song, Sarah. 2012. "The Boundary Problem in Democratic Theory: Why the Demos Should Be Bounded by the State." *International Theory* 4(1): 39–68.
Stuckey, Mary E. 2020. "'The Power of the President to Hurt': The Indecorous Rhetoric of Donald J. Trump and Rhetorical Norms of Democracy." *Presidential Studies Quarterly* 50(2): 366–91.
Talisse, Robert. 2007. *A Pragmatist Philosophy of Democracy*. New York: Routledge.
Talisse, Robert. 2022. "Review of *Making Constituencies: Representation as Mobilization in Mass Democracy* by Lisa Jane Disch." *Perspectives on Politics* 20(3): 1071–2.
Taylor, Charles. 1994. "The Politics of Recognition," in Amy Gutmann (ed.), *Multiculturalism: Examining the Politics of Recognition*. Princeton: Princeton University Press, 25–73.
Thompson, Abigail. 2014. "Does Diversity Trump Ability? An Example of the Misuse of Mathematics in Social Sciences." *Notices in the American Mathematical Society* 61(9): 1024–30.
Tóth, Csaba. 2014. "Full Text of Viktor Orbán's Speech at Băile Tuşnad (Tusnádfürdő) of 26 July 2014." *The Budapest Beacon*. https://budapestbeacon.com/full-text-of-viktor-orbans-speech-at-baile-tusnad-tusnadfurdo-of-26-july-2014/
Tufekci, Zeynep. 2017. *Twitter and Tear Gas: The Power and Fragility of Networked Protest*. New Haven: Yale University Press.
Tuck, Richard. 2016. *The Sleeping Sovereign*. Cambridge: Cambridge University Press.
Tuck, Richard (forthcoming). *Active and Passive Citizens: A Defense of Majoritarian Democracy*. Tanner Lectures, ed. Stephen Macedo. Princeton: Princeton University Press.
Tully, James. 1995. *Strange Multiplicity: Constitutionalism in an Age of Diversity*. Cambridge: Cambridge University Press.
Urbinati, Nadia. 2012. "Competing for Liberty: The Republican Critique of Democracy." *American Political Science Review* 106(3): 607–21.
Urbinati, Nadia. 2013. "Introduction," in Hans Kelsen (ed.), *The Essence and Value of Democracy*. New York: Rowman & Littlefield, 1–24.
Urbinati, Nadia. 2014. *Democracy Disfigured: Opinion, Truth, and the People*. Cambridge, MA: Harvard University Press.
Urbinati, Nadia. 2019. *Me the People: How Populism Transforms Democracy*. Cambridge, MA: Harvard University Press.

Valentini, Laura. 2012. "Justice, Disagreement and Democracy." *British Journal of Political Science* 43: 177–99.
Van Crombrugge, Ronald. 2021. "Are Referendums Necessarily Populist? Countering the Populist Interpretations of Referendums through Institutional Design." *Representation* 57(1): 109–30.
Van Reybrouck, David. 2016. *Against Elections*. London: Bodley Head.
Vasić, Miljan. 2022. "How Realistic is the Modeling of Epistemic Democracy?" *Critical Review* 34(2): 279–98.
Vergara, Camilla. 2020a. *Systemic Corruption: Constitutional Ideas for an Anti-oligarchic Republic*. Princeton: Princeton University Press.
Vergara, Camila. 2020b. "Populism as Plebeian Politics: Inequality, Domination, and Popular Empowerment." *Journal of Political Philosophy* 28(2): 222–46.
Viehoff, Daniel. 2014. "Democratic Equality and Political Authority." *Philosophy & Public Affairs* 42(4): 337–75.
Viehoff, Daniel. 2019. "Power and Equality." *Oxford Studies in Political Philosophy* 5: 1–38
Waldner, David and Lust, Ellen. 2018. "Unwelcome Change: Coming to Terms with Democratic Backsliding." *Annual Review of Political Science* 21: 93–113.
Waldron, Jeremy. 1999. *Law and Disagreement*. Oxford: Oxford University Press.
Waldron, Jeremy. 2006. "The Core of the Case Against Judicial Review." *Yale Law Journal* 115: 1347–406.
Waldron, Jeremy. 2016. *Political Theory: Essays on Institutions*. Cambridge, MA: Harvard University Press.
Wall, Steven. 2007. "Democracy and Equality." *Political Quarterly* 57: 416–38.
Warren, Mark E. 2008. "Citizen Representatives," in Mark E. Warren and Hilary Pearse (eds), *Designing Deliberative Democracy: The British Columbia Citizens' Assembly*. Cambridge: Cambridge University Press.
Warren, Mark. 2017. "A Problem-Based Approach to Democratic Theory." *American Political Science Review* 111(1): 39–53.
Warren, Mark. 2019. "How Representation Enables Democratic Citizenship," in Dario Castiglione and Johannes Pollak (eds), *Creating Political Presence: The New Politics of Democratic Representation*. Chicago: Chicago University Press, 39–60.
Warren, Mark E. and Pearse, Hilary (eds). 2008. *Designing Deliberative Democracy: The British Columbia Citizens' Assembly*. Cambridge: Cambridge University Press.
Weale, Albert. 2018. *The Will of the People*. Cambridge: Polity Press.

References

White, Jonathan and Ypi, Lea. 2016. *The Meaning of Partisanship.* Oxford: Oxford University Press.
White, Stephen K. and Farr, Evan Robert. 2012. "'No-Saying' in Habermas." *Political Theory* 40(1): 32–57.
Wike, Richard and Fetterolf, Janell. 2021. "Global Public Opinion in an Era of Democratic Anxiety." *Pew Research Center.*
Wike, Richard, Silver, Laura, Schumacher, Shannon, and Connaughton, Aidan. 2021. "Many in the US, Western Europe Say Their Political System Needs Major Reform." *Report: Pew Research Center*, March 31. https://www.pewresearch.org/global/2021/03/31/many-in-us-western-europe-say-their-political-system-needs-major-reform/
Williams, Bernard. 2005. *In the Beginning Was the Deed: Realism and Moralism in Political Argument.* Princeton: Princeton University Press.
Williams, Melissa S. 1998. *Voice, Trust and Memory: Marginalized Groups and the Failings of Liberal Representation.* Princeton: Princeton University Press.
Wilson, James Lindley. 2019. *Democratic Equality.* Princeton: Princeton University Press.
Wolkenstein, Fabio. 2019. "Agents of Popular Sovereignty." *Political Theory* 47(3): 338–62.
Wolkenstein, Fabio and Wratil, Christopher. 2021. "Multidimensional Representation." *American Journal of Political Science* 65(4): 862–76.
Woodly, Deva R. 2018. "The Importance of Public Meaning to Political Persuasion." *Perspectives on Politics* 16(1): 22–35.
Woodly, Deva R. 2021. *Reckoning: Black Lives Matter and the Democratic Necessity of Social Movements.* Oxford: Oxford University Press.
Wooton, David (ed.). 2003. *The Essential Federalist and Anti-Federalist Papers.* Indianapolis: Hackett.
World Values Survey. 2020. "Findings and Insights." https://www.worldvaluessurvey.org/WVSContents.jsp?CMSID=Findings
Yack, Bernard. 2001. "Popular Sovereignty and Nationalism." *Political Theory* 29: 517–36.
Yack, Bernard. 2006. "Rhetoric and Public Reasoning: An Aristotelian Understanding of Political Deliberation." *Political Theory* 34: 417–38.
Yazici, Hayati. 2017. *AK Party.* "İlk defa millet kendi anayasasını yapacak" [For the first time the people will make its own constitution], trans. Mert Onal. March 22. https://www.akparti.org.tr/site/haberler/ilk-defa-millet-kendi-anayasasini-yapacak/89136#1
Young, I. M. 2000. *Inclusion and Democracy.* Oxford: Oxford University Press.
Zakaria, Fareed. 1997. "The Rise of Illiberal Democracy." *Foreign Affairs* 76(2): 22–43.

Zerilli, Linda. 2016. *A Democratic Theory of Judgement*. Chicago: University of Chicago Press.
Ziliotti, Elena. 2020. "Democracy's Value: A Conceptual Map." *Journal of Value Inquiry* 54: 407–27.

Index

Abts, Koen and Rummens, Stefan 147
accountability mechanisms 156
affordances 185, 187
  see also technological affordances
Against Democracy (Brennan) 98
aggregation 18, 75–6
agonism 17, 83, 84–5, 194
agonistic democrats 13
algorithmic rhetoric 195
algorithms, democratization of 7
all-affected principle 149
all-purpose assemblies 205
all-purpose problem solving 113
all-subjected principle 149
American Political Science Association 200
analytic political philosophy 9
ancient Athens 36, 151, 152, 156
Anderson, Elizabeth 72, 116, 117, 119
antagonistic frontier, concept of 141, 142
anti-pluralism 19, 143
anticipatory representation 169–70
Antifederalists 101

Arato, Andrew and Cohen, Jean 130, 145, 147, 148
Arendt, Hannah 195–6
aristocrats 101
Aristotle 27, 72, 85, 154, 194–5, 228n1
Arneson, Richard J. 88
Arrow, Kenneth J. 75–6
assemblies 153
  see also citizens' assemblies
attachment 186
audience 194, 195, 196
audience autonomy 195
authoritarian populism 3–4, 5
authoritarianism 219, 220, 224
  external threats 219–20
  internal threats 219
authorship 55–7, 63, 68, 69, 70, 71
  co-authorship 67
autonomy 34, 56, 174, 192, 195
  see also political autonomy

backsliding 3–4, 25, 78, 138, 207, 219
Bagg, Samuel 71, 74
Balibar, Étienne 210, 211
Bell, Daniel 101–2

Bellamy, Richard 45
Benhabib, Seyla 194
Bernholz et al. 177
Between Facts and Norms (Habermas) 209
bias 94
Bickerton, Christopher and Invernizzi-Accetti, Carlo 61, 96
Big Tech 184–5, 188
Bird, Colin 11
Black Lives Matter movement 207, 208–9, 222
blockchain technology 188
boundary problem 149–50
bounded communities 186
Brennan, Jason 98–9
Brennan, Jason and Landemore, Hélène 73, 89, 91
Brexit (2016) 135, 152
Brighouse, Harry 39
British Columbia Citizens' Assembly 202, 205–6
brute arbitrary force 32
Burke, Edmund 168–9

Calvert, Aubin and Warren, Mark E. 191
Calvin, John 50
Canovan, Margaret 129, 135
Celikates, Robin 22, 212, 213–14
cellphone journalism 189
Chambers, Simone 179
China
  corruption 90, 103
  democracy 29
  meritocracy 90, 101, 102, 103
  performance scales 90
Christianity 36
Christiano, Thomas 15, 41, 43–4, 45, 48, 51

Christiano, Thomas and Bajaj, Sameer 9
Christopher, Griffin 38
Cicero 195
circumstances of politics 45–6
citizen apathy 221
citizen competence 7, 74, 93–6
  realistic assessment of 93–4
citizen contestation 66
citizen deliberative initiatives 178–9
citizen incompetence 93–5, 97, 98
  restrictions on 99
  voter incompetence 96
citizen initiatives 203–4
citizen oversight juries 86
citizen representatives 153–60
citizens
  authors of laws 59
  disillusionment with democratic institutions 221
  equal status 49
  freedom of 63
  majority rule 66
  moral reasoning 51
  political knowledge, lack of 221
  realistic democratic theory 74–5
  susceptibility to manipulation 95
citizens' assemblies 68, 130
  agential component 159–60
  critics of 161
  definition 153
  deliberation 158, 159, 206
  diversity 158
  equality 158
  impartiality 158
  track record 158
deliberative democracy 179
democratic theory 205
future-oriented policy 206

lottocratic chambers 160
  on climate change 206
  policies 159
  popularity of 153, 159
  problem solving 158, 205–6
  public trust in 207
  random selection 153, 159
  representing the people 157–8
  trust 157–8, 207
civic virtues 72–3
civil disobedience 22, 198, 207–17
  bottom-up citizen participation 199
  breaking the law 209
  citizens 214
  civil rights era 215
  contemporary interest in 207
  as a contested concept 209
  democratic innovation and 198–9
  direct action 200
  exercise of disruption 216
  as a form of coercion 215, 216
  as a form of persuasion 215, 216
  future oriented 199
  justification for 209
  legitimacy of 213
  liberal view of 212
  literature 198
  nonviolence 214–15
  radical democracy 212–14
  reevaluation of 207
civil rights era 215
civil society 166, 167, 186
civil war 78
climate change 88, 90, 91–2, 192, 206
climate crisis 6, 184, 213
coercion 32, 33, 56
  civil disobedience 215, 216

coercive power 52
coercive turn 22, 216
Cohen, Joshua 51, 52, 179, 229n2
Cohen, Joshua and Fung, Archon 182, 209
collaborative governance 203
collective action 32, 42, 49
collective competence 96
common good 59–60, 61, 75, 76, 162
  partisanship 163–4
common will 183
communication theory 192
communicatively fluid sovereignty 146
competence 93–6
  see also citizen competence
competency tests 99, 100
competent citizen *see* citizen incompetence
competitive elections 17, 60, 77, 156, 157, 161
Condorcet Jury Theorem (CJT) 18, 107–11, 122
  independence 108–9
  sincerity condition 109
Condorcet, Marquis of 107
Confucianism 101, 102, 103
Connolly, William 210
consensus 162
consent 52, 154
consequentialism 119
constituencies 172–3
constituent power 131, 135, 145, 211
constituted power 131
constitutional constraints 138
constitutional democracy 147, 209–10
constitutionalism 134, 147
constitutions 137–8, 210

constrained democracy 19, 133–8
constructivism 153
constructivist turn 172–5
contemporary democratic theory 12–13, 24, 29, 93
  democratic skepticism 93
  mutual justification 52
  populism 148
  realism 73
  representation, challenges to 169
  voter incompetence 96
    epistocracy 96, 98–101
    meritocracy 96, 101–3
    technocracy 96, 96–8
content-independent value *see* intrinsic value of democracy
contestation 66, 68, 69, 80, 81, 85
  control over government 80
  court challenges 80
  protest and street politics 80
contestatory proceduralism 16, 70, 71, 143
correct answers 109–10, 122
correct outcomes 116
correctness view/theories 106, 117, 122
correspondence 56–7
corruption complaint 151
counter-democracy 16, 67–8, 69
Covid-19 pandemic 6
critical realism 82
critical theory 223
crowdsourcing 204

Dalton, Russel 201
decision procedures *see* procedures
deep fakes 189
deep pluralists 45–7

deliberation 48, 84–5, 116, 158, 181
  citizens' assemblies 158, 159
    diversity 158
    equality 158
    impartiality 158
    track record 158
    hypothetical terms 159
    uniqueness of 159
deliberative bodies 153
deliberative democracy 12, 21, 49, 51, 177–85
  communication theory 192
  deliberative initiatives 178–9
  democratic legitimacy 179
  early critiques of 190
  macro level 179
  as radical democracy 209–10
  revivalism and 193–4
  rhetoric and 189–90, 192–3
  role of protest 208
  systems approach 193
  theories of 49–50
  tradition of 193–4
  two-track theory of 179–80, 180–1
deliberative democrats 84, 116
deliberative logic 216
deliberative mini-publics (DMPs) *see* citizens' assemblies 153, 202, 204, 205
deliberative opinion formation 184
delicate model of representation 168, 169
democracies
  economic growth 90
  performance of 90
  short-termism 92
democracy
  avoiding violence 77–8
  competitive election 77
  conceptions of 11–12

Index

in crisis 1, 2–8
  input perspective 7–8
  institutional/norm perspective 3–4
  outcome perspective 5–6
  subjective/attitudinal perspective 4–5
definition 211
elected rulers 77
epistemic benefits of 119
epistemic potential of 125
ethics-first views 79
features of 211–12
future of 225, 226
global desire for 1
indexes 2
justification for 14–15, 24–35
  instrumental value 14, 26, 31–2, 125
  intrinsic value 14, 15, 25–6, 27–8, 38–9, 88–9, 125
  legitimacy 14–15, 32–4
  outcomes-based views 14, 26, 28, 29–31
  procedural and proceduralism 28–9
  procedures 25–6
  value of 14–15, 25–7, 32–4, 51, 119
Kantian approach 34
minimalist theories of 135–6, 138
reputation 220
saving 13–14
shared commitments 120
sinking trust in 5, 20, 25
telic concept 126
threats to 226–7
transfer of power 78, 79
"Democracy's Value: A Conceptual Map" (Ziliotti) 26
democratic affordances 185–6, 187
Democratic Authority: A Philosophical Framework (Estlund) 120
democratic backsliding *see* backsliding
democratic constitutionalism 147
democratic decisions 29, 68, 69, 92, 109, 110
  Mizak on 115
democratic deficit 97, 98, 138, 147–8
democratic equality 116
democratic freedom 58
democratic innovation 5, 21–2, 187, 200–7
  bottom-up citizen participation 198–9
  categories of 202–4
  civil disobedience and 198–9
  criteria for evaluation 205–7
  definitions 200–2
  disillusionment with traditional institutions 201
  future oriented 199
  input values 205
  literature 198, 201, 204
  output values 205
  theoretical debates 200–2
  throughput values 205
Democratic Innovations: Designing Institutions for Citizen Participation (Smith) 200–1
democratic pluralism 19, 142–8
democratic procedures *see* procedures
democratic republics 28–9
democratic theory
  contemporary *see* contemporary democratic theory
  definition 8–11

democratic theory (*cont.*)
  epistemic approach 92–3
  history of 24
  populism and 128–33
  see also normative theory
democratization 220
descriptive representation 170–1
Dewey, John 115, 116, 118–19
dictatorships 90
differentiation 140
digital communities 186–7
digital design 188
digital enclaves 182–3
digital participation 204
digital public sphere 21
  centrifugal dynamic 182–3
  deliberative democracy 177–85
  inclusiveness 184
  manipulation and misinformation 7
  privatization of communication 183
  regulation of 185
  sharing private opinions 183
  trustworthy sources of fact and information 184
direct action 216
direct democracy 59, 62, 101, 134, 151
direct legislation 203–4
disagreement 43, 44, 47, 119
  equality and 41–5
  political parties 165
  public reason and 50–3
  restraint 51
Disch, Lisa 172, 173
disinformation 182
dispersed popular sovereignty 70, 143, 146–7, 148
dissent 118, 119
Diversity Trumps Ability Theorem (DTA) 18, 111–14, 229n5
  all-purpose assemblies 113
  cognitive diversity 113
  conditions 112
  deliberation 113
  extensions of 113
  sortition 113–14
  wisdom of crowds 112
domination 65, 80
  agents 81
  constitutional constraints 81
  minority rule 81
Dryzek, John 192
Du Bois, W. E. B. 196

e-democracy 204
e-voting 188
e-voting tools 204
economics 97
economists 97
efficiency 97, 98
egalitarian democrats 37–41
  citizens 49
egalitarian social justice 37
egalitarian theories 15
Eisgruber, Christopher 137
elected representatives 20, 39, 40, 101
elections 65, 79, 83
  agonistic struggle 84
  aristocratic nature of 20, 152
  avoiding violence and bloodshed 78, 83
  competence of elected officials 101
  competitive 60, 77, 157
  contestation 66
  core of democracy 69
  empowering opposition groups 83
  establishing distinctions 154

free and fair 27, 30, 48, 69, 79, 82
freedom 58
meritocracy and 101
regular 63, 65, 79
role of money 155
transfer of power 79
tyrannies 102
value of, questioning 93
wealthy and powerful candidates 155
will of the people 76
see also sortition
electoral competition 61, 83
electoral cycles 92, 206
electoral democracy 20, 67, 70, 84, 152
elitism 20
meritocrats' view of 102–3
myopia 206
electoral politics 160–1
electoral systems 76
electoral turnover 77–8, 136
elitist theories 135–6
Elstub, Stephen and McLaverty, Peter 201
embodiment 132, 144, 146
emotion 195
empirical political science 10, 161–2
empirical theory 90–1
empty signifier 141
empty space (Lefort) 144, 146
endogeneity 173, 174, 175, 181
enemies of the people 135, 142, 145
enfranchising lottery 99
epistemic approach 92–3
epistemic competence 99
epistemic considerations 121–2
epistemic democracy 13, 31, 105–27

Condorcet Jury Theorem (CJT) 18, 107–11, 122
critics of 117
Diversity Trumps Ability Theorem (DTA) 18, 111–14, 229n5
epistemic proceduralism 120–4
pragmatism 114–20
epistemic democrats 6, 18, 125, 126
epistemic forces 123
epistemic proceduralism 120–4
epistemic quality 180
epistocracy 6, 17, 18, 96, 98–101
epistocrats 97
arguments against 99–100
equal freedoms 57
equal opportunity to influence argument 39–40
equal participation 180
equal respect 28, 37, 38, 41, 46, 49
equal status 49, 53
equal voting rights 38, 39
equality 15, 36–54
deep pluralists 45–7
disagreement and 41–5
egalitarian democrats 37–41
mutual justification 47–50, 50–1, 52, 53
political 4
public reason and disagreement 50–3
equality democrats 126
Erdoğan, Recep 130
Estlund, David 120–2, 229n4
"ethics-first" theory 74
ethos 195
experimentalism 118, 186
experts and expertise 94, 96, 97
Extinction Rebellion 199

Index

Facebook 184–5, 186
facilitated deliberation 202
factionalism 164
facts 10
fairness 25–6, 46, 47–8, 119, 123
fake news 189
fallibility 116
Federalists 101, 155
financial crisis (2008) 5, 98
Fishkin, James 159
Floyd, George 189, 207
For a Left Populism (Mouffe) 83–4, 139
Forestal, Jennifer 185–7, 188
formal equality 40
formal theory 9–10
framing 95, 173, 191
free and fair elections 27, 30, 48, 69, 79, 82
freedom 16, 55–71
  as authorship 55–7
  autonomy 56
  correspondence 56–7
  good of 58
  Kelsenian proceduralism 57–64
  laws and 56
  levels of 63
  majority rule 62
  as non-domination 64–9
  self-determination 56
Freedom House 2
freedom ideal 61
Freeman, Samuel 137
fully dispersed sovereignty 146
fundamental equality 36
Fung, Archon 179

game theory *see* formal theory
Garsten, Bryan 189, 192–3
Gastil, John and Wright, Erik Olin 160–1
gatekeepers 182

general will 59, 60, 75, 76, 229n3
Geuss, Raymond 74
global democracy 225
globalization 140
good argument (*logos*) 194
good government 102
good performance 125
Goodin, Robert E. and Spiekermann, Kai 107–8, 109
Goodman, Rob 195
Green, Jeffrey 85
grievances 140–1
Gutmann, Amy and Thompson, Dennis 51
gyroscopic representation 169, 170

Habermas, Jürgen 145–60, 182–4, 190, 209
  communication theory 192
  radical democracy 210
  two-track model 179–80, 180–1
happiness 27
Hendriks, Frank 205
hierarchy 43
Hong, Lu and Page, Scott 111
Honig, Bonnie 188
Hooker, Juliet 215
Huq, Aziz 6

identity 95, 187
identity politics 222
illiberal democracy 133–4, 143, 147
impartiality 160, 162
impossibility theorem 75–6
inclusion 222
inclusiveness 118
independence 108–9
Indigenous peoples 202
individual rights 147

inequality, social and economic 4
information communication 7
in-group/out-group identification 95
initiatives 203, 204
input perspective of democracy 7–8
inquiry 115–16
institutional/norm perspective of democracy 3–4
instrumentalism 16–17
  epistemic democracy *see* epistemic democracy
  performance skeptics *see* performance skeptics
  realism *see* realism
instrumentalist view of democracy 14, 26, 31–2
interests 63
  equal advancement of 43–4
  unequal advancement of 43
interference 64–5
intermediary institutions 148
internet 178, 185, 187–8
intersubjectively dissolved popular sovereignty 146
intrinsic value of democracy 14, 15, 25–6, 27–8, 38–9, 88–9
Invernizzi-Accetti, Carlo and Oskian, Giulia 61
iron law of oligarchy 211

judgment 196
juries 109
justice 15, 43, 162
  formal conception of 44
justification turn 52

Kantians 34
Kaufman, Alexander 212
Kelsen, Hans 57–8, 60, 61
  majority principle 61–2, 63

majority rule 65
majority voting 66
parliamentary democracy 62
Kelsenian proceduralism 16, 57–64, 70
  common good 61
  institutions 63
  majority rule 63–4
  opposition to outcomes-based view 58
  parliamentary democracy 58
King, Martin Luther Jr 214–15, 215, 216
Knight, Jack and Johnson, James 117–18
Kohn, Margaret 188
Kolodny, Nico 40

Laclau, Ernesto 19, 129, 139–42, 144, 210
  democratic people 141–2
  grievances 140–1
Lafont, Cristina 56, 228–9n1
Landemore, Hélène 92–3, 112–13, 205
laws 32
  authorship of 56, 59
  freedom and 56
  interference 64–5
  justification of 210
  purpose of 59
Lefort, Claude 144
left-wing populism 19, 84, 138–42
  progressive causes 142
  technocratic governance 142
legitimacy 120–1, 180
  of democracy 14–15, 32–4, 52
  inclusive reason giving 179
  versus value 32–4
liberal republicanism 13
liberalism 134, 140, 143
liberty *see* freedom

Index

Livingston, Alexander 22, 118, 198, 207, 216, 216–17
logical truth 111
logos 195
lottocracy 156, 157, 158, 160
   arguments against 159–60
lottocratic chambers 160

MacGilvray, Eric 116, 118–19
Madison (in Wooton) 101, 154–5, 230n1
Maduro, Nicolas 130
majority principle 61–2
majority rule 46, 63, 63–4, 65, 66
majority will 63
Manin, Bernard 154
manipulation 108, 174, 182, 192
   problems of 7
Mansbridge, Jane 169–71, 175
marginalized groups 194
markets 97, 98
mass democracies 151
McCormick, John 13, 85, 86
meritocracy 17–18, 96, 101–3
Michels, Robert 211
Mill, John Stuart 72
Mills, Charles 223
minimal realism 17
minimalism 17
   procedural views 61
   theories 135–6, 138, 160
minimalist realism 77–82
minority groups
   majority rule 66
   rights of 16, 30, 63–4, 70
mirroring 157
misinformation 189
   problems of 7
Mizak, Cheryl 115, 116, 124
mobilization 163, 174, 189, 227
models-of-democracy approach 12–14

Modi, Narendra 130
Montesquieu 154
Moore, Alfred 187
moral equality 36, 119
moral theory 9
moral value 79
moralism 74
motivated reasoning 94
   biases 94
   motivated reasoners, humans as 94
Mouffe, Chantal 19, 86, 129, 130, 138–9, 210
   democratic politics 85
   electoral politics 86
   left-wing populism 83–4, 138–9
   the "people" 84, 85, 139
   right-wing populism 84, 130, 138–9
Muirhead, Russell and Rosenblum, Nancy 165
multiculturalism 222
mutual justification 47–50, 50–1, 52, 53, 167

Neblo et al. 204
neo-republicanism 64, 85
neoliberalism 84, 139
networked communication 182, 183
neutrality 162
Niko, Kolodny 38
non-derivative value *see* intrinsic value of democracy
non-domination
   freedom as 64–9
   realism and 80–2
non-domination theory 16
non-embodiment question 132
nonviolence 214–15
   mythologizing of 215

romanticization of 215
sacrifice 215
normative democratic theory *see* normative theory
normative theory 6, 10, 18–20
 critical theory and 223
 defining 8–11
 democratic innovation 198–9, 200–7
 empirical theory and 90–1
 expansive and inclusive idea of 8–9
 fact/value distinction 10
 legitimacy 33
 moral content 9
 myth of 74
 non-domination 80
 performance 89–90, 90–1
 political parties 161–2, 166
 populism 129
 rational and enlightened citizen 74
 realism 9
 reasonable disagreement 42–3, 50
 responsiveness 171
 tripartite methodological division 9

objective common good 60
Ochoa Espejo, Paulina 146
oligarchization 219
 of electoral institutions 4
 of representative democracy 5
oligarchy 82, 83, 86, 156
 external dimensions 220
 internal dimensions 220
 states 211–12
 worry about 221
On Populist Reason (Laclau) 139
one person, one vote 28, 40, 47, 93, 102, 160
open democracy 12–13
opposition 80–1
 democratic role of 81–2
 orators 194–5
Orbán, Viktor 130, 134
organized distrust 67–8
outcome perspective of democracy 5–6
outcomes 28, 46
 bad 26, 28, 30, 61
 deliberation 48
 democratic 30, 44–5
 equality 44–5
 evaluation of 29
 good 26, 30, 31, 50
 limits on 30
 outcomes-based views 14, 26, 28, 29–31
 from procedures 25, 44, 45, 56, 57
 will of the majority 62
overrepresentation 203

pandemic politics 92
parliamentary democracy 16, 57, 58, 62
parties *see* political parties
partisan realists 17, 82–6
partisanship 83, 153, 161, 164
 common good 163–4
 elements of 163
  caring/taking sides 163
  generalizable principles 164
  mobilization for causes 163
  pluralism 164
 negative connotations 163
 rehabilitation of 163
party democracy 17, 61, 69, 163, 164
 pluralism 165
party platforms 166

party politics 164
  divisiveness 165
pathos 195
peaceful coexistence 79
Peirce, Charles Sanders 115
people-as-plebs 86
"people," the 131, 230n1
  conception of 139
  constitutionalizing of 137
  construction of 139, 141
  contemporary populism 144
  definition 132
  democratic pluralists' view of 145
  dilemmas about 132–3
  dispersed and diverse plurality 146
  embodiment 144
  enemies of 135, 142, 145
  majoritarian-decision procedures 135
  majoritarian institutions 134
  mobilization of 141
  Mouffe, Chantal 84, 85, 139
  political equality 132–3
  populism and 134
  populist conception of 143, 144–5
  power 141, 144
  procedure of decision making and opinion formation 146
  representatives of 134
  rule of 131
  ultimate authority 131, 134
  ultimate sovereignty of 136–7
  will of 138
People's Tribunate 86
people's will 45, 75, 134, 135
performance 219–20
performance measurement
  bad outcomes 91–2
  democracy versus non-democracy 90
  good outcomes 91
performance skeptics 17, 88–104, 125
  citizen competence 93–6
  epistocracy 98–101
  measuring performance 89–93
  meritocracy 101–3
  technocracy 96–8
Perón, Juan 129
persuasion *see* rhetoric
Peter, Fabienne 119–20, 122–4
Pettit, Philip 13, 65, 70
  communitarian option 65–6
  contestation 66, 80, 81
  equally shared control 65
  non-domination 66–7, 80
Pineda, Erin 217
Pitkin, Hannah 172
Plato 93
Plattner, Marc F. 220
plebeian democracy 17, 83
plebeian democrats 86
plebeian neo-republicans 85–6
plebiscites 134, 151, 152, 203
pluralism 41, 45–6, 60, 69, 119, 164
  political parties 165
plutocracy 220–1
polarization 95, 163
policy agendas 155–6
political autonomy 63, 66, 69, 70, 126, 130
political communication 94–5, 193–4
  Habermas's two-track model 180–1
  mediation of 177
  medium 177
  message 177
  public sphere 180

political competence 93–6
political elites 152, 174
political equality 36, 40, 85, 102, 119, 132, 157
   definition 36
   formal 51
   public affirmation of 39
   public recognition 49
   social equality and 38
political leaders 168
political liberalism 51
political moralism 73–4
political parties 20, 62, 161–2
   bulwark against domination 81
   crisis of party democracy 162, 166
   dimensions of 163–4
   function of 164–6
   intra-party democracy 166–7
   mediating society and state 165–7
   messaging 167–8
   normative democratic theory 162
   partisanship *see* partisanship
   pluralism and disagreement 165
   political philosophy 162
   regulating rivalry 165
   transmission belts 166
political philosophy 8, 38, 52, 73, 84, 93, 100
   core principles 162
political power 39, 52
   bottom-up 166
   equality of 38
political preferences 94–5
political problems 114
political questions 89, 106
political representation 19–20
political rule 32
political struggle 39, 85
political theory 8, 73

political truths 106, 117
political virtues 72–3
politics 74, 77–8, 79
   moral principles 83
   nature of 140
   power struggles 82
   rhetoric and 193
politics of distrust 68
popular assemblies 203
popular culture 155
popular sovereignty 19, 129, 131, 145, 230n1
   constitutionalizing 136–7
   constrained democracy 133–8
   dangerous fictions 135–6
   democratic pluralism 142–8
   dispersed idea of 146
   downstream view 131
   hypothetical idea of 146
   radical democracy 210
   upstream view 131, 146
popular will 61, 134, 135
populism 3–4, 18–19, 68, 84, 128–50
   conception of the people 144–5
   constitutional change and amendment 135
   constrained democracy 133–8
   criticisms of 129
   definitions of 144
   democratic pluralism 142–8
   democratic theory and 128–33
   illiberal democracy 133–4
   phenomena of 130
   popular sovereignty 131
   primary danger of 133
   replacing differentiation and powerless grievances 140–1
   see also left-wing populism; right-wing populism
populist complaint 151
populist parties 136

positivism 10
post-truth 7
power 141
power of the people 129
power struggles 77–8, 85
    exclusion of the wealthy 86
pragmatism 106, 114–20
    criticism of 119–20
    experimentalism and reflexivity 118
preference formation 76–7, 173, 174
priming 95, 191
principle/agent relationship 169–70
The Principles of Representative Government (Manin) 154
problem solvers 111, 112, 113, 114
problem solving 48–9, 50, 84, 116–17
    in DTA 112, 116
    political 114
procedural-based theories 28–9, 29–30
procedural democracy 16, 57–8
procedural equality 44
proceduralism 28–9, 30
    Kelsenian 57–64
    Urbinati's defense of 62–3
    see also Kelsenian proceduralism
procedures 14–16, 25, 30
    common good 75
    control from state interference 67
    deep pluralists' view 46, 47
    equality 39, 44, 47
    fairness of 122, 123
    flipping a coin 29, 38, 78, 89, 121
    formal 40, 49
    freedom 61

good consequences 31
inclusiveness 116
instrumental 26, 31
intrinsic value 25–6, 27–8, 39, 44
justification for 100
majority-decision 46–7
minimalist realistic defense of 79
mutual justification 47, 48, 49
outcomes 56
procedural-based theories 28–9
Proceeding of the National Academy of Sciences (Hong & Scott) 111
promissory representation 169
propaganda 108, 182
protest 208–9
    justification for 208
    legitimate limits to 208–9
    right to, protection of 208
    roles and functions of 208
    see also civil disobedience
Przeworski, Adam 77–8, 79, 80, 83, 136
public affirmation argument 38, 39
public figures 168
public justification 52, 167, 194
public opinion 171, 180, 181
public policy 166
public reason 50–3, 137–8, 167, 168, 190
    criticisms of 52–3
    ethic of citizenship 52
public speech 194
public sphere 21, 133, 177–97
    civil society and the state 186
    communication in 183
    digital infrastructure of 182
    digital platforms 180
    inclusiveness 183

Index

multiple and conflicting opinions 183
orators 195
political communication 180
rhetoric 189–96
technological affordances 185–9
transformation of 184
see also digital public sphere
pure epistemic proceduralism 122–3
pure proceduralism 30–1, 47, 122

race 223
racial contract 223–4
racism 224
radical democracy 209–11, 211
   civil disobedience 212–14
   constituent power 211
   states 212
radical plebeianism 13
radical realism 82
Rancière, Jacques 210, 211–12
random selection 20, 112, 113, 153, 156–7, 157
   DMPs 202, 203
   see also sortition
randomly sampled opinion polls 158
rational ignorance 94
Rawls, John 38, 124, 190, 194
   burdens of judgment argument 42, 228n1
   civil disobedience 213
   justification 52
   public reason 50–3
realism 9, 16, 72–87
   in democratic theory 73–7
   meanings of 73–5
   minimalist realism 77–82
   non-domination and 80–2
   partisan realists 82–6
realist democratic theory 17, 83

realist logic 216
realists 9, 31, 126
   see also partisan realists
reason giving 179
reasonable disagreement 42–3, 119–20, 124
reasonableness 50, 162
recognition 186, 222
Reddit 187
redistributive authoritarianism 125
referendums 134, 151, 152, 203, 204
reflexivity 118
regime types 77
regulated rivalry 165
relational egalitarians 43
relational equality 37
relational social justice 38
representation 7–8, 151–76
   constructivist turn 172–5
   entrepreneurial function of 173
   feedback loops 171, 174–5
   Mansbridge's typology
      anticipatory representation 169–70
      gyroscopic representation 170
      promissory representation 169
      surrogate representation 170–1
   normative theories of 8
   parties, partisans, and partisanship 161–8
   political elites 152
   principle/agent relationships 169–70
   responsiveness 171
   sinking trust in 151–2
      corruption complaint 151
      populist complaint 151

representation (*cont.*)
  sortition 153–60
  standard view of 168–9
    delegate model 168, 169
    trustee model 168, 169
representative democracy 139–40
  crisis of 140, 155–6
  elected officials 39–40
  grievances 140–1
representative institutions 134, 156
  loss of trust in 19–20
representatives 62
republican theories 13
republicanism 64
republics, seventeenth-century 154
responsiveness 8, 20–1, 76, 149, 171, 173, 174
  crisis of 152
  democratic institutions 155
  "Rethinking Representation" (Mansbridge) 169
revisability 116
revivalism
  audience 194
  deliberative democracy and 193–4
  judgment 196
  oratory skills 194–5
  rhetoric and 192, 193–4
rhetoric 13, 21, 189–96
  ancient traditions of 193
  definitions 190
  deliberative democracy and 189–90, 192–3
  revivalism and 192, 193
  strategies of persuasion 190–1, 194
  types of 190–1
rhetorical bargain 195
right to be heard 118–19

right-wing populism 19, 84, 130, 139
  xenophobic character of 139
Rock, Chris 155
Rogers, Melvin 196
Rosanvallon, Pierre 67–8, 70, 146, 147, 147–8
Rosenblum, Nancy 165
Rostbøll, Christian 67, 146
Rousseau, Jean-Jacques 55–6, 57, 58–60, 62, 65–6, 69–70, 229n3
rule of the people 131, 132, 133, 146
ruling wills 62–3

Saffon, Maria Paula and Urbinati, Nadia 60–1
Sánchez-Cuenca, Ignacio 97
Saturday Night Live 155
Saussurean semiotic theory 141
Saward, Michael 172–3
Scheuerman, William 209, 214
Schmitt, Carl 141
Schumpeter, Joseph 17, 61, 77, 82
scientific procedures 91
self-determination 56, 70, 71
  civil disobedience 213
self-government 56, 58, 59, 65, 80, 126
  arguments against 75–6
  elected majorities 67, 70
self-rule 44, 56, 70, 71
  people as agent of 84
  see also authorship
self-selection 203
Servetus, Michael 50
Shapiro, Ian 77, 80, 83
  non-domination 80
  opposition view 80–1
shared goals 119

short-term profit margins 206
sincerity condition 109
Singapore 102, 103
Smith, Graham 200–1, 201–2
social bias 108
social choice argument 76
  see also formal theory
social contract tradition 223
social epistemology 123
social equality 36
  distributional terms 37
  political equality and 38
  relational terms 37
social forces 123
social groups/movements 160
social justice 41, 93, 220
  theory 37, 38
social media 182
social movements 199, 222
sortition 113–14, 153–60
  criticism of electoral representation 154, 161
  defenders of 155
  early democracy and 154
  endorsement of 160–1
  favorable features 157
  policy agendas 155–6
  rejection of 154
  technocracy 159
  see also elections
sovereignty of the people 147
space metaphor 188
stagnation 201
Stanford Encyclopedia of Philosophy (Christiano and Bajaj) 9
status 39
strategic voting 109
stratification 202
subjective/attitudinal perspective of democracy 4–5
success
  external standards of 116
  internal standards of 116
suffragette movement 39
Supreme Court 137
surrogate representation 169, 170–1
systemic error 108
systemic prejudice 108

Talisse, Robert 115, 116
Taylor, Charles 126
team booster 95
technocracy 6, 17, 96–8, 140, 143
  sortition and 159
technocrats 97, 98
technological affordances 185–9
A Theory of Justice (Rawls) 38
totalitarian regimes 90
transfer of power 78, 79
transnational democracy 225
true belief 115, 116
Trump, Donald 130, 226
trustee model of representation 168, 169
truth 42, 115, 123, 124
Tuck, Richard 66
Tully, James 210
Turkish Constitution (2017) 131
Twitter 186

ultimate authority 131, 134
uncontrolled interference 65
universal franchise 46
universal suffrage 93, 99, 100
unruly speech 194
Urbinati, Nadia 16, 57, 58
  party democracy and elections 68–9
  proceduralism 62–3

value of democracy 14–15, 25–7
  versus legitimacy 32–4

value relativism 60
Vergara, Camilla 85, 86
violence 31, 74, 77–8, 79, 80
virtual civil society 186
voter ignorance 98, 156
voter incompetence 96
  epistocracy 98–101
  meritocracy 101–3
  technocracy 96–8
voter turnout 40
  sinking 5, 162
voters' competence 107
voting rights 49, 53

Waldron, Jeremy 15, 41, 43, 45, 46, 48, 61, 123

"circumstances of politics" 45–6
Web3 188
Weber, Max 32–3
welfare state 139–40
White, Jonathan and Ypi, Lea 164
white supremacy 214–15, 224
Wikipedia 187
will of the majority 138
will of the people 138, 147, 159
Woodly, Deva 191
Wooton, David 101
World Values Survey (WVS) 1

Zakaria, Fareed 133
Ziliotti, Elena 26